# PORSCHE 911

CHRIS HARVEY

The Oxford Illustrated Press

The Oxford Illustrated Press



ISBN 0 946609 69 1

**Published by:**
The Oxford Illustrated Press Limited, Sparkford,
Near Yeovil, Somerset BA 22 7JJ, England.

Haynes Publications Inc
861 Lawrence Drive, Newbury Park, California 91320 USA.

**Printed in England by:**
J.H. Haynes & Co Limited, Sparkford, Nr Yeovil, Somerset.

**British Library Cataloguing in Publication Data**

Harvey, Chris
The Porsche 911 in all its forms.
1. Porsche 911 cars, to 1984
I. Title
629.2'222
ISBN 0-946609-69-1

**Library of Congress Catalog Card Number**
88-81060

# Contents

# Acknowledgements

Little did I know when the first edition of this book was written in 1979 that the Porsche 911 had so long to live. Even the men who made it were adamant that it would soon be replaced by a combination of the new four and eight-cylinder Porsches. But there was one person, in particular, who believed that the 911 could go on to what now seems near-immortality: its creator, Ferry Porsche. He kept what has become the world's greatest sports car in production long enough for it to see a new lease of life, appealing not only to people whose enthusiasm borders on the fanatical, but a whole new wave of fans to replace those who have gone since the car first appeared in 1964.

Initially I had to thank Mike Cotton, then of Porsche Cars, Great Britain, who also ran the Porsche Club of Great Britain, for much of my help, as well as his secretary, Julia Brown. I still thank them, but now they have moved on, I have to thank in particular, Jeremy Snook, Corinna Phillips and Melanie Hill, representing the British arm of Porsche, for their invaluable help with the revised book, and Chris Branston, chairman of the British Porsche Club, for his continuing encouragement. My thanks again, to David Edelstein, who gave so much help, and I am even more indebted to Josh Sadler and Steve Carr of Autofarm. They imparted a lot of the wisdom accumulated over years of involvement at Autofarm with 911s young and old, and even sold me what is now a Carrera RS . . . since then Autofarm, John Greasley and Bob Watson have helped keep this, the cover car, on the road and raise my enthusiasm for Porsche 911s to new heights. My only regret when driving a new one is that I cannot afford both!

One of the biggest challenges when compiling a book like this is finding illustrations that have not been published before. The hours, days and weeks that have gone into finding good new pictures of the Porsche 911 in all its forms were countless. It was a task that could never have been accomplished without the help of Porsche Cars, Great Britain, Paul Skilleter, Jeremy Coulter of *Classic Cars,* Ian Fraser of *CAR* magazine, Owen Barnes, Bob Young, Maurice Rowe of *Motor,* Warren Allport, formerly of *Autocar,* Maurice Selden, John Dunbar and Kathy Ager, then of London Art Technical, with special thanks to Vic Elford's son, Martin, of LAT, who printed many of the pictures. My thanks also to my wife, Mary, who shot and printed the Hilton Press Services pictures that I could not take myself, and to Mike Valente for taking the cover picture when he was with *Classic & Sportscar*.

My thanks also to Oxford Illustrated Press for having the courage to publish such a beautiful book initially when all around were saying: 'How can we cut costs?' Porsches have never compromised on quality. Neither have Oxford Illustrated Press . . . so it is good to see both the car and the book enjoying a strong future together.

Chris Harvey
Hethe,
December 1987

# Colour Plates

**Plate One** One of the first two-pedal Porsches, a 1968 911L Sportomatic.
**Plate Two** Jean-Pierre Hanrioud driving his 911S into thirteenth place in the 1967 Monte Carlo Rally.
**Plate Three** Classic of classics: the 1973 2.7-litre Carrera RS.
**Plate Four** Bjorn Waldegaard storming to fourth place in the 1978 East African Safari Rally with a special 911 SC-engined Carrera.
**Plate Five** Bjorn Waldegaard using all his skill to win the 1968 Swedish Rally in his 911T.
**Plate Six** A 935 driven at Le Mans by Jean-Louis Schlesser in 1979.
**Plate Seven** A 2.8-litre Porsche 935 shared by Bob Akin, Rob McFarlin and Roy Woods at Le Mans 1979.
**Plate Eight** The ultimate development of the 911 in the 1970s: The 930 3.3-litre Turbo during performance testing.
**Plate Nine** A popular modern road car: the 1976 Carrera 3.
**Plate Ten** The 911 Turbo—or 930—that caused a sensation when it was introduced in 1975.
**Plate Eleven** The most extraordinary of the early 935s, the special-bodied 'Moby Dick'.
**Plate Twelve** The focus of much attention at Le Mans in 1979: the 935 driven into second place by American film star Paul Newman with Rolf Stommelen and Dick Barbour.
**Plate Thirteen** Porsche perfectionism at its best: a view of the production line at the factory in 1968.
**Plate Fourteen** The 2.7-litre 911 that *Motor Sport* used for their road test in 1974.
**Plate Fifteen** First of the long-wheelbase 911s, a 1968 911E.
**Plate Sixteen** Bjorn Waldegaard driving his 2.7-litre Carrera in the European Rallycross championship at Lydden in 1974.
**Plate Seventeen** The popular Porsche Carrera RS on the 1977 Donegal Rally.
**Plate Eighteen** Manfred Schurti and Helmuth Koinigg driving a Turbo RSR into sixth place in the 1974 Nurburgring 750 kilometre race.
**Plate Nineteen** Porsche 911s have proved to be one of the most popular racing cars in America. Peter Gregg's early example is seen competing in the 1969 Watkins Glen Six-Hour race won by a Porsche 908.
**Plate Twenty** Josh Sadler competing at Silverstone in his 911.
**Plate Twenty-One** Three Porsche 911s lined up for a stage in the 1969 Tour de France.
**Plate Twenty-Two** What more impressive rear end to a car than that of a 930?
**Plate Twenty-Three** Supercar of the Seventies: the Porsche Carrera 3 Sport.
**Plate Twenty-Four** Hard to tell apart . . . a lightweight Carrera RS in the foreground and a touring model in the background.

**Plate Twenty-Five** One of Porsche's greatest . . . Jody Scheckter in a 3.0RSR at the Nurburgring in 1974.
**Plate Twenty-Six** Luxury racer . . . the Porsche 934.
**Plate Twenty-Seven** Ultimate 935 . . . John Fitzpatrick's spaceframe example at Brands Hatch in 1982.
**Plate Twenty-Eight** Ever popular and practical Porsche . . . the 911SC coupé.
**Plate Twenty-Nine** The open 911SC introduced a new dimension into modern Porsche motoring.
**Plate Thirty** One of the ultimate Porsche road cars . . . a 3.5-litre RSR.
**Plate Thirty-One** Ever popular open-air Porsche . . . the Targa in Carrera form.
**Plate Thirty-Two** Porsche still make great hill-climb cars.
**Plate Thirty-Three** The Group B Turbo provided superbly economical international racing for drivers like Claude Haldi, pictured at Le Mans in 1983.
**Plate Thirty-Four** Finland's Matti Alamaki piles on the 750 bhp of his 935-powered rallycross Porsche at Lydden in 1984.
**Plate Thirty-Five** Back in action . . . the historic ex-Elford and Faure 911S driven in the 1985 Coronation Rally at Eppynt by Pete Russell and Steve Foster.
**Plate Thirty-Six** The Carrera RS is still winning in the 1980s . . . with Tony Dron at the wheel in the Porsche Challenge.
**Plate Thirty-Seven** Typically close-packed action in the Porsche Challenge for production cars.
**Plate Thirty-Eight** Modified Porsches have a championship of their own in Britain
**Plate Thirty-Nine** Rally supercar . . . the 911SC/RS of Bernard Beguin in the 1985 Rally D'Antibes.
**Plate Forty** Exclusive Porsche . . . the Turbo SE.
**Plate Forty-One** Wild Porsche . . . the 959 stars in the North African desert.
**Plate Forty-Two** The Porsche 961 charges on at Le Mans in 1987.
**Plate Forty-Three** Economy Porsche . . . Dage Sport's Turbo SE lookalike.
**Plate Forty-Four** Practical and economical powerplant . . . the 1987 Carrera.
**Plate Forty-Five** The 1987 Carrera Sport interior.
**Plate Forty-Six** Benign Porsche . . . the 1987 Carrera Sport.
**Plate Forty-Seven** Porsche's greatest road car? The 959

# The Car for all Seasons

There's nothing quite like a Porsche 911. Every one of the 250,000 made is a car with an extraordinary character. You either love it or hate it. There's no emotional compromise with a Porsche 911. The early ones understeered, oversteered, cost a fortune in fuel, started and stopped like nothing else on earth, cornered well and spun even better. The later ones are softer, more frugal and forgiving, reaching their climax in the 959 which holds the road fabulously well on its way to a maximum speed of nearly 200 mph. But old or new, the front seats of a 911 are superb, the luggage space is restricted and the back seats a challenge even for a contortionist. There are dozens of optional extras to confuse the customer and, no matter what anybody says, the engine is in the wrong place.

What makes a Porsche 911 so attractive and why has it such a fanatical following? First, it has incredibly sensitive handling. With the combined weight of the engine and transmission concentrated at the back, the rear end typically swings round very fast when cornering, particularly on the very early cars, which had narrow tyres and little grip. This characteristic can be used to advantage by a very good driver, but it is a deadly seductress for one who isn't. A touch too much, or too little, on the accelerator and the ordinary driver could be out of control, especially in the wet. The only safe way for him to drive a 911 is slow into a corner and fast out. Fast in and fast out needs the touch of a master.

Mind you, it is getting easier to drive a 911. Modern rubber gives them far more grip and more than 20 years' development has minimised the tail-happy characteristics. But the bite is still there, especially in the heavy and powerful Turbo. The one 911 that goes beyond these barriers is the extraordinary 959, featuring a four-wheel-drive system with adjustable dispensation of power and torque for the ultimate security on any surface. This is the car that points the way ahead for at least another decade of 911 development.

Meanwhile the average 911 is still a throwback to the days when rally drivers used the tail-happy handling to great effect, swinging their cars round endless hairpins, and driving with a combination of superb throttle control and extremely sensitive steering. The steering on a 911 is light and precise, partly due to so much weight being concentrated at the back. Drop the clutch at exactly the right number of revs and the 911 takes off like a rocket. Too few or too many revs and it's a waste of time. The engine either stutters as though it is going to stall or the tyres spin madly with the car hardly moving.

One of the star attractions of the Frankfurt Motor Show in September 1963 was a brand new primrose yellow Porsche—the 901 which was to become the 911.

Many of the 911's best qualities—such as traction, ease of control and precise steering—have been developed on roads like this in the Monte Carlo Rally.

A famous picture that sums up everything about the 911 series in competition: the day that Herbert Muller and Gijs van Lennep won the world's last great open road race, the Targa Florio in 1973 with a Carrera RSR.

With the older 911s on their narrow wheels and tall tyres, spinning was a matter of course when taking off fast. Now you can stall the car, too, such is the grip of its wide wheels and low-profile rubber. It's things like this that make a 911 so sensuous. Get it right and every moment is supremely satisfying; get it wrong and it's frustrating. If you're the sort of person who is willing to keep trying until you get it right every time then you're the sort who loves a Porsche 911. But if you want a car that will do it all for you with hardly any contribution from yourself, then it wouldn't suit you at all. Some people spend a lifetime trying to get it right, and some just give up and buy a different car. The only 911 which makes a move towards doing it all for you is the 959, and that goes so fast that the driver really is a vital accessory . . .

The second reason for the Porsche 911's continued popularity is that the performance is phenomenal. Even the most mundane 911 goes like a bat out of hell, with the faster examples showing that they have already reached the physical limits that lesser cars will never achieve. This performance has become ever more manageable over the years. The first Porsche 911s introduced in 1964 had high-revving engines with relatively little pulling power, or torque, low down in their range. This was especially noticeable with the high-performance S model introduced in 1967. The engine's capacity was gradually increased to make it more flexible and the performance went up with it until the 911 hit a high spot with the Carrera RS launched in 1972. This has remained a classic, possibly the best 911 ever if nimble high performance is the absolute standard.

After that, the performance of many rivals deteriorated in the face of power-sapping exhaust emission regulations, although the Porsche 911 held its ground with ever larger engines, and ultimately, turbocharging to counter other 'safety' laws which made it heavier. The fabulous Turbo, the first version of which was introduced in 1975, is typical of Porsche. The German firm intended only to produce a small number to qualify the model for sports car racing, but the customers liked it so much that it has stayed in production every since—despite Porsche having introduced new front-engined, water-cooled cars, such as the 928, when it seemed that ever more stern laws covering exhaust notes would kill the 911. Like the Carrera RS of 1973, the Turbo really is a racing car for the road.

The third reason is that the quality of a Porsche 911 is incredible. The factory is a perfectionist's paradise with the firm's pride in its product showing in every nook and cranny of a 911. Like the performance, it's a quality that started off good, but with no regulations to sap it, has got better and better. The early cars—in common with the majority of their rivals—suffered badly from corrosion after six or seven years. Gradually,

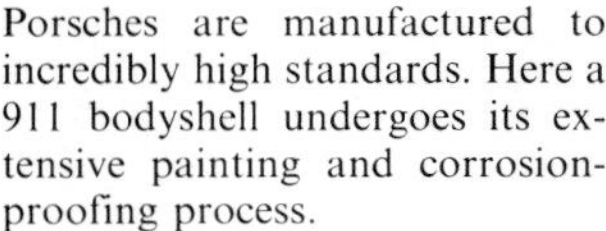

Porsches are manufactured to incredibly high standards. Here a 911 bodyshell undergoes its extensive painting and corrosion-proofing process.

undersealing was improved to combat this, then the very metal from which the cars were made was changed until ultimately, in 1975, the entire body was made from galvanised steel to make the 911 far more resistant to the normal ravishes of salt-laden roads—so much so that Porsche now guarantees the metal against perforation for 10 years. The same standards have always been applied to the mechanical side, with the result that 911s are renowned for covering huge mileages with few replacement parts being needed. Such is the quality of a Porsche.

The development of the 911, from the prototype called the 901 in 1963, into the 1980s has been a constant search for perfection: a triumph of engineering over outdated basic design. How did the 911's engine get in the wrong place? It all goes back to the rear-engined Volkswagen designed by the first Professor Ferdinand Porsche in the 1930s. It was relatively low-powered as contemporary standards of roadholding were not very good, but its advantages outweighed its disadvantages: the traction could be very useful on poor roads and on the steep hills of Professor Porsche's native Austria. By using a flat, horizontally-opposed, cylinder formation, the car's centre of gravity was kept low and air cooling saved an awful lot of complication. When the first car to bear his name was designed by his son, Dr (later Prof) Ferdinand Porsche in 1947, bits and pieces of old Volkswagens were all that was available to the Porsche family, who had by then decided to make a living by building their own cars rather than just designing them for other people. The first Porsche had a Volkswagen engine turned around to sit in the middle of the car. This was because it was designed for competition and a mid-engined configuration gave the best weight distribution, making it therefore in theory, the ideal position. The second Porsche, which was called the Type 356 after its design office number, had a rear-mounted engine like a Volkswagen, because it was designed for touring. Its handling was inferior because most of its weight was in the back, but Porsche considered that the extra room liberated for its occupants was more important. The engine stayed at the back of the touring Porsches until the introduction of new models from 1969. Porches that have been designed purely for competition, notably the 904, 906, 907, 908, 909, 910, 917, 936, 956 and 962, have used the mid-engined configuration.

Porsche first tried changing the basic lay-out of their touring cars by putting the engine in the middle with the 914 in 1969, and by putting it in the front with the 924 in 1975, the 928 in 1977 and the 944 in 1982, but still the customers clamour for 911s, so the traditional touring Porsche—which like all Porsches up to the 924 has also been used with great success in competition—stays in production with the factory saying that they will carry on with it while there is still a demand for at least 2,500 a year. With sales steady at between 10,000 and 13,000 a year that looks like being a long time. In these circumstances, Porsche's development engineers have looked upon the car's lay-out as a challenge to be overcome rather than an impossible problem. There can be no better proof of their ability than the way in which they have taken the ill-handling pre-war design and turned it into one of the world's greatest sports cars.

The ultimate development of the 911 theme was 'Moby Dick', a turbocharged type 935 pictured at Le Mans in 1978 with its close relation, the type 936 sports racing car.

The demands of American crash regulations killed some sports cars and caused the design of many to be dramatically altered: but not the 911, the definitive shape of which has survived even the advent of reinforced bumpers. The car pictured here is a 911 SC.

The first 911s were nervous cars that often had to have lead ingots bolted in their front bumpers to help balance the weight of the engine at the back. Their tyres were too narrow to stop the tail swinging out at the slightest provocation, but their 4.5-inch treads were the widest that the tyre manufacturers would recommend at the time for 15-inch diameter wheels, which were necessary to give the car a good ride. The first 911s had a bodyshell of immense strength that was made from steel rather than alloy to save money in what would, inevitably, be an expensive car. Sadly, it suffered terribly from rust after a few years, but this was eventually minimised with the galvanised 911s.

Each year, the engineers whittled away at the weight at the back of the 911 and transferred what they could to the front. But their first really significant change was when they lengthened the wheelbase late in 1968 to improve weight distribution. With the longer wheelbase and improved tyre technology allowing the use of wider treads, the 911's handling has been steadily improved ever since. It hit a high spot with the Carrera RS in 1972—the first Porsche road car to have wider wheels at the back than the front, and a rear spoiler to increase downforce. Since then it has been a case of conserving—and improving—the 911's best points within an increasingly more luxurious package. Porsche 911s started to become more luxurious in the 1970s because their prices had been forced up, which pushed them into a different market; the original, stark, sports car had to become more comfortable. At the same time, advances in the world of electronics and

Porsche showed the way the 911 would develop with a Studie model four-wheel-drive turbo-charged cabriolet at the Frankfurt Show in 1981.

lubrication made the later 911s far more economical to run.

As this process was starting, Porsche tended to concentrate on racing their mid-engined machines for maximum publicity and development experience. Engines and transmissions aside, these cars bore little resemblance to contemporary versions of the 911. As a result, initially the competition activities of the 911 were confined chiefly to rallying and races for Grand Touring cars, rather than the glamorous top-line track events. However, a change in top management led to Porsche concentrating on the 911 in competition rather than on the fantastically expensive 917 prototype sports cars. So relatively late in its life, the 911—which had been conceived as a potential competition car and now has proved to be one of the most versatile—became a really formidable competitor in top-line racing. Various aspects of the 917's development, such as turbocharging, ventilated brakes and advanced aerodynamics, were adapted to the basic 911, with the result that in its most extreme form, as the 935, it became one of the most successful endurance racing cars ever built!

Then just when it looked as though the 911 might be replaced by the new front-engined production cars, another change of management—inspired by its creator, 'Ferry' Porsche—led to its revival in first, completely open form

The 959 took four years to develop from its Turbo base but became the world's greatest sports car in 1987.

to complement the existing Targa variant with a roll hoop, and then into the most exciting version ever, the fantastic 959, already hailed as the best sports car in the world.

The way Porsche's corporate mind is working . . . the 964 model that will be launched during the 1989 model year will be called the Carrera 4 and feature a 963-inspired four-wheel-drive system as an additional model to the existing range.

# The Early 911s

It all started so simply: there was only one Porsche 911 from which to choose. It was based on the 901 prototype, which had been designed on principles laid down by—then Dr, now Professor—Ferry Porsche, son of the firm's founder. He had been closely involved with the development of the Type 356, which had established Porsche's name among the top flight of sports cars. The body was, in turn, designed by Ferry's son, also called Ferdinand, but known to everybody as 'Butzi' Porsche. One of Ferry Porsche's standpoints was that the new Porsche must be about the same size as the existing Type 356. It must also be a two-plus-two and as Porsche had made their name with rear-engined air-cooled cars, that's how the new 901 turned out. Ferry Porsche allowed a longer wheelbase—87 inches—than that of the Type 356 because it would make the car more comfortable in terms of ride and interior accommodation, without increasing its outward size much. Butzi Porsche was so successful at carving away the 356's bulbous curves to form the definitive 911 shape that the result was 2.4 inches narrower and only 6 inches longer. This stretching and squeezing was aimed at enlarging the interior space without increasing wind resistance. A true measure of Butzi's success can be seen from the length of time the 911 shape has been in production.

The 901 had a wheelbase of 7 ft 3.05 ins, length of 13 ft 7.9 ins and width of 5 ft 3.4 ins. Everything about the 911-to-be was aimed at saving space. Torsion bar suspension was retained all round and the engine was still hung at the back with its tall cooling fan behind the rear axle so that the car could have vestigial rear seats. Putting the engine as far away from the car's occupants as possible also had the beneficial effect of isolating them better from the noise: an important factor with an alloy engine that has no water jackets to absorb some of the sound.

The front suspension was carefully designed so that it did not encroach too much on the front luggage boot space. This had to be big enough to carry a set of golf clubs (chiefly to please American customers), yet small enough not to cause too much wind resistance. In ultimate competition form, the car's relatively large frontal area (17.9 sq ft), which was partly increased by wide wheels, was to prove something of a handicap.

The rear torsion bars ran across the frame in a tube with wheel location by trailing arms to avoid using space that could be devoted to the rear seats. Additional wheel location was provided by a bracket mounted low down. A contributory factor that influenced the design of the rear suspension was that the tubular shock absorbers fitted could be mounted behind the wheel centre

One of the first 911s imported into Britain was the Porsche distributor's demonstration model, registered GVB 911D, which was to become a famous car in its own right, seeing action not only on the road but on racetracks and in off-road events. It also holds fond memories for the author as the first 911 he drove.

for greater travel, and hence, more effective control. MacPherson struts, incorporating the shock absorbers and lower wishbones, operating on torsion bars running parallel with the frame were used at the front. An anti-roll bar was fitted at the front only to counteract the natural tendency for a rear-engined car to oversteer. Ferry Porsche insisted that the steering had to be rack-and-pinion like the best of their contemporaries. As a result, the pinion was mounted in the middle of the rack with two universal joints in the steering column. This meant that cars could be built in left-hand and right-hand form with the minimum of alteration. This lay-out also had a tremendous advantage from the safety angle. The steering column would simply fold up in the event of a frontal impact, rather than spear the driver like some cars with solid columns.

The braking system was carried over from the established Type 356 Porsches: it used Ate discs all round, 9.25 inches in diameter at the front and 9.57 inches at the back, which incorporated two built-in drums for an efficient handbrake. Cars with rear disc brakes have long suffered from illegally-weak handbrakes when deprived of the binding effect of drums for a mechanical linkage. Cast iron calipers with two pistons and quick-change pads on a single-circuit hydraulic system were used for the foot brakes to save the cost of alloy fittings when the potential price of the 901 in production began to worry Ferry Porsche. For the same reason, steel road wheels were retained, of 15 inches diameter and 4.5 inches width.

Butzi Porsche's flowing lines, engineered by Erwin Komenda, fitted around this package very well. The body/chassis unit was of thoroughly modern conception: an integral structure based on Porsche's time-honoured platform chassis. Steel was used throughout to make production easier and to ensure the rigidity which is essential for good roadholding with modern suspension systems. The sheer strength of this most basic of the car's structures, which depended on the floor and sill members, was such that it was possible to reduce accident repair costs by fitting bolt-on front wings. It also meant that an open top version could be made later with the minimum of alteration to increase the 901/911's potential market. Measurements of 4 ft 5.3 ins and 4 ft 4 ins were used for the front and rear track within the overall width of 5 ft 3 ins and maximum height of 4 ft 4 in—just about as small as you could make a two-plus-two grand tourer!

More power was needed to keep the 901 ahead of the rapidly-developing saloon cars such as Jaguars and Mercedes than could be extracted from the existing flat four-cylinder engine in the Type 356, so Porsche's designers started work on another. Their existing racing units were too complicated to use in a volume-production GT, so they decided to simplify one of the best—the flat eight used in the 1962 Formula One car. Two cylinders were deleted to save weight and reduce rear-end overhang, while still ensuring smoother running than that which could have been obtained with another flat four. The horizontally-opposed cylinder lay-out had to be retained for reasons of space and to keep the car's centre of gravity as low as possible. This entailed the use of forced-feed lubrication because of oil surge problems

The interior of an early 911 showing its wood-rimmed steering wheel.

A typical example of Porsche attention to detail: the protective flap fitted to the filler cap orifice.

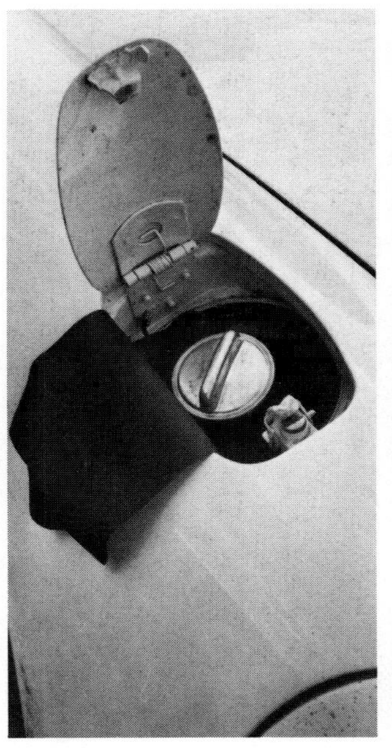

The trunk of a 911, shown complete with comprehensive toolkit, can hold a surprisingly large amount of luggage despite the car's low frontal area.

inherent with such shallow-sump configurations. On a vertically-mounted engine the oil rests at the bottom and can be stopped from slopping around too much: this is much more difficult when the engine is effectively laid on its side. Hence the use of dry-sump lubrication such as that on racing cars.

This kind of sophistication added to production costs, so it was decided to use single overhead chain-driven camshafts as the best compromise in terms of cost, noise, power, and future development potential. Twin overhead cams were too expensive and alternative systems of driving the cams—such as gears, shafts, or belts—were either too noisy or had not proven themselves sufficiently. A 2-litre capacity was selected to produce enough performance with economy, although provision was made at the design stage for the engine to be stretched to ever-increasing capacities later in its life.

Aluminium was used wherever possible in the engine's construction (except for the cylinder walls themselves, which were of cast iron to save wear), so that the critical overhanging weight could be kept down and the operating heat dispersed more easily. The aluminium crankcase was split along the seven-bearing crankshaft's centre line. Bolts held it together with long studs to the individual cylinder heads. Three-bearing camshaft boxes containing the valve gear were bolted to the cylinder heads. The exhaust valves were sodium-filled for better cooling with conventional lock nuts and screws for adjustment carried on the rockers. The connecting rods were made from steel and the pistons were cast in alloy. The fully-balanced forged crankshaft had a pinion at the back between the seventh and eighth bearing to drive a shaft which operated the camshaft chains, oil pressure and scavenge pumps. The oil extracted from the crankcase passed through a radiator in the engine-cooling fan's blast on the way to a catch tank located in the right-hand rear wing housing. This fan, driven by a belt off the back of the crankshaft was an alloy axial device that did many things. The air it sucked in was ducted through a one-piece moulding that covered the top of the cylinders and heads. Some of this air was diverted to heat exchangers surrounding the exhaust manifolds. It then passed on through flap valves into the atmosphere or into silencers in the sills before reaching the cockpit to provide heating. The flap valves were operated by the driver, but he or she couldn't control the temperature of the engine (which was dependent on driving conditions so the flaps needed a lot of attention to adjust the amount of air that entered the car). To add to the fan's responsibilities, an alternator was incorporated in its hub: waste not, want not!

By 1968 and the introduction of the B series cars, the 911's interior showed signs of constant development.

The air extraction vents above the rear window of a 1968 911E.

Ventilation was aided by opening rear window quarter lights.

Interior ventilation was through a grille at the base of the windscreen and via vents above the dashboard with extraction by slots above the rear window, or by simply opening the rear side window. A gasoline-fired heater was also available that switched on automatically when the cockpit temperature dropped to an uncomfortable level. This was mounted next to the 16.4-gallon tank in the boot.

The 1991 cc engine (with bore and stroke of 80 mm x 66 mm and 9 : 1 compression ratio), developed 130 bhp (DIN) at 6100 rpm and 128 lb/ft of torque at 4200—pretty peaky. A rev-limiter set at 7100 was contained in the distributor of the single-plug ignition system. Initially, two triple-choke 40 PI Solex carburettors were used with a Bendix electric fuel pump scavenged by twin mechanical pumps driven off the back off the left-hand camshaft.

A five-speed gearbox had to be used because of the high state of tune of the engine. This took the form of a transaxle with one aluminium casing housing an 8.5-inch diameter Fichtel & Sachs single disc diaphragm clutch, differential and main gear clusters. A front cover contained the first and reverse gears, a speedometer drive and the front of the gear change mechanism. Gear ratios could be varied at will, although changing second gear meant replacing the input shaft as well. Initially, the 901/911 was fitted with 3.09, 1.89, 1.32, direct and 0.76 : 1 ratios with a 4.43 spiral bevel crownwheel and pinion. Porsche split-ring synchromesh was fitted and the drive shafts had Hooke joints at the wheel ends with similar joints allowing axial movement as well at the differential end. The gear lever worked through a conventional H pattern with first and reverse on a plane to the left of the H.

The interior was typically Porsche with excellent individual front seats which folded back so that they could be used for a rather cramped sleeping

Profile of a 1969 911T showing its standard steel wheels.

Head-on view of the 1969 911S.

The interior of the 911T was not so plush as that of the more expensive models and was correspondingly lighter.

Door trim of the 911T.

position. The back rests of the tiny rear seats folded forward to provide additional luggage space. Originally it had been intended to provide an opening rear window to give easier access to the luggage area, but Reutters, who were making the body, said that it would be impossible to seal it properly. Hindsight has proved them wrong.

There was a full set of instruments with a rev counter dominating the display. Four other gauges recorded speed, oil pressure and temperature (with 130 degrees C as the critical mark) and quantities of fuel and oil. The oil level could be checked on the gauge after half a minute's idling when the engine was fully warmed up as there was no dipstick. A wood-rimmed steering wheel completed the rather stark interior.

Series production started in September 1964 alongside the existing Type 356C. Almost as soon as production started, Porsche changed the model's designation to 911 following complaints from Peugeot, who had registered type numbers with a zero in the middle as a trade mark in France. Racing Porsches, such as the 904 built at the same time as the 911 retained their middle zero because Peugeot did not have any competition cars. The Type 356C was discontinued in March 1965 and replaced in the next month by the Porsche 912, which amounted to a Porsche 911 with the early car's 1600SC four-cylinder engine. This was replaced in 1969 by the 914, a mid-engined Porsche made in collaboration with Volkswagen that was a long way from the 911 concept, making a brief re-appearance in 1976 as the 912E (which was a basic 911 with a four-cylinder Volkswagen-based engine). These cars were intended as cheaper versions of the 911 and were simply not in the same class, so they are not included in this book.

When production of the Type 356C ended, Porsche were left without a convertible, so Butzi Porsche designed the optional Targa top for the 911, which was introduced in September 1965. This distinctive body style, which was inspired by the 'Surrey' split hard top on the English Triumph TR sports car, had a massive permanent hoop forming shoulders the shape of the car's roofline. A metal panel above the front seats could be detached and, initially, a plastic rear window behind the hoop could be unzipped. Alternatively, it could be left in place to prevent chilling draughts swirling around the occupants' necks. It was a typically well-engineered Porsche compromise to provide the attractions of a convertible without risking sacrificing the rigidity of the coupé's body structure. Like the steering column, the hoop had an added attraction from the safety angle, providing protection for the occupants in the event of the car being overturned. Nevertheless, some potential customers considered that the car was not a proper convertible because of the hoop and Porsche sought to make a virtue out of its necessity by giving it a polished stainless steel finish as a total contrast to the body colours.

The engine was heavier than expected, at 406 lb complete with clutch, and the resulting extra weight at the back (58 per cent of a 19.5 cwt dry weight total), gave Porsche many problems. Naturally the cars tended to oversteer dramatically, especially when going through bends at high speeds when the narrow tyres lost adhesion. To counteract this, the Porsche engineers built as much understeer into the suspension as was possible without making the car too difficult to drive at low speeds when the rear tyres were gripping. In addition, some cars suffered badly from throttle steer in corners, and then there were quite different handling characteristics for left-hand or right-hand bends. This was because they were built to series production line tolerances rather than to the degree of accuracy achieved by the highly-skilled technicians making prototypes. Porsche had to resort to bolting cast-iron ingots into the ends of the front bumper on more difficult cars to balance some of the rearward weight. These 'reinforced' front bumpers had the added advantage of cutting down on the tendency of the lightly-laden front wheels to aquaplane on heavy surface water. But such backyard techniques did not fit in with Porsche's engineering ideals, and a new solution was devised as soon as possible.

The Solex carburettors gave problems, too, for despite having been designed for the engine, no amount of adjustment and development would rid them of a flat spot between 2500 rpm and 3000 rpm. In February 1966 they were replaced by two triple-choke Weber 40 IDA carburettors, which cured the problem with no loss of power, but cost more. The engine also became a good deal more flexible although a new set of gear ratios had already been fitted to improve tractability right up to the new 6800 rev limit.

Once these problems were solved, Porsche concentrated on extracting more power from the engine so that they could offer a wider range of models. Racing versions of the engine were producing a reliable 210 bhp at 8000 rpm, so Porsche felt justified in offering a slightly-detuned version. The compression ratio on this engine was raised from that of the standard engine to 9.8 : 1 by the use of higher-crown forged pistons (fitted with nitrided connecting rods), new camshafts which gave a much-increased valve overlap, bigger valves and ports, and slightly-modified Weber 40 IDS carburettors and a freer-flowing exhaust. This was the engine that produced 160 bhp (DIN) at 6600 rpm (with a new maximum of 7300), that was to power the 911S model introduced in July 1966. Torque was still on the low side at 133 lb/ft at 4200 rpm. The engine could be readily identified by an air duct shrouding made from red plastic rather than the black of the standard 911. The most powerful engine in the 911 range has been identified in this way ever since.

To cope with the extra performance, the suspension was revised with a larger—15 mm rather than 13 mm—front anti-roll bar and a new one (16 mm in diameter), at the back, with Koni adjustable shock absorbers all

Electronic ignition was fitted from the B series cars.

Neat and tidy stowage for the spare wheel, jack, battery and windscreen washer reservoir.

round. Ventilated brake discs were fitted with new alloy wheels of distinctive 'five-spoke' appearance to improve cooling. The new wheels also improved roadholding by reducing unsprung weight and because of their new 5-inch tread width. All models received constant velocity joints in their drive shafts at the same time.

These were the O-series models, taking their designation from the initial use of the O type number. In August 1967, a new range was introduced for the 1968 model year, bearing A-series chassis numbers with the German coachbuilder Karmann building some of the coupé bodies, such was the demand. This line was headed by the 911S with a more luxurious version of the standard 911 being introduced as the 911L (for Lux), and supported by a lower-powered and more spartan (and therefore lighter) version using what amounted to the cheaper 912's trim, but with the 911's running gear, called the 911T (for Touring). The 911T also had cast iron cylinders to save money, which were acceptable because of the lower stresses involved. This engine also had a cheaper crankshaft without counterweights, and had cast iron rather than steel rockers. These cheaper rockers proved extremely successful and were adopted throughout the range a few months later. The 911T's compression ratio was lowered to 8.6 : 1 and milder camshafts used, but the expensive Weber carburettors were retained to qualify it for competition. In this form it was rated at 110 bhp. Straight-line performance was not much reduced because of the car's lighter overall weight. Solid brake discs, steel wheels, a lighter front anti-roll bar, and a four-speed gearbox from the 912 with ratios of 3.09, 1.63, 1.04 and 0.79 helped to keep the price down. Porsche were anxious to keep the power outputs at intervals consistent with their differing price bands, so the 911L stayed at 130 bhp and the 911S at 160. All models were available in coupé or Targa form. Dual circuit braking was fitted to meet American safety regulations as were recessed door handles with push button catches and front seat belt anchorage points. Quartz halogen fog lights improved forward vision and new windscreen wiper arms which were placed in front of the driver were finished in matt black to prevent distracting reflections from chrome.

Porsche also produced a limited number of competition models based on the 911T but fitted with the 911S engine and transmission for maximum performance with minimum weight in 'standard' classes. They also produced 20 911R competition models with the 210/220 bhp power unit from the mid-engined 904 GTS model, glass fibre doors, lids, front wings and bumpers, and Perspex side and rear windows. Six-inch and 7-inch alloy wheels were fitted from the 904 GTS. Other items, such as the oil tank—which was located in front of the right rear wheel—were moved around for better weight distribution. These were also fitted with the four-cam 906 sports racing engine. To add to the confusion, the basic two-cam 911L and 911T could also be ordered with 911S options and could have other parts swopped about generally; the 911T, for instance, was frequently fitted with the five-speed gearbox.

This vast range of permutations on the 911 theme was increased by the option of semi-automatic, or Sportomatic, transmission on the 911T, 911L and 911S. Gear selection was simple with this system. It had a conventional synchromesh gearbox in series with a torque converter and a normal clutch operated by a vacuum-controlled lever. The lever was worked, in turn, by a switch at the bottom of the gearlever. This meant that as soon as the driver moved the lever, the clutch was disengaged. In practice, the system was so sensitive that it only needed a touch to trigger it off, so it was essential to keep hands and knees well clear of the gearlever until it was actually necessary to change. The resultant action was, however, smoother than most people could manage with a manual transmission providing the linkage was adjusted perfectly.

The gearlever was marked L, D, $D_3$ and $D_4$ in a conventional H pattern with R for reverse back on the left and P for Park in front of it. The factory advised using D for a normal standing start and then changing up through the gears; but if you felt lazy you could take off in any of the higher gears. Alternatively, if you were feeling full of fun, you could blast off in L—which was officially only for 'ascending or descending steep grades, or for driving on sand or ice'—and whistle through the gears with the traditional Porsche slicing motion. Remember though to let go of the gearlever with each change, otherwise you may have nothing more than a box full of neutrals.

Performance was affected only by the initial delay in taking off due to the torque converter having to build up pressure. Fuel consumption was a little heavier because of the power losses inherent with such a device. This transmission was an immediate success with the people who bought 911Ts and 911Ls in America, but it never really found favour with 911S owners, who preferred the competition-style clutch and manual gearbox. Generally, European buyers were less affectionate towards the Sportomatic option, delighting in the use of Porsche's well-synchronised manual box on all models.

Very few 911Ss from this series found their way to America as their exhaust systems did not meet the new environmental regulations introduced in 1968. As a result, only the 911T and 911L were exported to America at that time. The 911S also suffered from spark plug fouling unless it was driven hard all the time, and this was only improved when Bosch developed a new plug for it. The 911Ts and 911Ls imported by the Americans from this series also had a tendency to backfire on deceleration and generally make strange noises from the exhaust pipe. This was because they used an air injection system to meet the Federal emission laws. They were fitted with a pump which fed air at low pressure into the exhaust manifolds and thus reduced the carbon dioxide content of the exhaust gases. The backfiring and funny noises were a result of this system.

On the credit side, handling was improved by the substitution of 5.5-inch rims for the old 4.5-inch rims with the same 165 HR 15 tyres. Great efforts were made also to improve quality control on bodyline assembly following numerous complaints of excessive wind noise, and from the front edges of the doors in particular.

Dramatic improvements were made in the B-series cars introduced for the 1969 model year. Mechanical fuel injection was fitted to the top two models to increase power by 10 per cent and help meet US exhaust regulations without all the popping and banging. As a result the 911L's designation was changed to 911E—for Einspritzung, or fuel injection. These models also received electronic ignition systems and an oil cooler in the left-hand front wing when viewed from the front.

The wheelbase was extended 2.24 inches by the simple expedient of increasing the length of the trailing arms and moving the wheels back while leaving the engine and transmission in their original place. The drive shafts, which had already been running at a slight angle in the Sportomatic models, accepted this distortion readily when they were fitted with larger constant velocity joints. Magnesium was used in place of aluminium for the engine casing (saving 22 lb), and twin six-volt batteries replaced the single twelve-volt battery in the nose for better weight distribution. As a result, it was changed to 43 per cent front, 57 per cent rear, according to factory figures. The wheel rim widths were increased to 6 inches and lower profile 185/70 VR 15 tyres were fitted to 911E and 911S models to improve handling. Fourteen-inch alloy wheels were listed for customers more interested in comfort than ultimate performance. They were fitted as standard on American 911E and 911S models and on European 911E Sportomatics with the new 15-inch wheels and 185/70 tyres as an option. These 15-inch wheels and tyres were fitted as standard on European 911E manual cars and 911Ss, with the 14-inch wheels as an option. The 14-inch wheels could also be fitted to the 911T, which otherwise had 15-inch x 5.5-inch steel wheels with 165HR tyres as standard or the 15-inch alloy wheels and 185/70 VR tyres as an option.

An optional 'comfort' package became available for the 911T, giving it, in effect, a 911E or 911S interior and fittings, plus Boge self-levelling hydro-pneumatic front struts and ventilated discs with alloy calipers. These struts replaced the front springs, shock absorbers and anti-roll bar. When a lot of weight was put in the front boot, for instance, the nose would go down and rise to the right height again within a mile, as various valves and passages within the struts re-arranged the fluid with a pumping motion. These struts were fitted as standard on the 911E and very early 911S B-series cars. The aluminium calipers had to be used with them on the 911T because they were specially designed to operate in conjunction with the struts. In practice, these

Power unit of the early Porsche 911S.

Boge units were not so successful for handling as the earlier system and they wore out relatively quickly, so all 911s went back to torsion bars, conventional shock absorbers and an anti-roll bar after three years. The Boge struts remained as an option on the 911S until then, however.

The steering rack was given a slightly lower ratio to help dampen road shocks, but the overall steering ratio felt much the same because of the adoption of a smaller, leather-covered steering wheel like that fitted to 911S models.

Larger brake calipers were fitted to reduce pad wear with aluminium as standard on the 911S, no matter what struts were fitted, and thicker ventilated brake discs were used on both the 911S and 911E. These increased the front track by 0.4 inches and the wheelarches were flared slightly to cover the tyres which were of flatter tread profile. One-piece front wishbones were substituted at the same time.

The heating and ventilation was improved by fitting a three-speed fan and the Targa top was also revised to improve comfort. It was fitted with a wrap-round glass window instead of the plastic panel which had proved difficult to zip up and often leaked. Air extraction slots were let into the rollover hoop to assist ventilation. All cars received electrically-heated rear windows, quartz halogen headlights and hazard warning lights with a more powerful alternator to help the batteries cope with the extra demands.

A hand throttle was fitted between the front seats to make starting easier and numerous small changes were made to the trim, aimed at improving comfort and safety. These included moving the fusebox from the interior to the front luggage boot, fitting recessed inside door catches, a dipping mirror, thicker carpets and a new oil pressure-cum-oil level indicator.

Further dramatic, but not so extensive changes, were afoot for the C series introduced for the 1970 model year. The engine's cylinders were bored out from 80 mm to 84 mm to give a capacity of 2195 cc. As a result, torque was improved to 131 lb/ft (DIN) on the 911T, 141 on the 911E and 147 on the 911S, at 4200, 4500 and 5200 rpm respectively. Power was raised to 125, 155 and 180 bhp at 5800, 6200 and 6500 rpm. Besides a capacity increase, different camshafts were fitted to each engine although they now all shared the same big-valve heads, which had their plug inserts cut directly into the aluminium rather than using Helicoil inserts. Triple-choke Solex carburettors were phased in to replace the expensive Webers on the 911T. To cope with the extra power and torque, an 8.86-inch clutch was fitted and at the same time the gearbox was redesigned. In addition the transaxle casings were cast in magnesium to save the weight which had been marginally increased by the bigger engine. The 911T also received the same ventilated brake discs as the top models because of its increased performance, although iron, rather than alloy, calipers were used to cut costs. On the 911E and the 911S, the engine lid and rear panels were made from aluminium rather than steel to reduce overhanging weight. All models were offered with a ZF limited slip differential of either 40 per cent or 80 per cent slip factor as an optional extra which could improve roadholding and traction.

Also, the front suspension's top anchorage points were moved forward on all cars to make the steering lighter and reduce feedback to the steering wheel. Significantly, the chassis was give a coating of Tectyl oil-based anti-corrosion fluid which was far more effective than that used before. The interior was remodelled yet again with repositioned indicator and wiper levers that could be operated without taking a hand off the steering wheel. The screen wipers received a 'pause' facility and the heated rear window two settings for mist or for ice. Rear window wipers were fitted as optional extras to many cars, and the Targa models received a lighter and easier to stow and unfurl roof. In addition a lightweight version of the 911S was homologated for competition to replace the 911R. These cars were known as 911 STs. The standard 2.2-litre capacity was particularly beneficial in this respect because it allowed the engine to be bored out to the limit for the 2.5-litre competition classes without rendering the 911 ineligible.

Few alterations were made for the D series cars built for the 1971 model year, other than building much of the bodyshell from galvanised steel to combat corrosion, along with detailed changes to the fuel injection and ignition to meet ever more restrictive exhaust emission regulations in America.

# The Perfectionist Porsches

The introduction of the E-series cars for 1972 represented a pinnacle in Porsche's ambitious drive to improve the 911 regardless of cost. The modifications carried out to the cars were also significant in that they were aimed far more at improving the car for road use than for competition. The Porsches made between 1972 and 1974 were real road burners that recognised for the first time that competition cars now belonged to a world apart, although ironically the most extreme version of these cars, the Carrera RS was also one of the marque's most formidable competition machines.

The new 2.4-litre engines represented a complete change in 911 philosophy. A bigger capacity was needed to combat the power-sapping effects of U.S. emission regulations, so the stroke was increased from 66 mm to 70.4 mm. This object had been achieved on earlier 2.4-litre 911 racing engines by increasing the bore, a solution more compatible with high revs. By increasing the stroke instead, Porsche also created an engine that had a lot more torque rather than substantially more power at the top end of its range. This made the car easier to drive in the heavier traffic that was fouling up America and Europe. Porsche also re-designed the cylinder heads so that their revised engines could be run with relatively low compression ratios in anticipation of the subsequent reduction in the quality of fuel offered by the petrol companies. Fuel consumption suffered, but at least the cost of the petrol used by the new engines was lower. From that day in September 1971 when the new 2.4-litre 911s first appeared, filling station attendants have never ceased to be amazed at these Porsche drivers' insistence on filling up their cars with two-star petrol!

The new compression ratios ranged from 7.5:1 for the 911T to 8:1 for the 911E and 8.5:1 for the 911S. Solex 40 TIN carburettors were retained on the least powerful U.S. model, which was re-christened the 911TV, whereas other 911Ts bound for America were fitted with fuel injection and called 911TEs. Outputs worked out like this:

Bhp 911TV; 130 (DIN); 911TE 140; 911E 165; 911S 190, produced at 5600, 5600, 6200 and 6500 rpm: torque 911TV 145 (DIN); 911TE 145; 911E 152; 911S 159 at 4000, 4000, 4500 and 5200 rpm.

The extra power and torque put an additional strain on the transmission, so the transaxle was redesigned at great expense (despite the fact that it had just been reworked in magnesium). It was an era of 911 development regardless of cost. The new, stronger, transmission that had a three-piece rather than a barrel-type housing, was most easily distinguished

The E series Porsche 911, typified by the 911E pictured here, was developed almost regardless of cost.

The British versions of the 911E were normally fitted with numerous options such as the rear windscreen wiper shown here.

from inside the car by an about-change in the gearshift pattern. The new casing was designed for either four or five forward speeds. On the five-speed version, top gear was now forward and to the right of the old H-pattern. This pleased the speed-limited American market, whose customers had complained that they spent more time in the bottom three ratios than the top three, so it would be better if first and second gears were in a direct plane, leaving their rarely-used fifth speed out on a limb. Gear ratios were also lowered a little at the same time to promote greater flexibility at the expense of all-out speed. Lower gear ratios and lower compression ratios inevitably meant higher fuel consumption, so a new 22.4-gallon tank (with a space-saving deflated spare tyre in a well moulded into the tank) was introduced as an option that would enable the 911 to maintain its old range of around 300 miles between filling stations.

The eternal quest for perfection by the Porsche development engineers was never more evident than in the re-location of the oil tank ahead of the right rear wheel in the manner of the 911R with an elaborate alloy oil cooler in the left-hand front wing, as viewed from the front. The object was the same—to improve the weight distribution—but the cost on such relatively small production run cars was high: the E-series bodies had to have a separate lid on the rear wing to give access to the tank. The rear seats were also moved back a few millimetres at great cost. Another visible alteration on the E-series 911s was an aerodynamic front lip, which was standard on the 911S, and optional on other models. The idea behind this was to keep the 911's nose down without increasing drag so that a tendency to aquaplane over heavy surface water could be combatted without slowing down the car.

The cost of these modifications was high, so the 911E's running gear and trim were downgraded to 911T standards, with the old 911S items (such as full instrumentation, alloy wheels and so on) offered as options at an extra cost. New options included the Boge struts on all models with a reversion to torsion bars and conventional dampers as standard. The hydro-pneumatic struts had shown themselves to be fast-wearing and expensive to replace.

These were the heaviest 911s yet. They weighed an average of 21 cwt because of a general strengthening to take the extra power and meet American safety regulations. Their bigger engines also made them the fastest production 911s so far but they were soon to be put in the shade by the car which many enthusiasts consider to be the ultimate 911—the 2.7-litre Carrera RS introduced in October 1972. The engine was of the same stroke as the 2.4-litre, 70.4 mm, but had a larger bore, up from 84 mm to 90 mm. This gave a capacity of 2687 cc and was the largest bore yet seen in a 911 engine, short-stroke 2.5-litre racing units included. Experience with these engines had shown that they could not be bored out beyond 87.5 mm without inviting trouble from the reduction in thickness of the Biral cylinder insert material. Therefore an expensive, but hard-wearing, process developed on

Detail view of the optional rear wiper on a 911T with washer nozzle to the left.

The Targa-topped version of the F series 911T.

The removable Targa top could be stored either in the trunk or, if that was filled with luggage, on one of the rear seats.

the 917 racing car was used. This was a nickel-silicon carbide plating for the aluminium cylinders that needed to be only a fraction of a millimetre thick, enabling the bore to be increased beyond the limits imposed by the thick Biral inserts within the restriction of the existing cylinder studs. The Nikasil plating also reduced friction, enabling the engine to produce more power. Otherwise the Carrera engine was similar to that of the 1972 911S, producing 210 bhp (DIN)—20 bhp more—with 188 lb/ft of torque. A five-speed transaxle with oil pump was fitted as standard, with an extra strong clutch spring and a gearlever with a shorter movement.

The extra power and torque would not have been enough to give the Carrera RS a dramatically better performance than the 911S had it not been for drastic weight-saving exercises and better wheels and tyres.

Everything reasonable was done to lighten the car. Thinner than standard sheet steel was used for the body with glass fibre on unstressed parts such as the rear lid, and the bumpers of competition versions. Special thin

Interior of the F series 911T.

The F series Carrera RS showing its front and rear spoilers.

glass was used and the interior was spartan to put it mildly. There was no sound damping, carpets or back seats. The door opening mechanism was replaced by a cord and catch and the luxurious front seats were replaced with lightweight ones. Numerous small fittings, such as the front lid counterbalancing springs, were deleted and a great deal of weight was saved by using normal paint on the underside rather than Porsche's usual underseal. All told the car weighed not much more than 19 cwt. At the same time, touring versions were offered with the standard 911S interior, including electrically-operated windows.

Lightweight Bilstein shock absorbers were fitted, with stiffer anti-roll bars, 18 mm at the front and 19 mm at the back instead of 15 mm all round with wider, 7-inch rear wheels instead of 6-inch ones. Low-profile Pirelli CN36 radials were fitted, 185/70 at the front and 215/60 at the back. The rear suspension pivot mounts were also changed to accommodate the movement of the wider tyres. The result was the fastest-cornering 911 yet, a figure of 0.912 g having been recorded. The Carrera RS could be easily identified by the bulging wheel arches needed to clear its wider rear track (4 ft 6.9 ins) and the 'ducktail' rear spoiler, which worked in conjunction with a revised version of the 911S-style front lip.

The spoiler performed a similar function to that of the lip, which incorporated a number plate housing, reducing lift dramatically at the back and cutting drag a little at the same time.

There was a notable absence of badges and unnecessarily heavy ornamentation on the car, although the Porsche design department excelled with flamboyantly-painted Carrera signs and stripes along the lower edges of the body. It was about this time that many teams racing 911s started to adopt the most lurid colour schemes to distinguish their cars from those of their rivals because there were so many 911s on the tracks at that time.

Powerhouse of the 2.7-litre Carrera.

Much to Porsche's surprise, these cars sold so well that they were able to produce a second series for 1973. Originally, it had been intended to make only 500 to qualify the 911 for international Group 4 special GT racing, but the second run of 500 promptly qualified it for the less-competitive Group 3 category. No sooner was that run completed than Porsche found themselves in a quandary. They had produced only 1,000 sets of special panels—and other items such as an alloy front crossmember—plus a few spares. But still the demand for the Carrera RS continued. Few customers, however, wanted the basic lightweight edition, the vast majority ordering their cars with RS Touring options. At first it had been possible to fit this luxury option after the car was assembled, but now it was obviously far more economical to produce the Carrera RS with the 911S interior from the start, and simply strip it out and replace it with lightweight parts for the odd customer who wanted that specification. The wisdom of this plan was emphasised by the fact that the Carrera RS could not be sold in their biggest market, the United States, which had to be content with the 911S. So after most of the lightweight parts had been used up on a further 36 cars, Porsche switched Carrera RS production to a basic 911S shell, complete with its heavier steel panels and front crossmember. These cars, which went on to chassis number 1590, were known internally as the 911SC for 911S-Carrera, and were fitted with full Carrera RS running gear and badges.

Initially it had been possible to register these F series cars, along with other series production 911s, individually through the local Stuttgart taxation office. The sharp-looking edge of the spoiler would have given problems over legality had the car been presented in the normal way to Germany's national road licensing authorities. However, the Stuttgart office could pass only 1,000 such vehicles, and when Carrera RS production was in its later stages, many cars were produced without the spoiler, only to have them fitted as an accessory later by their owners!

On the more conventional side, the F series cars produced for the 1973 model year had their oil tanks back in the old position! Apparently, some petrol filling station attendants had mistaken the flap for a petrol (or water!) filler, and, in any case, Porsche engineers had started worrying that it might not meet looming American side-impact regulations. The rear seats remained in their new position, however, which meant that some of the cost of the tooling involved in this sheet metal change could be regained over the life of future models. Moving the oil tank backwards and forwards was a complete waste of money, however, although it was made larger on the second time round, and fabricated from stainless steel. This meant that the F series cars' service interval could be extended from 6,000 to 12,000 miles and potential problems caused by internal corrosion of the oil tank reduced. Similar criticism of the short life of the exhaust system was countered by making it from stainless steel so that it was not subject to so much corrosion. In addition, the sills were made from Thyssen zinc-coated steel, which was much more resistant to corrosion than the material used earlier.

Softer Boge dampers were fitted all round with revised mounting points at the rear to make the car's ride more comfortable, with anti-roll bars being retained only on the 911S as standard.

The trim was changed on the F series cars, too. It was made from flame-resistant materials to satisfy new American safety regulations, and several chrome parts were replaced with more fashionable matt black decorations, made from plastic, which was lighter and cheaper in any case. The 911S front lip was fitted as standard on the 911E because that model was almost as quick, and American-specification 911s had rubber bumper guards to meet crash regulations. Air conditioning was offered as an option and the heating and ventilation system further improved.

There was good news for British, Australian and Japanese customers: the Targa option became available with right-hand drive for the first time with the F series. The 911E was fitted with aluminium wheels of a new star pattern with 6-inch rims as standard. These replaced the Mahle magnesium wheels and were also fitted to the 911T when ordered as an option to the standard steel wheels. Part of the way through the 1973 model year, the 911Ts bound for America were fitted with K-Jetronic fuel injection, which cost less and was better suited to increasingly more stringent emission laws. This meant fitting milder cams to the 911TE, with the resultant loss of power being compensated for completely by raising the compression ratio to 8:1. The only difference in performance was that peak power was now developed at 5700 rpm and torque was up 3 lb/ft.

Even as these standard production Porsches were being watered down by American regulations, the hot ones were being made even hotter. The 911 RSR introduced for the 1973 competition season amounted to a 2.8-litre production racing car (see chapter six), with its ultimate development, the 3.0-litre Martini-backed 911 RSRs raced by the works that year. This engine was to be the forerunner of the latter-day 911s, excellent cars but not such classics as the E and F series 911s, because they had to cater for so many compromises.

# The 911 Grows Up

The G-series Porsches for the 1974 model year were the cars that many people were convinced could never be produced. Not only did they look very much like the previous 911s, but they met the drastic new American crash regulations! Porsche bumpers had always been on the flimsy side, and because they were built into the front and back of the 911, it was difficult to see how they could be made to withstand a 5 mph impact without the lighting and other legal necessities being damaged (which is exactly what the new concrete block and pendulum-reinforced safety regulations demanded).

Most other sports car manufacturers produced such weird and wonderful devices to withstand such impacts, that they ruined the appearance of their cars, and in at least one case knocked the bottom out of the performance and upset the handling. That the Porsche 911 continued with hardly an outward change was a tribute to the styling department and engineeers responsible for the new bumpers. And they did it so simply. They just redesigned the bumpers along their old lines in aluminium to absorb the impacts and mounted them on alloy shafts running into the already very strong hull. Hydraulic dampers to return the bumpers to their original positions were available as an option that was soon to become mandatory in America. These were the first of the Porsche dodgem cars!

Meanwhile the Carrera RS's 2.7-litre engine capacity had shown itself to be such a success that it was adopted for all G series cars, except the RSR covered in chapter six. The 911T was dropped from the range with the cheapest model now being known as just the 911, the middle model becoming the 911S and the top performer the Carrera (without the RS for *Rennsport* tag—circuit racing—as it was now purely a road car). In 911 form, the engine produced 150 bhp (DIN) at 5700 rpm, with 174 lb/ft (DIN) torque at 3800 rpm from an 8:1 compression ratio, with 175 bhp at 5800 rpm and 175 lb/ft at 4000 rpm for the 911S, and the existing 210 bhp for the Carrera. All engines were now fitted with the K-Jetronic continuous fuel injection except that of the Carrera, the radical valve timing of which dictated the continued use of the old purely mechanical fuel injection. For this reason, all American G series Carreras were fitted with the 911S engine to meet emission regulations. A cheaper steel hoop also replaced the alloy oil cooler. This Carrera also became the first to be offered with the option of a Targa top.

The top now became available in two forms, the standard one with a single plastic panel (which proved difficult to seal at first), and the second, at extra cost, in the old metal folding format. There was no alternative but to

The G series 911, fitted with optional alloy wheels, showing its new bumpers to good advantage.

use the folding top when the 911 was fitted with optional air conditioning because the extra equipment was mounted under the front lid where the Targa top panel was normally stored when not in use.

Electric windows were standard on the Carrera, and optional on the 911 and 911S. The rear spoiler was no longer available on German Carreras, but could be ordered as an option on 911s bound for other markets. It was replaced later in the G series by a rubber-edged rear spoiler which was matched with a rubber-edged front lip.

Considerable changes were made to the interior, partly to meet new American safety regulations. Cheaper, but more comfortable, 'tombstone' high-backed front seats with fixed headrests replaced the old ones which had adjustable headrests. A special steering wheel became available for tall drivers who had complained that there was not enough room for their legs, and the steering wheel was redesigned in anticipation of possible American air-bag restraint regulations. Black fittings continued to replace brightwork in the interior, although chrome was still available on the exterior as an option. All sorts of minor pieces of trim were uprated, and electric windows were standardised on the Carrera.

All cars were fitted with a 21.1-gallon fuel tank to maintain their range and a single 12-volt battery replaced the twin 6-volts in the nose now that

The interior of the G series 911 was redesigned to meet American safety regulations.

The high-backed seats of the G series 911 offered more support without seriously restricting visibility.

The rear seating of the G series 911 remained as restricted as ever.

problems of balance had been largely overcome. A gigantic 2.25-gallon screen wash reservoir was also fitted in the nose.

More rigid alloy rear suspension arms were adopted with larger rear wheel bearings to cope with the extra power and torque from the 2.7-litre engine. Anti-roll bars, which had modified mountings, were available in a variety of diameters to suit owners' tastes in ride and roadholding.

The five-speed transmission was fitted as standard on European Carreras and as an option on the 911 and 911S. American Carreras had the four-speed transmission as standard with the fifth gear as an option and the Sportomatic gearbox was offered on all models. Its gearlever was made less sensitive to accidental bumping and a new, lighter-to-operate, clutch linkage was fitted to all models except the powerful European Carrera. The brake pedal on all models was lengthened from 9.1 inches to 9.8 inches to give more leverage. Cast iron calipers were fitted to the 911 and 911S to cut costs.

Despite the complexity of these changes, the inherent good design of the Porsche 911 shell and brilliant development engineering were emphasised by a rise of only 10 lb in overall weight for these bigger-engined cars. But such development is only possible at great expense, so the cost of a 911 was already hitting new heights, having moved from a middle-priced sports car into the same league as the exotics.

As such, the Porsche's competition consisted chiefly of larger-capacity cars that were starting to suffer from the economies of a fuel-starved world.

The engine room of the 2.7-litre 911.

The 911SC in coupé and Targa-topped form.

Interior of the 911SC.

The space-saving spare wheel as fitted to a 911SC.

Therefore, there seemed to be little future in increasing the 911's engine capacity substantially, but it was evident that more power would have to be extracted if this Porsche was to remain competitive—and as it was still selling well by comparison with other exotics, this would have to be done by methods other than boring, stroking and redesigning an engine that already gave problems with weight behind the rear wheels. Turbocharging was the obvious answer.

The works therefore ran the turbocharged Carrera RSRs (see chapter six) in international racing in 1974 as a test bed for their dramatic new H series turbocharged 911 introduced for the 1975 model year. This was to be what amounted to a Carrera RSR 3.0-litre with a turbocharging system which had been under development on Porsche's 917 racing cars since 1969. The changes were so extensive that this new model was designated the 930, but as it was still a 911 at heart and as Porsche continued to call it simply the Turbo it is part of this book.

The main problem with the KKK turbocharger installation was typical of all such devices: when the throttle was closed, there were no exhaust gases to keep the turbocharger spinning and it quickly dropped from its 80,000–100,000 rpm.

When the throttle was opened again it naturally took a little time to get back to full operational speed. This delay could prove embarrassing, particularly when a lot of torque was needed when leaving a bend.

The 3-litre engine was chosen for the new Turbo for this reason. It had been completely reworked to give a 95 mm bore for the Carrera RSR 3.0 with a capacity of 2994 cc. It had been necessary to use aluminium, rather than the lighter magnesium of the 1970s, for additional strength. This was eminently suitable for a turbocharged engine producing far more power and torque, and running hotter than the existing 2.7-litre.

Much of the frustration was taken out of the turbo-lag by a fitting called a 'wastegate' which had been developed on the 917 and the turbocharged Carrera RSR. This controlled the inlet pressure by means of a flap valve—or wastegate—thus allowing the turbocharger to regain speed much more quickly than had it been subject to inlet pressure while idling. The turbocharger boosted the intake at a maximum of 11.5 psi. The engine had been modified by fitting new four-bearing camshafts with a 6.5:1 compression ratio to enable it to work well with the existing K-Jetronic fuel injection and turbocharger. But because it had a theoretical maximum

The ultimate road-going Porsche 911, the Turbo or Type 930.

compression ratio of 11.7:1, it was necessary to use 97-octane fuel. Useful power could be felt upwards of 1500 rpm instead of most of the power cutting in with a bang in the manner of racing turbocharged units more concerned with ultimate power at the top end of their range. It was felt that sudden surges of power and torque should be avoided for relatively inexperienced drivers with such a fast car. In this guise, the European Turbo's engine developed 260 bhp (DIN) at 5500 rpm with 253 lb/ft of torque at 4000 rpm just before the wastegate opened. American Turbos had to have a thermal reactor in their exhaust system to reduce emission, and as a result produced only 245 bhp at the same revs. A major drawback to the fitting of a thermal reactor was that the additional plumbing needed meant that the engine had to be removed to change a sparking plug. Even though removing the engine on a 911 is a relatively quick job, it meant that the car had to be taken into a garage for such a minor repair.

The cross-drilled brakes developed from the type 917 racing car and fitted to the late Turbo.

A new transaxle with only four speeds was developed to take the extra power and torque of the Turbo because the engine was so flexible. It was possible to fit a heavier-duty 9.5-inch clutch because this transmission was so much stronger. The rear suspension was also strengthened to take the extra power and torque by fitting larger cast aluminium trailing arms and bigger wheel bearings. It was also intended to uprate the braking system by fitting 917-style ventilated and cross-drilled 12-inch discs, but production difficulties delayed the introduction of the cross-drilling. One of the chief problems was the cross-drilled discs tended to crack easily. Nevertheless, the front suspension was modified to give some anti-drive characteristics in view of the intended extra braking power.

Apart from that, the Turbo was substantially the same as the Carrera RSR it was intended to help qualify for Appendix J racing. It had a recessed 'picnic table' spoiler needed to qualify the larger profile of the racing RSR for competition and extra wide wheel arches would allow the fitting of really wide wheels for track use. It was not possible to fit the same wheels for use on the road as there would have been a likelihood of aquaplaning in wet weather on everyday tyres. As a result the widest possible wheels for safe road use were 7 inches at the front and 8 inches at the back. To enable these wheels to fill the arches, the hubs were fitted with spacers. Had it not been necessary to use such wide wheel arches for the purpose of homologating the Turbo in GT racing, a more conservative track could have been used with the result that the road-going cars would not have had such a high drag factor and would have been capable of an even higher maximum speed. Dunlop 185/70 and 215/60 tyres were fitted on 15-inch wheels at first for the American market, so that the car rode at the correct height for their bumper regulations. Lower-profile Pirelli P7s (of 205/50 and 225/50 section) were fitted in Europe where there were no such bumper height restrictions. The Pirelli tyres offered greater grip, and with them the Turbo became the fastest-cornering production Porsche to date. These tyres gripped the road so well, however, that it was difficult to spin the rear wheels, so that the acceleration times up to 60 mph were not so fast as the narrower-wheeled Carrera. The turbo-lag emphasised this.

With such mechanical sophistication, the Turbo was much more expensive than a normal 911, so it was decided to give it top-quality interior fittings as well. These included air conditioning and a much-improved heating system operated by a thermostat control in the car's interior. This enabled the driver to dial his desired level of cooling or warmth between zero and ten. The thermostat worked with twin sensors inside the car which made constant adjustments to the outlet valves. Its task was made easier because the turbocharger kept the heat exchangers at a more constant temperature than on the normal 911. Leather was used extensively in the Turbo's interior with deep pile carpets and heavy soundproofing. Because the turbocharger's turbine absorbed a lot of the exhaust noise, this model became by far the quietest and most civilised 911 yet. High-pressure spray nozzles were fitted to the front bumper to clean the headlights while the car was in motion, and a rear window wiper was fitted as standard. The only item obviously missing from the Turbo was a pressure boost gauge.

Porsche were of the opinion that having just spent a great deal of money on turbo-power, the new owner would not be impressed to see how little boost was needed for much of the car's normal running time!

The Turbo, at around 25 cwt, was a lot heavier than the earlier 911s, which explained why the lightweight Carrera was virtually as fast despite having a smaller, normally-aspirated engine. It must be admitted, however, that it only achieved this speed with a great deal more drama.

As Porsches moved into the top price bracket, most of the other changes in the H series cars were aimed at improving comfort. The heating system was revised and third and fourth gears on the 911S four-speed box, and fourth and fifth gears on the five-speed box were raised slightly for a more relaxed performance. Sound insulation was improved and alloy wheels were fitted to all cars for the first time. Californian Porsches had to have different emission equipment, which reduced power a little more than on the other American Porsches (known as 'forty-nine state cars'). These cars all had an engine whose output was rated at 165 bhp at 5800 rpm with 166 lb/ft of torque at 4000. The basic 911 was no longer marketed in America.

The Sportomatic transmission was modified to take advantage of the better torque band of the European engines. It meant that one of the ratios could be abandoned and the remaining gears strengthened to cope with the increased torque. The new shift pattern had first and second gears in line with top to the right and forward. Reverse and park were on the left.

All Carreras were given the Turbo-style 'picnic table' rear spoiler and the front lip lost its rubber. The operation of the standard heating system was

The 3.3-litre Turbo engine and its installation.

improved and the automatic heating control was offered as an option. The Turbo's headlight-cleaning system was also made an option on the rest of the range, as was the electrically-operated sunroof which had been available before only on the top models. The alternator was uprated to 980 watts to help it cope with the extra demands which included those of a fan in the heating system.

The I series cars introduced for 1976 were especially significant in that they featured total galvanisation of the steel used in the bodyshell. Now that everything structural was made of galvanised steel of varying thicknesses, Porsche were able to give a six-year guarantee against underbody corrosion: a historic achievement unmatched by any rival at the time. The steel cost slightly more and there were problems with zinc fumes given off during welding, but the result was a considerable boost to marketing as the cars now enjoyed either a far higher resale value or simply lasted longer for those who wanted to hold on to them. Sound-proofing was further improved at the same time as these major changes in the body's construction.

The existing 911S was dropped for 1976 with the 911 remaining as the basic model. Its 2.7-litre engine was uprated to 165 bhp at 5800 rpm and 174 lb/ft of torque at 4000 rpm with an improved oil pump. Costs were kept down by using a cheaper cylinder-coating process known as Alusil in preference to Nikasil, which was retained for the Carrera and Turbo. A supplementary air slide was fitted to improve hot starting. The Carrera became the middle model with an 8.5:1 compression ratio version of the Turbo's 3-litre engine. It was fitted with the normal K-Jetronic fuel injection so the valve gear and timing had to be modified to suit its characteristics. In this form, the engine produced 200 bhp at 6000 rpm with 188 lb/ft of torque at 4200 rpm. This tamer version of the Carrera was called the Carrera 3 in Europe and the 911S in America, where the Turbo became known as the Turbo Carrera or simply 930. The 911S (née Carrera) was offered with the options of Turbo wheels, tyres and bodywork.

The Turbo was fitted with a by-pass valve to prevent sudden build-ups of pressure and the boost raised at the same time to 14.5 psi. The pressure now built up from 2500 rpm rather than 3000 rpm and the car became much easier to drive on a slippery road.

All Turbos were fitted with an electrically-operated and heated exterior driving mirror and their automatic temperature control listed as an option on the cheaper models. The 911 received revised cast iron front brake calipers to take the same size pads as the Turbo. The extra weight was negated by lighter tyres which had now become available. In addition, all models were now fitted with a new cooling fan which had five blades rather than eleven. This meant that it could be driven at a higher speed and the internal alternator's output boosted as a result.

Cars bound for America could also be ordered with a Tempostat cruise control which would keep the car going at any chosen speed until it was cancelled either manually or by accelerating and braking. It could be reset instantly to its original reading by a lever. This device was controlled by pulses from an electronic speedometer and proved popular for long, boring, motorway journeys at the 55 mph blanket speed limit.

Lots of small improvements were made to the J series for 1977 with one major change in options—a 'Comfort' pack for the American 911S, which was also available on the 911 and Carrera 3 in Europe. This comprised softer Bilstein shock absorbers, 14-inch Fuchs alloy wheels with Uniroyal Rallye 240 tyres (that had been used on the short-lived 912E in 1976), electric windows and an automatic speed control. This Tempostat speed control was not available as part of the European Comfort package. These options smoothed out the ride of the 911, but imposed a speed limitation of 130 mph because of the tyres. This meant that cars with this package of options had a speed limiter in the distributor and markings on the speedometer at 130 mph. They were inclined to wallow more than the stiffer-sprung, larger-tyred 911s and showed a tendency to oversteer like the earlier cars.

The gearbox on all manual cars was modified to accommodate twin baulking segments in the first and second ratios with revised first-gear cogs to ease engagement from neutral. The Turbo gearbox's synchromesh was improved.

All I series 911s without automatic temperature control were fitted with improved heater controls. Eye-level ventilation, and better thief-proofing locks and knobs made their appearance on all models and Targas lost their quarter lights, which were not now deemed necessary for ventilation when the top was fitted.

The range was extended to five models for Europe: the 911 in its basic form with 165 bhp, available only on special order in Britain; the 911 Lux with 165 bhp and more luxurious fittings; the Carrera 3 with 200 bhp, Koni dampers and wider wheels, arches and tyres; the Carrera 3 Sport, which had Bilstein shock absorbers, and Pirelli P7s with wide rims, arches and spoilers, and special seats; and the Turbo.

'Nuff said . . .

Left-hand-drive versions of the 911S with Sportomatic transmission were fitted with a brake servo. Porsche purists were very much against brake servos because they said that the over-light devices normally fitted to American cars took away any feel there was in the brakes. They appreciated the sensitive feel of a 911's brakes and did not want them 'ruined' by a servo for the softies. However, the Porsche factory considered that the sort of people who bought Sportomatic 911s would appreciate some assistance with the brakes when they were cold or operating at low speeds, when heavy pressures were needed. Commendably, their servo was as good as the rest of the car, providing relatively unobtrusive assistance.

This servo was also fitted to left-hand-drive Turbos. The pressure needed to depress the clutch pedal was lightened to match, by fitting an over-centre auxiliary spring in the release mechanism. Larger wheels were fitted, of 16 inches diameter like those first used on the racing 934. An advantage was that they allowed more rubber to be put on the road with better control through stiffer sidewalls. Pirelli P7 tyres of 205/55 section front and 225/50 rear were fitted as standard.

The Turbo's three-piece front anti-roll bar was replaced with the one-piece 20 mm fitting from the other 911s and the rear trailing arms made in two pieces with an eccentric screw adjustment to make it easier to raise or lower the ride height.

The interior was improved by fitting a new console with provision for cassette tapes and separate fresh-air and blower controls with centre outlets for fresh air.

Major changes were made to the range for the K series in 1978 when a new basic model, the 911SC, was introduced to replace the normally-aspirated cars. The 911SC was really a Carrera 3 with its engine slightly detuned by fitting softer camshafts, which had the advantage of giving it more torque. In this form, it produced 180 bhp at 5500 rpm with 195 lb/ft of torque at 4200 rpm in European form and 166 bhp with 170 lb/ft at the same revs in American tune using an 8.5:1 compression ratio. Part of the reason for the reduction in power was because of the substitution of contactless capacity-discharge ignition to reduce maintenance and the fitting of an air pump to reduce pollution.

The five-speed gearbox was fitted as standard to achieve maximum performance and the brake servo was fitted to all models. A special clutch-disc hub was incorporated in the transmission to eliminate the 911's characteristic gear chatter at low revs, and the eleven-blade fan was re-introduced to cut the noise level.

At last the Turbo was given the 917-style cross-drilled brakes, the cracking problems having been solved, and four-piston calipers. The engine was uprated to 3299 cc by increasing the bore and stroke to 97 mm x 74.4 mm, now that the brakes could cope. It had 300 bhp at 5500 rpm (265 bhp at the same revs in American form) and 303 lb/ft of torque at 4000 rpm (290 in America). This was achieved with a 7:1 compression ratio and a new, larger bearing crankshaft, that was also fitted to the 911SC. An intercooler was fitted to the Turbo's intake system to improve the turbocharger's efficiency and the entire engine moved back 30 mm to allow space for the new clutch-disc that its transmission shared with the 911SC. The 3.3-litre 930 became more tail-heavy as a a result and the tyre pressures had to be increased from 34 psi to 43 psi to cater for this. At the same time, the rear spoiler was redesigned. The pressure plate and clutch housing were revised in cast iron to cope with the extra torque and the 911SC was also listed with Turbo running gear as an option.

Few changes were made to the 911SC for the 1980 model year other than ignition modifications that raised power to 188 bhp for cars sold outside the United States, with American versions on 180 bhp. The European modifications also allowed the compression ratio to be lowered from 9.3:1 to 8.6:1. and raised the maximum torque to 195 lb/ft at 4,300 rpm. The Sportomatic transmission was abandoned through lack of demand in the United States, the country for which it had been intended. In these forms, the 911 series and its variants were given new chassis numbers, reverting to the A series, with designations starting 91 (followed by A and the individual number) for the 911SC and 93 for the Turbo. The Turbo had to be withdrawn from sale in the United States at the end of 1979, however, because of ever-tightening sound and emission regulations although it continued to be sold in Canada.

# The Latter-Day 911s

The Porsche 911 and its turbocharged variants looked like being phased out in favour of the water-cooled cars in the early 1980s. A new Porsche-engined 944 was close to introduction to supplement the Audi-engined 924 and the 928 flagship. The main problem with the relatively low-priced 924 was that it cost a lot to produce at the Audi works. Porsche managing director Professor Ernst Fuhrmann had reasoned that if he could liberate enough capacity at Porsche's Zuffenhausen factory, he could produce the 944—which shared components with the 928 and could replace the 924—much more economically. The only way in which he could find room was to cut back on the 911. The 911, however, was still selling well at 11000 units per year, so the company's main shareholders, the Porsche and Piech families, were reluctant to kill it. A compromise was reached when Fuhrmann retired early and his replacement, Peter Schutz—who had a good knowledge of the vital American market—followed Ferry Porsche's incentive and launched a new programme to develop the 911.

Initially, these developments were confined to extracting yet more power from the normally-aspirated 911SC's engine for markets other than the emission-restricted North America and Japan. This meant fitting new pistons to raise the compression ratio to 9.8:1, which, with further revisions to the ignition and K-Jetronic fuel injection settings, produced 204 bhp slightly higher up the rev range at 5900 rpm, 195 lb/ft of torque still being available at 4300 rpm. These changes meant, however, that four-star petrol was needed again, rather than the two-star diet introduced on the 2.4-litre models. Earlier practice was followed by replacing the oil cooling serpentine in the front wing with a radiator that was fitted at the same time to the Turbo. The performance of North American and Japanese versions of the 911SC was also improved by raising the compression ratio to 9.3:1 in company with appropriate modifications to the ignition and injection settings. In this form, the engines produced 172 bhp at 5500 rpm with 175 lb/ft of torque at 4,200 rpm.

They retained the same transmission, but in the considerably more-powerful European editions, the fifth gear ratio was raised from 0.821:1 to 0.786:1 to improve economy. Coil springs were adopted in the clutch disc hub of all versions of the 911SC, however, to dampen gear chatter at low engine speeds. Rubber damping still proved adeqate on the Turbo, however, because its hub was bigger. In addition, the Turbo was fitted with a new twin-pipe exhaust system to reduce noise by 2.5 per cent at no cost to the

Hood up and hood down, the 1981 Porsche Turbo Cabriolet Studie.

power output. The 911SC rear suspension was also made a little stiffer by using 24 mm, rather than 23 mm, diameter torsion bars. Apart from new interior materials, black window frames, a new central console and 15-inch diameter steering wheel, the only visual changes to the new B series cars for the 1981 model year were repeater lights on the sides of the front wings for the indicators needed to meet new legislation in most markets.

In Germany in particular, special bodywork conversions on cars like

Porsches were becoming very popular. So from the autumn of 1981 the Zuffenhausen restoration department decided to do some of their own for the odd customer who could afford it. The obvious line to adopt was that of the 935 competition cars, in which the front wing profile followed that of the bonnet. The Porsche restoration shop started by taking brand new Turbos, stripping off the wings, and fitting new ones. These had the 'flat nose' profile at the front with 928-style pop-up headlamps and a line of seven louvres behind them. Side skirts were then fitted to match new rear wings with massive air intakes ahead of the rear wheel arches. A new front spoiler with built-in fog lights and central wire mesh grille completed the effect. The coachwork was then hand-finished to a very high standard—for what would be a very high price—and the engine uprated with a larger turbocharger, higher-lift cams, and modified exhaust to give it 330 bhp with similar torque to the standard 930. Production of this Porsche 911 Turbo Special Equipment model would, necessarily, be very limited.

Minor changes only were made for the C series in the 1982 model year. The alternator was uprated from 980 watts to 1,150 in keeping with the extra electrical equipment—such as hi-fi stereo—likely to be fitted to cars of the 1980s. Cosmetic changes were confined to black wheel centres with polished silver rims and new interior materials, including special leathers. The Sport option now listed a deeper-section high-downforce Turbo-style front air dam and larger rear wing, with forged alloy wheels carrying low profile tyres. This

The renaissance of the 911 began in 1981 with the uprated 204-bhp SC, pictured on the left alongside the beefy Turbo.

The Targa-topped 911SC continued to be a good seller in 1981, especially in North America, where it matched the sales of coupés.

The 911SC cabriolet, introduced at the Geneva Show in 1982, was an immediate success as the first completely open Porsche since the 356 series ended in 1965.

option also had far better gripping sports seats. The six-year corrosion warranty was also extended now to seven years.

The long-awaited 911 Cabriolet—first seen as a 'Studie' prototype with four-wheel-drive at the Frankfurt Show in 1981—was introduced six months later at the Geneva Show in March 1982. In essence it was a Targa with the roll hoop removed, the floorpan having been strengthened to make up for any loss of rigidity. The folding fabric roof was not power-operated, but based on the Volkswagen Golf convertible's cantilever mechanism. This was exceptionally easy to use and ensured a good weatherproof fit. The plastic rear window could be unzipped—officially so that it should not be damaged when the hood was stowed—but effectively to improve through-flow ventilation. Frameless side windows dropped down flush to the door tops, but the hood had to stay above the waistline when lowered because there was insufficient room inside the rear body panels. The angle of the rear seat squabs also had to be raised a little to make room for the hood. A neat cover could be clipped over the furled top. Fixed quarter lights deflected air passing around the windscreen, and the automatic heater control was replaced with a manual version that worked better with the hood down. Otherwise the Cabriolet's specification was the same as that of the normal 911SC.

During the year the 911SC's distinctive sound was muffled a little more by a new primary silencer—chiefly to meet tougher Swiss noise regulations—and the heater system's override lever was deleted.

Provision was made for rear seat belts and four radio/stereo speakers were adopted was standard.

Faster versions of the normally-aspirated 911 and the 928 were about to be launched, so the Turbo's performance was improved for the 1983 D series model year by raising the torque from 303 lb/ft at 4000 rpm to 318. This was achieved chiefly by re-routing the wastegate's 'dump pipe' past the silencer so that it ejected straight into the atmosphere. Modifications also had to be made to the ignition and fuel injection settings, the warm-up regulator and distributor were changed, and a new fuel distributor was fitted with a capsule valve for better full-throttle response.

Durability was improved by fitting force-fed timing chain tensioners. The earlier tensioners relied on their own oil-damping reservoirs that typically needed replacing every 40,000 miles when the seals leaked.

The Turbo's interior heating and ventilation was also improved by fitting two extra fans to force air into the footwells.

The full fruits of Ferry Porsche's decision to continue 911 development then became apparent when the new E series Carrera was introduced in September 1983. The most obvious change was in the engine, which was uprated to 231 bhp with its capacity increased to 3164 cc. This was achieved by using the Turbo's 74.4 mm throw crankshaft with the 911SC's 95 mm bore cylinders. Porsche resisted the temptation to increase the volume to that

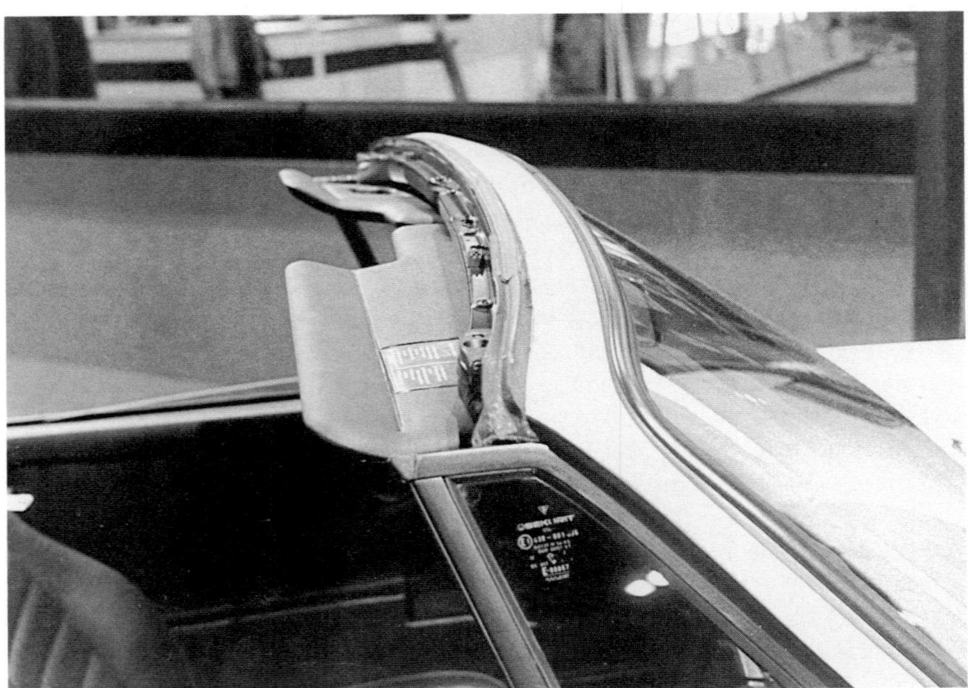

The 911SC Cabriolet featured neat high-backed seats to meet whiplash regulations and a tonneau cover for the hood when it was furled. When raised the hood slotted into a top rail on the windscreen.

of the Turbo because the 3.2-litre's torque—209 lb/ft at 4800 rpm in European form—was at the limit of the 911 series transmission's range. But naturally, there was more than that to the changes . . .

Porsche were determined that the fuel consumption should not suffer and adopted a new Bosch DME (Digital Motor Electronics) management system. This combined a computerised ignition control with LE Jetronic injection. The system was programmed to cut off fuel supplies as soon as pressure was released on the accelerator at more than 1080 rpm. A similar cut-off also regulated maximum revs to 6520 per minute. Numerous other microcomputer programmes—contained in a control box under the driver's seat—kept the engine working to optimum efficiency. The result was that the fuel consumption improved even though the compression ratio was raised to 10.3:1 for more power. Internal changes included adopting larger ports, 40 mm for the inlet and 38 mm for the exhaust. A further regulator reduced the idling speed to 800 rpm. Other detail changes included following the 3.3-litre Turbo's example in omitting the head gaskets, and fitting force-fed timing chain tensioners.

The exhaust system was also changed to a freer-flowing unit with larger diameter pipes (and correspondingly bigger double-skinned heat exchangers) linked to a silencer increased in size to keep down the noise. There had to be a penalty, of course: the new engine weighed 210 kg against 190.

Cars exported to the United States, Canada and Japan had to be detuned to accept catalysts. In these forms, the compression ratio was reduced to 9.5:1, giving an output of 200 bhp at the same 5900 rpm and 185 lb/ft of torque at 4800 rpm which meant that they could run on 91-octane unleaded petrol. These cars kept the same overall gearing as the European SC, the new Carrera's fourth and fifth ratios being raised from direct to 0.966 and 0.763 to 0.786 with the normal 3.9:1 final drive.

A new flywheel with calibrated pickups for the DME system was fitted to all Carreras.

The transmission had to be made more durable to cope with the higher power and torque output. This was achieved in competition style by incorporating a pump to circulate the lubricating oil through serpentine piping on the outside of the gearbox casing. If the optional limited slip differential was specified, the increased weight of its components was compensated for by using steel rather than iron for the cast gear cage. It had the additional advantage of being stronger as well.

Braking was improved by using 3.5 mm thicker front discs with the pressure-limiting valve from the 928S incorporated to counter front-wheel locking on slippery surfaces. The Turbo's 8-inch servo was also standardised in place of the earlier 7-inch unit.

Cast alloy wheels of a similar 'telephone dial' pattern to those of the 928 were offered as standard, with the traditional forged wheels as a high-priced option. Detail changes included Turbo-style heater controls and an improved wind deflector in the optional sunroof and better sealing for the Targa top. Fog lights were incorporated as standard in the front spoiler with a new Carrera badge on the engine cover. American models had an upshift indicator in the rev counter.

Almost since the Turbo had been introduced, Porsche owners had been specifying or converting normal 911s to similar-pattern bodywork and running gear. This trend was recognised by offering a new Super Sport model that was, in effect, a Turbo fitted with the Carrera engine and transmission—as an extra cost option for the basic range. At first this model was available only in coupé form. In addition, plain engine lids without spoilers continued to be offered as an option on all cars other than the Turbo, which needed its 'picnic table' spoiler to cover the intercooler.

Improvements on the 928S also resulted in the Turbo receiving that model's central locking system, with electrically-operated front seats as standard. At the same time, an expensive alloy detachable hardtop was made available for the Cabriolet. It followed the same lines as the coupé's roof, but

The Turbo's performance was made even more smooth and refined by raising the torque to an immensely-strong 318 lb/ft for the 1983 model year.

All models of the 911SC—including the Cabriolet—were offered with a Sport package including a similar spoiler to that used on the Turbo.

the exact dimensions were so critical that the car had to be returned to the factory for hand-fitting.

Meanwhile the seat's backrests were made 40 mm higher for the 1985 F series model year with electric operation for height and rake with the option of heating. The Turbo's central locking system also became an option. The gear lever was shortened to reduce movement by 10 per cent in keeping with contemporary modern practice and the radio aerial concealed in the windscreen; the screen's washers were also electrically-heated to combat freezing.

The Carrera continued to be improved in detail for the 1986 G series model year, with revised shock absorber settings and new anti-roll bars and rear torsion bars that worked better with the latest tyres. An even shorter—again by 10 per cent—gearshift was offered as an option. But the most obvious changes were in the interior: there was a new dashboard featuring larger fresh air vents, new grilles and switches, and a more precise temperature control. Its sensor was now relocated on top of the fascia rather than above the screen and the sun visors were modified to incorporate vanity mirrors with retractable covers. The front seats were also mounted 0.75 ins lower with an increased range of adjustment to allow more legroom,

Alternatively, the 911SC could be ordered without the spoiler, which became a popular configuration on the Cabriolet because it emphasised its clean lines.

A variety of changes to the 1983 model year Turbo included twin exhaust outlets which helped raise the torque.

recognising that the rear seats were hardly ever used. At the same time a more powerful, intensive, windscreen washer unit was adopted.

The Turbo Special Equipment was at last listed as an official model and received wider, 245/45 VR16, tyres on 9J back rims in company with the standard Turbo—which now had the Carrera's interior improvements—and Targa and Cabrio versions of the Super Sport Carrera.

Late in the year the Cabrios received electric roof operation. This was an exceptionally sophisticated system featuring not only powered lifting and lowering for the hood, but latching and unlatching as well. All the driver had to do to operate the hood was press a rocker switch. This activated microprocessors which controlled two drive motors in a well behind the rear seat backs for folding or extending the hood through gearing and flexible shafts. Two further electric motors in the hood's windscreen rail worked latching pins. The complexity of the mechanism was well illustrated by the use of 13 movable struts and a roof frame and control arms with 22 joints. In normal conditions, this operation could be completed with the plastic rear window in place, although it had to be unzipped to avoid damage in freezing weather. For safety's sake, the hood could be lowered or raised only when the car was stationary. In addition, the microprocessors were programmed to abort action at any stage where a fault was evident.

The most important changes for the 1987 H-series model year centred on hydraulic clutch operation—making the action lighter—and a new gearbox for the Carrera with its change pattern revised to place reverse in the

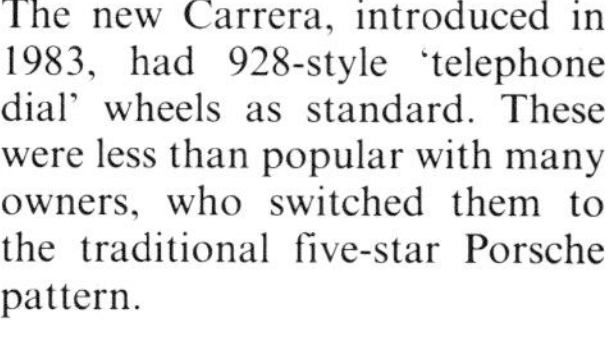

The new Carrera, introduced in 1983, had 928-style 'telephone dial' wheels as standard. These were less than popular with many owners, who switched them to the traditional five-star Porsche pattern.

The original five-star Porsche wheels in forged alloy 16-inch form with low-profile tyres—as fitted to this 1984 Carrera—not only improved the appearance, but the handling, too.

left-forward plane rather than the right rear. This was aimed at avoiding the possibility of touching the reverse gear operation on the downward change from fifth gear to fourth.

Wider, 195/65VR15, tyres replaced 185/70 section ones at the front of the standard model with neater styling at the back. This entailed removing the fog lamp from under the left end of the bumper and replacing it with twin lamps, and two reversing lights integrated into the red reflector strip. Other detail changes included a more convenient switch for the electrically-operated exterior mirrors, a point of light in the door handle which reflected in the dark, making it easier to find with the illuminated key, and improved door seals for the Targas. Fully-adjustable electric seats received a new lumbar control.

The power output of the Carrera with a catalytic converter was raised from 207 bhp to 217 on the new unleaded Eurosuper fuel. This model was also fitted with an oil cooler fan, thermostatically controlled and mounted in the right front wheel arch when viewed from the driver's seat.

The corrosion warranty was also stepped up to 10 years now that Porsche had been able to evaluate the life of early all-galvanised cars.

Development of the 911 took a massive step forward with the introduction of the 959 early in 1987. Its concept was so advanced that spin-offs from the limited run of 250 cars looked good to influence lower-priced 911s for at least 15 years.

The 959 had taken a long while to develop, however, despite an appearance which was hardly changed from that of the Gruppe B show car that had been revealed four years earlier. The low-drag body—which had a coefficient of only 0.31—used a Turbo galvanised steel floorpan clad with Kevlar plastic and aluminium external panels. The roof, mounted on a steel structure, wings, engine lid, spoilers and underbody panelling were made from the immensely-strong Kevlar while traditional aluminium was used for the doors and luggage boot lid. A Securiflex windscreen helped reinforce the shell and provided good protection against glass shattering. The roof was further stiffened with hard foam and the floor with Nomex cloth. Like the 928 and recently-introduced 944 Porsches, the nose was made from tough deformable elastic polyurethane which provided good deformable impact resistance. In this form the 959 met the normal Porsche warranty conditions.

Most of the development time had been taken up by the engine, derived from the competition 935, 956 and 962 cars. Porsche's chief, Peter Schutz, had decided that American customers for such an expensive car would not tolerate the inferior power output normally associated with having to run on their compulsory lead-free petrol. So more than a year was spent adapting the 962 engine and its management system to run on RON95 fuel. By then Peugeot's 205 Turbo 16 rally car had become so formidable that it was apparent that the much heavier 959 would not be competitive in the average international rally, so the majority of the production run would have to be road cars. That meant another six months had to be spent developing power steering. But at least the use of the 962 engine had one inherent advantage: it

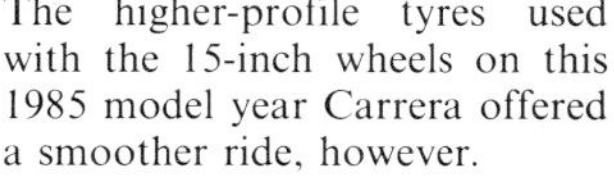
The higher-profile tyres used with the 15-inch wheels on this 1985 model year Carrera offered a smoother ride, however.

The Carrera Sport featured a spoiler of the same basic shape as that of the SC, but pared back more neatly on its underside.

Cautious arrival in Britain . . . one of 12 right-hand-drive Turbo Special Equipment models built in 1986.

had water-cooled cylinder heads, which made the task of operating the heater and air conditioning units far easier than with the normal air-cooled unit. Temperature maintenance, boosted by an electric water pump, now became independent of engine revs and much more competitive with the systems used on other very expensive road cars.

Apart from additional controls for the four-wheel-drive system and suspension, the interior was remarkably like that of the normal Turbo. There were instruments for the water temperature in the cylinder heads, oil temperature, oil pressure, fuel level in the large 18.8-gallon tank, and turbocharger boost (from 0 to 2.5 bar), plus two which showed the amount of lock on the control clutches. Rather like the Carrera RS of old, the 959 was offered in two specifications, one a Sport and the other a Comfort model, very much like the lightweight and touring RS. The main differences between the two 959s were that the Sport lacked the automatic and manual ride height control of the Comfort and was built without air conditioning, electric window winders and seat adjustment, and had less sound-proofing.

The 1986 model year Carrera had revised shock absorber settings and new anti-roll bars to take advantage of the latest low-profile tyres.

The Super Sport Carrera became available with cabriolet bodywork in 1986 to provide yet another variant on the 911 theme.

The result was a saving of more than 1 cwt over the normal total of 28 cwt.

On the central console of the more popular car with the Comfort package were located two large rotary switches, one for regulating the stiffness of the dual Bilstein coil-spring damper units with soft, normal and hard settings, and the other controlling ride height, up, down and intermediate, which ranged from 120 mm for fast driving to 180 mm for bumpy surfaces. No matter what the setting, the suspension—by wishbones front and rear—automatically dropped to its lowest level for maximum stability and minimum air drag at speeds above 90 mph. Camber changes with the ultra-low profile tyres—235/45VR17 at the front on 9J rims and 275/40VR17 rear at 10J—prevented any lower ride height. An extra stalk on the steering column could be used to select one of four transmission programmes, for dry, wet, or icy and snow-bound roads, and for maximum traction.

When set in traction, all four wheels were connected by locking up two multi-plate oil-fed clutches in the driveline. This gave a 50/50 torque split for maximum traction in sand, mud or deep snow. In the other three modes, there was no fixed division of torque, but a variable one determined by each corner's individual needs, which were monitored by sensors in the hollow-spoked central-locking magnesium wheels. These sensors—which also kept check on tyre pressures—fed information to a central computer which operated the engine-driven four-cylinder, radial-piston self-levelling and suspension-controlling pump, and electric motors within the shock absorber rods. Although the 959 was fitted with a steering rack, hydraulically-powered by a vane-type pump, the ratio—18.2:1—was the same as that of a normal 911.

A third electrically-driven five-piston pump powered the anti-lock braking system which used ventilated discs all round—12.67-inch front, 11.97-inch rear—and competition four-pot calipers.

The engine was the familiar flat six with a capacity of 2847 cc achieved from a bore of 95 mm and stroke of 67, which would allow the weight of competition versions for Le Mans to be reduced to 1100kg—or 21.5 cwt. The chief characteristics of the engine were a two-piece pressure cast aluminium crankcase, with a forged steel nitrided seven-bearing crankshaft, titanium connecting rods, forged alloy pistons, Nikasil air-cooled cylinders, chain-driven single overhead cams, four-valve water-jacketed cylinder heads and five scavenge pump dry sump lubrication. Two-stage sequential turbocharging—with twin intercoolers, one in each rear wing—minimised lag and helped produce 450 bhp at 6500 rpm with 3263 lb/ft of torque at 5500 rpm from the compression ratio of 8.3:1 needed for unleaded petrol. The rev limiter was set at 7,600 with a maximum boost pressure of 2 bar at 4300 rpm. The 911's normal fan cooling combined with the alternator was supplemented by a water radiator and twin oil coolers in the nose.

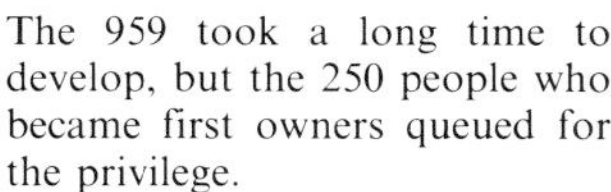
The 959 took a long time to develop, but the 250 people who became first owners queued for the privilege.

Porsche's latest 911 for the sporting enthusiast—the Carrera CS.

The close relationship to the Group C racing cars was emphasised by the pressure-regulated Bosch Motronic fuel injection and ignition unit. Pressure behind the throttle flap was used as a load signal, corrected by charge air temperature. Hydraulic valve play adjustment played an important role and helped keep this incredibly sophisticated car to a normal Porsche servicing cycle!

Retaining the rear-drive configuration enabled a relatively simple four-wheel-drive conversion to be made. The rear wheels were driven directly in the normal 911 manner, via a six-speed gearbox and rear differential. The gear ratios—which was shared with Audi's Quattro Sport—had an exceptionally low first gear to allow smooth take-offs on gradients as steep as 1-in-2.5 when the four-wheel-drive system would provide so much grip it would have been impossible to spin the wheels without dropping the clutch at near maximum revs. This transmission incorporated an output shaft to the front differential, which was rigidly connected to the magnesium castings and a single dry plate clutch by a central torque tube. This aluminium tube was shrouded to reduce noise and carried the gearlever for single-rod shifting.

The propeller shaft ran inside the tube, supported by four elastically-suspended, deep groove, bearings. An inlet in the underbody tray fed the gearbox's oil cooler. A Porsche control clutch, dubbed PSK, was installed between the gearbox and the front transverse differential, which was linked to the front wheels' conventional driveshafts through cast aluminium uprights and large-diameter bearings. The oil-bathed, steel-faced, clutch discs were arranged to slip to a variable degree dictated by the sensor-fed computer, which adjusted the oil pressure. A similar PSK clutch in the rear differential acted as a variable transverse slip limiter. By applying more pressure to the front clutch and reducing that on the rear clutch by an equivalent amount, power through the rear wheels is increased and vice versa.

In this form the 959 became a production reality and laid the foundations for continuing development of the basic 911 range. Meanwhile, in the spring of 1987, the Turbo was joined by two further variants, a Targa and a Cabrio—each with the slant nose Special Equipment option—which had the electrically-operated top as standard equipment. At the same time, the electrically-adjusted passenger mirror of the Cabrio was standardised on the Coupe and Targa. Interior changes included the option of crushed leather upholstery and more sophisticated stereo and radio equipment. Later in the year the Turbo was again made available for the United States with a catalytic converter model that produced 282 bhp at 5500 rpm. This model also formed the basis for variants exported to Canada and Japan with a further version under development when the converter became necessary in Europe.

Changes for the I-series model year in 1988 were confined to provision for an emergency manual winder crank should the electric windows give trouble. Some of the equipment that had been optional on the Carreras—the electric passenger's mirror, height adjustment for the passenger's seat, central locking, headlight washers, and intensive-wash unit for the windscreen, were made standard, along with forged alloy wheels carrying 195/65 and 215/60VR15 tyres. Sixteen-inch wheels with lower profile rubber remained as an option, along with the Turbo's uprated stereo and crushed leather.

At the same time, two significant new Carrera variants were introduced: the Club Sport and the Speedster. The Club Sport was aimed chiefly at enthusiasts who were by now paying substantial sums for 1972 and 1973 model Carrera RS cars and demonstrating that they could frequently outrun the heavier later 911s on the racetrack. On the one hand, Porsche were pleased to see their old cars still winning races, but galled by the fact that their new ones could not keep up. As a result they decided that there was a new market for a lightweight version of the Carrera. The Carrera CS as the new model became known was essentially a Sport model Carrera fitted with stiffer dampers and engine mounts to improve handling—at the expense of some of the smooth-riding ability—hollow inlet valves and a revised ignition setting to allow it to rev to 6840 per minute rather than 6250 and slightly higher fourth and fifth gear ratios—of 0.965:1 and 0.763. The dry weight was reduced to 2654 lb, on the British market example, however, from 2824 by deleting the rear seats, rear side panels, firewall trim, much of the sound-deadening material, heater fans and electric heater controls, glove box lock, passenger sun visor, door pocket lids, electric window winders, boot and engine lights and electrical seat adjustment. A far simpler radio with only two speakers, and push-pull heater controls, were substituted for the normal complex systems, along with thinner carpets. The chief penalty to counter its spartan appeal was the necessity to reduce the corrosion warranty to two years. Examples sold in Germany, however, were slightly heavier at 2583 lb

Drop-top for the Spyder form . . . the new Porsche 911 Speedster.

because they had to retain a catalytic exhaust converter.

Soon after, in time for the 1988 model year, Speedster versions of the normal Carrera and CS were announced. Like the Cabrio, these were open cars, but with modified windscreens, hoods and a plain engine lid. In the Carrera version, the windscreen angle was reduced by 5 degrees, and the normal Cabrio frame replaced by thin black anodised alloy, making it 3 inches lower. The hood line swept upwards, however, so that when it was erect, headroom inside was less than an inch lower than that of the coupé. The rectangular mirrors were also replaced by more dainty manually-adjusted and unheated eggshape editions. When the simple unlined soft top was furled, it disappeared under a flip-up plastic half tonneau panel of controversial hunchback lines. The rest of the interior amounted to a mixture between the conventional Carrera and the CS coupé. As in the CS, the seats were fixed in their lowest position, and were not power-operated, and the windows had to be raised and lowered manually. The dash-mounted heater and ventilation controls were also replaced by simple levers. Such weight-saving measures helped reduce the overall weight to 2552-lb—110 lb lighter than the Cabrio. The CS version of the Speedster—aimed at American car racing—was even more radical.

It involved removing the windscreen wipers, then the screen itself with a special toolkit. The passenger seat was then unbolted and a new all enveloping plastic tonneau substituted for the soft top cover. The CS full-length lid, which covered in the entire cockpit except for an aperture for the driver, used the same rear hinges, with the front located by the windscreen wiper axles. Entry was gained by lifting up the cover and getting somebody to clip it back on, wriggling through the driver's door, or leaping, cowboy-style in through the driver aperture. Further variations were planned for the 1989 model year with a plastic hardtop and a soft top.

# The Competition 911s

The rearward weight distribution that presented such problems with the 911 for use on the road has generally had the opposite effect in competition, where it has been a positive advantage. The resulting tremendous traction and controllability has led to a seemingly never-ending succession of victories in all manner of competitions; from circuit racing to rallying and even off-road events. In essence, the competition 911s split into the following groups: the early lightweight road and rally cars; the Safari and off-road specials; the track-racing Carreras; the rally Carreras; the club competition cars and the turbocharged machines culminating in the 953, 959 and 961.

The apparent versatility of the 911 is hardly surprising when it is realised that the car was designed from the start to be equally suitable for competition and series production. The majority of the 911's competitors have been competition adaptations of standard road cars but have usually been too much of a compromise to be successful in all quarters. The first 911 to be used in competition was a works Monte Carlo Rally car built for Herbert Linge and Peter Falk in 1965 that was, in effect, the 911S prototype. This had a 160 bhp engine with relatively few modifications for a competition machine: polished ports, higher compression ratio, wilder cams, platinum sparking plugs, Weber carburettors, lightened flywheel and free-flow exhaust. A lower final drive was fitted with a ZF limited slip differential and competition clutch. The suspension was uprated with Boge front struts and braking improved with larger rear calipers and front air scoops. Cars built to this type of specification with oversize fuel tanks, extra lighting and so on, were also used by private entrants in rallying before the 911S was introduced.

The 911's engine was uprated to 210 bhp for circuit racing with a magnesium crankcase and covers, improved induction and larger Weber carburettors, wilder cams, and the crankshaft and titanium connecting rods from a Porsche 906. These engines also had twin-plug heads, quite a simple modification on an air-cooled unit with no water passages to worry about. An engine of this specification also powered the Porsche 904/6 in which Umberto Maglioli and Linge finished third in the 1965 Targa Florio. They were beaten only by another Porsche using the eight-cylinder engine from which the 911's unit was developed and a Ferrari 275P.

This was the engine used in the four 911Rs built in 1967, which the engineers hoped would be put into limited production, but which the sales staff said could not be sold in sufficient quantity. Later, the Carrera was to prove them wrong on this point. The 911Rs had thinner-than-average gauge

One of the highly-successful Porsche 911T rally cars complete with steel wheels, driven by Bjorn Waldegaard into tenth place in the 1968 Monte Carlo Rally.

Porsche commemorated Vic Elford's winning drive in the 1968 Monte Carlo Rally with this proud display model at the Geneva Motor Show later in the year.

steel shells, glass fibre doors, lids and bumpers, and Perspex windows with a lightweight glass screen. The suspension was lowered and they were fitted with 6-inch Porsche alloy wheels at the front and 7-inch Minilite magnesium wheels at the back because such rims were not yet available in the 911S pattern. Racing tyres were fitted all round. The 911Rs had all sorts of small modifications, such as external fillers for long-distance fuel tanks, beside the re-located oil tank. The overall weight was around 15.5 cwt.

The 911 and 911L were also homologated for the modified touring car Group 2 class, and the 911T and 911S as Group 3 GT cars. The reason for qualifying the relatively mundane 911T in the higher category was that it was the lightest car in the standard 911 range, with a special 'basic' version being marketed with all the unnecessary items (such as interior parts) removed and 911S running gear! These 911STs weighed about 18.25 cwt. As on the 911R, anti-roll bars and dampers could be varied to suit individual events. A slightly-modified version of the 210 bhp engine, shared with the 911R and the 906, 907 and 910 sports racing cars, was also available for the 911T and the 911S; this had single ignition and standard-sized valves to meet touring car regulations.

Three 911 rally models were also built with the 160 bhp engine with 911S

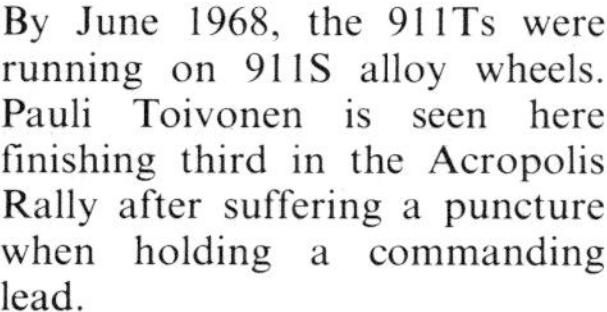

By June 1968, the 911Ts were running on 911S alloy wheels. Pauli Toivonen is seen here finishing third in the Acropolis Rally after suffering a puncture when holding a commanding lead.

suspension, brakes, wheels and so on. Two Sportkits were available for cars modified to this specification, giving 170 bhp and 175 bhp. These higher outputs were achieved with changes to the carburettors, ignition and exhaust systems, with the greatest power being achieved with an exhaust note that was illegal in some areas. Underbody shields were fitted to many rally cars, but it was not considered at first that these needed to be very extensive because the basic shell was extremely tough. As a result, fully-equipped Porsche 911 rally cars frequently weighed about the same as standard cars. They were homologated around the ton mark, whereas their competitors often weighed a great deal more by the time they had full rally equipment.

A wide variety of gear ratios could be ordered with a special shaft for owners who wished to alter the second ratio without changing the entire shaft, as would have been necessary with the standard gearbox. Limited slip differentials were listed and a variety of anti-roll bars. Little was done to the suspension generally, other than altering the ride height by adjusting torsion bar settings.

Porsche 911s used for off-road events such as Rallycross—a European

*Facing page:* Three extraordinary 911s were built for the 1968 *Daily Express* marathon rally. This event, which was in effect half race and half rally, run at high speeds for 12,000 miles from London to Sydney (with a nine-day sea trip from Bombay to Freemantle), was the subject of vast publicity—and much expenditure as a result by major manufacturers. The works 911 pictured here, driven by Terry Hunter and *Autosport* rallies editor John Davenport, featured a welded bar 'gate' to protect it from stray kangaroos, falling boulders, and similar obstacles anticipated en route. This gate was hinged at the front and folded forward for access to the trunk. As *Autosport* reported:

'The outermost steel tube on each side is continued upwards towards the windscreen top corner, mounted on the roof just behind the windscreen, and then continued along the roof line to end just below the rear window. These two tubes, two inches in diameter, form the roof rack sides, and six tubes welded between them form the floor of the rack. Onto this rack can be mounted four wheels and tyres at the front and, at the rear three twenty-litre jerrycans. With typical Teutonic efficiency, Stuttgart have arranged another task for these cans in an emergency: the right-hand one doubles as an oil tank should the standard tank be damaged . . . spare hoses of the correct length, which are stored inside the car, are then run from this tank to the engine oil inlet and outlet points. The centre jerrycan can be used as an emergency fuel tank should the 100-litre boot-mounted tank be damaged, and the specially-made lid of the can has a hose which runs through the boot lid to the fuel filter.

'Mounted on each side-member of the roof rack, by means of six spring clips, are the exhaust snorkels. When a deep ford has to be negotiated, these are attached to the two exhaust outlets which have clips already welded to them, and the snorkle hoses are run up to the roof rack. On the carburettor intake side, the air filter, which is completely sealed, has clips ready to take the intake hose (found inside the car) and this runs from the filter intake through a four-inch hole in the engine cover which is normally covered by a treacle tin-type can, and then onto the roof rack. The engine can then be run while submerged in water, the electrical side being water-proofed to Porsche standards.

'The interior of the car is very functional, with the standard 911S instrument layout for the driver, although the speedo is disconnected to relieve the Halda Tripmaster of unnecessary strain. Both seats recline, and the co-driver has a very necessary foot-operated horn button. The car jack, mounted alongside the passenger's seat, has a special attachment which converts it into a very efficient body jack. The rear fold-down seats have been removed to make room for the ten-litre water carriers, complete with drinking tubes, and in between these is mounted a Pyrene fire extinguisher which has an outlet leading directly to the clutch housing in order to remove oil from the clutch plates should it ever get there.

'General equipment includes a hacksaw (large), hand-axe (fierce), two-man woodsaw, and a lead lamp which plugs into the cigarette lighter. The winch is a cunning device and works by removing three wheel nuts from a rear wheel and attaching a drum, using the same three nuts. A two-ton breaking strain wire is already attached to this drum; the other end can then be attached to a solid object or to a stake supplied. First gear or reverse is then selected and the car winds itself out of trouble, the independently-operated

handbrake locking the other wheel should the limited-slip diff fail.

'Tools include a set of spanners which would be the envy of any racing mechanic, and a special tool for removing the guts of the front Koni shock absorbers, enabling a front shock absorber change in three minutes instead of the normal three hours, plus retrack and blake bleed. Spares are quite minimal: one drive shaft, one set of shock absorbers, one front stub axle, and the usual wiper blades, distributor and bulbs. Cables, coil, fuel pump, battery and electrical control box are duplicated in situ, ready to be plugged in.

'The food problem has been studied by the sponsors (Bio-Strath), and Michael van Straten, a dietician and the British importer of Bio-Strath, has produced a food pack which will be the envy of most crews. Apart from a daily bottle of Bio-Strath for each driver, there are various dried fruits, bananas, apricots, cheese and rye bread, and a variety of nuts and raisins. There is a special concentrated mixture to be mixed with the drinking water, and it is thought that the normal instruction "shake well before use" will not be needed!

'To overcome the problems of low octane fuel, Porsche persuaded Aral, the German fuel company, to produce some 80-octane juice, and the standard engine was tweaked to the fullest extent on this fuel with reliability in mind. It was found necessary to reduce the compression ratio to 8.6:1, and in this form, on 80-octane, the engine produces 162 bhp at 6400 rpm. However, on 100-octane fuel, it produces a staggering 175 bhp, which manages to propel the Porsche at a maximum speed of 126 mph (6600 rpm in fifth) which means a cruising speed of 126 mph. Not bad for an all-up weight of 32 cwt, including 27 gallons of fuel (277 lb), two drivers (too much), luggage (enough), and spares.'

These special two-litre 911Ss set off well with Hunter leading team-mates Sobieslaw Zasada and Wachowski and Ed Herrmann and Schuller into Belgrade before brake pipe trouble set all three back on the Turkish-Iranian border. More problems with the brake pipes delayed the Hunter car before it blew a piston, but Zasada—one of the most experienced long-distance drivers in the world—soldiered on to finish fourth behind winner Andrew Cowan in a Hillman Hunter. At least there was some reward for all the work that went into this rally.

mixture between circuit racing and special stage rallying—tended to be standard rally cars at this time with few modifications other than the removal of unnecessary objects such as the extra lighting needed for after-dark events.

Such was the pounding that they took in these events that they were soon reinforced to survive the 'yumping'. The author well remembers landing with a thump in a 911S in one early Rallycross and later discovering that the engine mounts had bent upwards. Fortunately this was not a major repair on a 911 as the engine could be easily removed and the brackets repaired and reinforced without a lot of trouble.

By 1968 and the advent of the A series, factory-pattern alloy wheels became available in widths of between 4.5 inches and 7 inches, but it was not until the introduction of the B series cars that the 911 became a much more practical car for competition, such was the improvement in weight distribution. The B series flared wheel arches helped a lot, too, as current regulations allowed them to be extended only 2 inches wider than standard.

The oil cooler in the right-hand front wing, which was fitted to most competition 911s, became standard and the Bosch plunger type fuel injection was modified to suit the characteristics of racing versions of the engine. The 1991 cc capacity was a handicap, however, as the international regulations allowed engines to be bored out only to their class limits, which was 2 litres in the case of the 911. If the engine capacity was increased beyond these limits, the car had to run in the prototype classes against much more formidable and specialised machinery. With the introduction of the C series for the 1970 season, however, the 2.2-litre engine (which fell into the 2- to 2.5-litre class) could go up to 2.5 litres providing this could be achieved by increasing the bore only. Similar modifications to those allowed for the 2-litre engines were used with the 2.2 litre, plus larger-bore cylinders. At first an 85 mm cylinder was marketed which allowed the capacity to be increased to 2247 cc and then, from March 1971, an 87.5 mm cylinder which gave 2380 cc. The 2247 cc racing engines produced 240 bhp and the 2380 cc 250 bhp.

Rally engines departed less from standard, producing 180 bhp in 2.2-litre form, except in exceptional circumstances when they gave 240 bhp from 2.25 litres with full Group 4 modifications which included twin triple-choke Weber 46 IDA carburettors. Reinforced clutches were fitted as a rule and the same wide range of gear ratios was available with the new C series magnesium gearbox.

Racing cars frequently used 7-inch rims at the front and 9-inch rims at the back while rally cars tended to stick to 6 inches all round. The racing 911ST used a thin-gauge steel shell, alloy doors and glass fibre bumpers, wheelarches and lids. Perspex was used for the windows and everything possible was done to reduce weight to around 16 cwt by removing interior fittings and dispensing with any attempt at undersealing. Cars to this specification, using rally engines, suspension and wheels, were also driven in

Later rally cars have generally been based on the 1973 Carrera 2.7-litre with mildly reinforced shells, full-length undershields, roll cages, raised suspension and so on, but relatively few modifications compared to those made by other manufacturers.

The Safari cars prepared for the 1973, 1974 and 1978 events were far nearer to the specification of the production Carreras than the marathon cars despite sharing a similarly-modified appearance. Most of the changes to specification centred around the suspension, which was reinforced and raised to give ten inches of ground clearance. Much original detail work went into these cars, however, as can be seen from the front lighting and trunk full of spares.

Tour de France cars, such as that prepared by Jean-Pierre Gaban for the 1970 event, were lightened as far as possible with the most successful being based on the 911R.

the 1970 Monte Carlo Rally by Bjorn Waldegaard and Gérard Larrouse. One particular 911ST was taken down to 15.4 cwt for Larrousse by the extensive use of titanium and glass fibre and fitted with a prototype 2.4-litre engine using a new long, 70.4-mm, stroke with the 85-mm cylinders. This produced no less than 260 bhp at 8000 rpm with 181 lb/ft of torque at 6500 rpm. Three cars were also built for the East African Safari with standard 2.2-litre engines.

A large variety of anti-roll bars and torsion bars was used front and rear to vary the cars' handling characteristics, with rally cars usually being set up to oversteer far more than racing cars. This was because rally drivers found their task much easier when they could whip the tail round at extreme angles while cornering, whereas racing drivers naturally favoured cars that followed a more consistent line through corners.

When the E series cars were introduced for the 1972 season, it was possible to increase the engine capacity to the limit of the 2.5-litre class by boring out to 86.7 mm, while retaining the new stroke of 70.4 mm. It had not been possible to bore out the Biral cylinders beyond 87.5 mm, so while the stroke was restricted to 66 mm as on the 2.2-litre engine, 2380 cc had been the maximum normal racing capacity. Unfortunately the 2494 cc engine that resulted from the 86.7 mm bore and 70.4 mm stroke proved unreliable at the normal Porsche racing revs of 8,000. The long-stroke crank was weaker than the earlier 66 mm version, so later 2.5-litre racing units used cylinders made from Nikasil. This meant that an 89 mm bore could be used with the safer 66 mm crank to give 2466 cc. In this form, the 2.5-litre engine proved far more reliable and produced just as much power—270 bhp at 8,000 rpm.

The stronger transmission introduced with the E series was also especially well suited to competition. First gear was cut into the main shaft with this gearbox, and although a similar number of ratios were available as before, the shaft had to be changed as well if it was necessary to vary the first gear ratio. Racing versions of this gearbox used a pump to feed oil under pressure to the most highly-stressed parts. Early cars using this transmission had gearbox oil coolers in the left-hand front wing. Later the engine and gearbox oil coolers were replaced with a single large radiator in an air dam at the front.

Special 911s were also run in the East African Safari Rally with 180 bhp 2.2-litre engines, raised suspension, comprehensive full-length undershields and outside protection, oversize fuel tanks and uprated torsion bars. These were real heavyweights, weighing around 24 cwt.

The 911 was proving popular in Rallycross for a variety of reasons, not least because of its excellent traction and the fact that it was air-cooled and

Rallycross cars, such as the Carrera pictured here at Lydden in 1974, which followed similar principles to the Tour de France cars, except that their suspension was strengthened in rally style. They tended to suffer more from bodily contact with their rivals, however, hence the lack of lighting equipment. The rivals at this time were frequently ultra-lightweight Porsche-engined Volkswagen Beetles.

MARTINI INTERNATIONAL CLUB
MARTINI
8T
Shell
BILSTEIN
BOSCH

*Facing page, top:* The mighty Turbo RSR, pictured here at the Nurburgring in 1974, had to use relatively narrow wheels in the wet to combat aquaplaning.

*Facing page, bottom:* One of the most luxurious racing cars ever—because of minimum weight regulations—was the 934, seen here at the Nurburgring in 1976.

*Right:* Purposeful prow of the 935/77A pictured on test at Silverstone in 1977. Pity the poor journalist strapped into the passenger's seat beside the driver (on the right hand side of the picture). He's about to be subjected to the most horrifying G-forces with no steering wheel or pedals to locate him as the car is hurled round corners at astonishing speeds even in the wet, such is the downforce exerted by the body profile and the grip of its giant tyres.

*Below:* Tail-end view of the 935/77A showing its highly-developed wing.

there was no water radiator to become clogged with mud! These were among the lightest of rally-style cars at around 16 cwt.

The classic Carrera RS 2.7-litre built in 1972, and developed from the 911ST, formed the basis of Porsche's assault on the international 3-litre classes. The RSR racing version of this car had Nikasil cylinders so that a 92 mm bore could be used to raise its capacity to 2806 cc, which gave it around 308 bhp with a damper on the end of its crankshaft to quell the vibrations which had caused so many problems with the 70.4 mm crank. The standard wheel widths and arches had been arranged so that it could use 9-inch wide wheels at the front and 11-inch wheels at the back. Twin-circuit ventilated and perforated brake discs from the Type 917 sports racing car were used with a balance bar to adjust the front to rear braking ratio. An extra deep air dam containing a massive oil radiator and a ducktail spoiler were used on the ultra-lightweight body. The rear wing became bigger as the 1973 season went on. The suspension was also modified to cope with the demands of the wide racing tyres. Rear suspension pivot points were changed to keep the heavily-loaded outside tyre as near vertical as possible in a bend, and the stub axles were located higher than normal on the front suspension so that the roll centre of cars lowered by this means was relatively unaffected. Special dampers were made with coil spring surrounds to allow more scope for suspension adjustment. Titanium hubs were also made to reduce unsprung and overall weight.

The engine had to be redesigned with the cylinder head studs further

The complex plumbing required by the 935/77A's turbocharging system is revealed when the 'rear bumper' is removed.

The air intercooler on the 935 that was to run into trouble with the regulations.

apart before the bore could be taken out to 95 mm for the full 3-litre capacity. This meant using aluminium for the castings rather than magnesium, which was not strong enough. In this form, the engine—with a capacity of 2994 cc—developed 315 bhp at first, which was increased to 330 bhp when sliding throttles were substituted for butterflies. The cars built for this engine in 1973 were eight Carrera 3.0 RSR prototypes. Extensive use was made of glass fibre and titanium in place of steel, which brought its weight down to around 16.5 cwt. The wheels became even wider at 10.5 inches front and 14 inches back. Nine GT racing versions were also built which weighed around 2 cwt more and stuck to 9-inch and 11-inch wheels with 230 bhp engines.

Porsche found themselves well set up for the 1974 racing season with the 3-litre cars, the Carrera prototype and the Carrera GT. In essence, these became the Carrera 3.0 RSR and the Carrera 3.0 RS. They managed to get the RS homologated in Group 3 as a logical evolution of the Carrera 2.7 RS, after showing evidence that 100 had been completed. Half of these were built as racing cars from the start. They looked quite like the G series 911 except that they had even wider wings to accept 8-inch front wheels and 9-inch back, plus a large flat 'picnic table' rear spoiler. This enabled them to be fitted with 10.5-inch front and 14-inch rear wheels within racing regulations in RSR form. Two rear spoilers were supplied for German cars, one for use on the road which meant that its form had to be contained within the car's platform shape, and the other—which projected over the rear bumper—for racing. These new spoilers were also attractive from the production point of view in that they were wholly contained within the engine lid rather than involving the rear wings as well, as they did on the Carrera prototype.

The rear suspension mountings were revised so that they could be used with racing tyres without modification and lowered front struts were supplied as an extra. The aluminium engine was homologated, producing 230 bhp in road-going form. Numerous competition modifications were supplied as standard, which put up the price considerably, but meant that anybody wanting to race such a car—and practically every customer did!—would have to spend little extra on it. In fact, it cost very little to convert it to RSR specification, which meant further engine modifications, a special clutch and wider wheels. The RS fittings included a crack-tested crank and connecting rods, lightweight flywheel, 917 braking, limited-slip differential and gearbox oil pump, large front-mounted oil cooler and glass fibre front lid.

An interesting parallel development in 1973 was the Carrera 2.7 for the 1974 East African Safari Rally. This car featured a mildly reinforced shell—Porsche's basic 911 structure was still standing them in good stead—with strengthened and raised suspension. The engine was a standard 2.7-litre Carrera unit with a stronger clutch and low gear ratios, pressure lubrication, and front wing-mounted oil cooler. Standard 6-inch alloy wheels were used all round and shields fitted under the body. These modifications were few, however, compared to those made by other manufacturers, and the Safari Carrera weighed only around 20 cwt, showing how strong the standard car was. Two works Porsches used in the 1978 East African Safari were Carrera RSs with their suspension raised to give a 10-inch ground clearance, and powered by 911SC engines. They weighed about 23 cwt. Meanwhile, Rallycross Carreras, run over similar but far shorter and less demanding courses, were down to around 17 cwt.

Little competition development has taken place since at the factory with normally-aspirated 911s because of the decision taken in 1973 to develop the 917's turbocharging system for the road. The Carrera RSR was used as a guinea pig for this purpose in 1974. The current Group 5 regulations imposed a 3-litre limit on engine capacity with turbocharging being evaluated as being worth 1.4 times normal capacity. This meant that a turbocharged car could compete only if its engine was of 2143 cc or less. Porsche juggled with their bores and strokes and found that by using the original 911 66 mm crank with an 83 mm bore they could produce a 2142 cc engine. A magnesium crankcase was strong enough to last six hours in such a unit, so this was used for all races except Le Mans, where an aluminium casting was substitued. Nikasil

Tail-end treatment throughout the years: the first spoiler on the Carrera prototype in 1972 led to the adoption of the duck's tail device in production.

Two 3.0-litre Carreras appeared at the Austrian 1000-kilometre race in May 1973. One, pictured here, had vertical fins grafted on to the tail (which projected a long way back) and were linked by an extended engine lid. This car also had modified suspension with transverse tubular struts running from the lowest part of each wheel hub carrier to the point between the differential housing. It was the start of development which led to the Turbo RSR.

The most extreme development of the wings, or spoilers, as fitted to the Turbo RSR in 1974.

*Below right:* Yet another development of the rear wing seen at the Nurburgring in 1976.

*Below left:* Works wing as used at the Nurburgring in 1976.

cylinders were used with the 906's titanium connecting rods and enlarged oil pumps from the 908 sports racing car. Low-compression, 6.5:1, pistons were used with a KKK turbocharger from one bank of the 917's twelve-cylinder engine and a waste gate. To be competitive against normally-aspirated 3-litre racing engines, this unit had to produce around 480 bhp. In the event, it gave a reliable 450 bhp in its initial form, so the weight of the 911 Carrera Turbo as it was designated—or Turbo RSR to avoid confusion—had to be reduced below the 16.5 cwt achieved in 1973.

One solution would have been to have built a spaceframe car with a glass fibre body which made it look vaguely like a 911, but this idea was vetoed by the Porsche chiefs, partly because they were having to keep a close eye on budgets at a time when the world was in the throes of an energy crisis. In the end, a standard RSR shell was retained although it was much modified. The fuel tank was moved to the passenger compartment so that its changing load did little to influence handling. This meant that the nose could be redesigned as Group 5 cars did not have to carry a spare wheel. As a result the front was considerably lightened and new ducting was made to improve brake cooling. The rear end was lightened as well by fabricating an aluminium tube sub-frame to carry the engine, transmission and rear suspension in place of the heavier steel cross members and side sections. An aluminium roll cage was fitted which meant that the scuttle structure could be lightened. Around 1.5 cwt was taken off the body by these methods.

The suspension remained basically the same except that titanium coil springs were used as the only springing medium. This saved the weight of the steel torsion bars and meant that lighter wishbones could be used. All this saved another 0.5 cwt. Because the Turbo RSR was intended only as a racing machine, the designers did not have to worry about the luggage and interior space occupied by the bulkier coil springs. Anti-dive and anti-squat geometry was built into the suspension to help cope with the extra power and braking efficiency. The bodywork was made from thinner-than-normal glass fibre with an enormous wing at the back.

Trouble was experienced at first with excess heat generated by the air the turbocharger compressed at 18.5–20 psi. The top of the cylinders got so hot that problems were expected, so Porsche fitted an intercooler to the pipe that delivered the air from the turbocharger to the inlet manifold. This was located under the rear deck between the arches supporting the wing. Initially the car's weight was brought down to 14.75 cwt, but it was not strong enough at this figure, so it ended up at 16 cwt—just about low enough for it to remain competitive with 450 bhp. Cooling was further improved during the season to extract an eventual 516 bhp. Other developments included the early fitting of 17-inch wide wheels at the back.

The Achilles heel of this proved to be the Carrera's type 915 transmission, which just could not cope with the 406 lb/ft of torque for a prolonged period. As a result, the new, stronger, transmission was developed for the road-going Turbo to come.

The next competition development along these lines was the Type 934. Thirty-one cars built to this specification were based on the standard Turbo (Type 930) with the addition of the number 4 showing that they were to run under Group 4 rules in 1976. This class for special GT cars imposed more severe limitations on development than the Group 5 rules under which the Turbo RSR had raced. Wheel widths were restricted to 13 inches for 2- to 3-litre cars and 14 inches for 3- to 5-litre cars. Twin ignition systems like those used on racing Porsches were banned and wings and spoilers were limited in size. Cars of between 4 and 4.5 litres—the class into which the Type 934 fell—had to weigh at least 22 cwt. As this was only slightly less than that of a standard Turbo, the 934 raced with virtually full road-going equipment, including electric windows and much of its trim—surely one of the most luxurious racing cars ever built!

The suspension was basically the same as that of the standard Turbo, except that coil springs supplemented the torsion bars in a similar manner to those on the early racing Carreras. Wheel diameters went up to 16 inches to take improved tyres with less flexible sidewalls because they retained a similar rolling radius. These were necessary because widths of only 10.5 inches at the front and 12.5 inches at the back could be used. This entailed the fitting of five-pin drive BBS wheels because there were no 16-inch diameter Porsche wheels available at that time. Suspension mountings were reinforced to take the forces generated by the grip and rigidity of these new tyres.

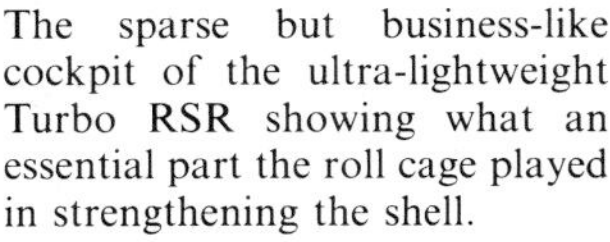
The sparse but business-like cockpit of the ultra-lightweight Turbo RSR showing what an essential part the roll cage played in strengthening the shell.

The K3 featured extensively-revised bodywork, including a re-angled rear deck with a massive wing. This 2.8-litre version, driven by Dudley Wood, Eddie Jordan and Glen Loxton to 16th place in the 1982 Brands Hatch 1,000-kilometre race, shows the typical turbo flame-out on the over-run into Paddock Bend.

The K3 used very wide wings to cover its tyres and provide more downforce, but the doors had to remain standard, so they were inset. This example, driven by John Cooper and Dudley Wood, is pictured before retiring with accident damage in the 1981 Silverstone Six-Hour race.

Front-running German Porsche team owner Reinhold Joest built a spaceframe 935 for the Italian driver Gianpiero Moretti using bodywork similar to that of the 1978 'Moby Dick' works car. Moretti used it initially in the American IMSA GTX class and then took it back to Europe when the introduction of the new Group C regulations meant that in the first year, 1982, grids had to be bolstered by IMSA cars and the earlier Groups 4, 5 and 6 machinery. Moretti is pictured here finishing seventh in the Silverstone Six-Hour race partnered by Mauro Baldi.

Porsche K3s were normally built around a standard Turbo bodyshell, but this example, driven by John Greasley at Donington in 1986, was lightened by the partial use of a spaceframe.

The engine was basically the same as that of a standard Turbo except that it had twin water radiators at the front instead of the air intercooler on the Turbo RSRs. This was because the bulky air intercooler could not be contained within the car's basic shape which had to remain unchanged under Group 4 regulations. In this form the engine produced a conservative 485 bhp at 18.5 psi boost although it could have been taken up to 600 bhp. The higher figure was considered to be too much for the tyres. The stronger new Turbo transmission was used with a limited slip differential.

The final development on the 911 theme has been the Group 5 racing Type 935 that first appeared in 1976. Like the 934, it was based on the standard Turbo, but far more extensively modified. The use of 19-inch diameter rear wheels with ultra-low profile 15-inch wide rear tyres and 16-inch by 10.5-inch front wheels allowed the engine to be taken up to 590 bhp at 21 psi with 630 bhp available for a short burst on 23 psi boost. The engine capacity, 2856 cc with a 92.5mm x 70.4 mm bore and stroke, was chosen because it kept the 935 within the 4-litre class at a calculated capacity of 3998 cc. The minimum weight for this class—19 cwt—was the most favourable for Porsche. The bare 935 weighed only 17.5 cwt which meant that it had to carry ballast. But by placing the ballast mostly in the nose and partly alongside the driver, the car's balance was much improved with a front-to-rear weight distribution of 47 per cent to 53 per cent. The fuel tank was located in the nose as part of this exercise, which was necessary because of more severe limitations on the rear wing shape than had been the case with the Turbo RSR in 1974.

A competition version of the standard Turbo transmission coped well

As late as 1984, Porsche 935s were still being campaigned in endurance racing. This is Vittorio Coggiola's IMSA GTX example taking 13th place in the Brands Hatch 1,000-kilometre race.

The class-winning Group B Porsche Turbo driven by John Cooper, Paul Smith and David Ovey into 11th place overall at Le Mans in 1983 proved especially good value—it cost less to buy and race than the cost of just the engine of one of the nine 956s that finished ahead of it.

with the 434 lb/ft of torque produced by the car's engine. The suspension was exactly the same as that of the Turbo RSR, except that it used production aluminium rear arms instead of the fabricated ones. The rear suspension also had an anti-roll bar adjustable from the cockpit like that on the Type 917/30 Can-Am car. Additional brake cooling ducts were built into the nose and the bodywork was as light as possible. Initially a Turbo RSR-style intercooler was fitted because it was much lighter than the 934-type water intercooler. However, this was soon outlawed because it did not fall within the original 911 silhouette. Therefore, at great expense, Porsche had to adapt the 934's waterworks to fit the 935. Extensive alterations were needed to the inlet system. Another interesting mid-season development was the chopping off of the tops of the front wings. It was discovered that it was possible to reduce drag in this way by a neat piece of Group 5 rule bending in which the regulations said that front wing contours could be modified to follow the bonnet line. This change of shape also improved stability. Fifteen of these cars were built in 1976 and 1977.

Another development in 1977 was the building of a 'Baby 935' for the German GT Championship. This ultra-light 935 weighed only 14.75 cwt and was powered by a turbocharged 1425 cc version of the 935 engine, producing

370 bhp. This enabled it to scrape into the hotly-contested 2-litre class with a calculated capacity of 1995 cc.

The engine capacity was increased to 3211 cc with a bore and stroke of 95.7 mm x 74.4 mm on the normal 935 to take it to 4498 cc and the limit of the 4- to 4.5-litre class for the 1977 season. This unit produced 630 bhp with twin turbochargers and the car was called the 935/77A. These were smaller 'blowers' than the single one used earlier and worked on each bank of cylinders. The advantage was that the engine produced better low-speed torque and throttle lag was reduced. A solid rear axle also became standard equipment to help drivers apply the power as soon as possible when leaving a corner—of vital necessity when they were struggling to cut into the seconds lost to turbo lag. The minimum weight in this class was 20.25 cwt.

An even more powerful Porsche, the 935/78 was developed for the 1978 season. This used four-valve cylinder heads to produce 750 bhp from the same capacity as the 1977 935. To squeeze four valves into the combustion chamber of each cylinder meant that the valves had to be made smaller. Air-cooled engines need large valves, so it was necessary to use water cooling for the heads—a complete departure from normal 911 practice. The works 935/78 was also fitted with spectacular extended coachwork and a high wing. As soon as the race crowds saw it in its white Porsche livery and lurid Martini sponsors' striping they christened it Moby Dick!

It was the final factory development of the 911 theme in Group 5 racing, although the Kremer tuning firm carried on improving the 935 with support from the factory for the 1979 season. The most dramatic result was the 935K3 which won at Le Mans. It took the FIA regulations governing Group 5 to their limit. One of the rules stipulated that the wings which covered the wheels could be modified for tyre clearance. This was interpreted in such a way that they became aerodynamic devices with prominent fences along the outside edges to prevent the airflow spilling over the side and reducing downforce. The doors could not be altered, however, so the wings and sills were built up as far as possible around them. The rear window had to be retained in its original position, but there was nothing to say that a second rear window could not be added above it. This meant that the K3's roofline could be extended to reduce drag. It was also discovered that almost any aerodynamic spoiler could be used at the back provided it was entirely hidden by the roof of the car when viewed from the front. As a result the K3 received a massive new spoiler which completely altered the appearance of the car—except from the front!

The revised roofline now allowed the K3 to use an air-to-air intercooler which was lighter and more efficient than the water-cooled unit. The power output remained the same with the air cooler, but a higher boost could now be run for a longer period because it ran at a lower temperature.

Lessons were also learned from the baby 935's construction. The K3's bodyshell was lightened in a similar manner and then strengthened with an intricate space frame that connected the roll cage to the suspension mountings. The result was not only lighter, but stiffer than the original shell. Two other cars were built to similar specifications by another privateer, Reinhold Joest, but these featured replicas of the Moby Dick bodywork.

The Kremer team then followed this lead with their K4 of 1981, effectively a K3 with Moby Dick bodywork, before the factory produced a new engine kit to take outputs up to 800 bhp for short periods. The kit consisted of stronger cylinder heads, pistons, liners and connecting rods, with a bigger oil pump, cooling fan intercooler and KKK turbochargers. The intention was to produce a more robust unit which would be run on higher boost levels for longer. A variety of engine capacities were used, the most powerful being a 3164-cc two valve fully air-cooled edition combining the 95mm bore of the 3-litre cars with the 74.4mm stroke of the 930 and Kugelfischer injection rather than the Bosch, which had smaller inlets. Maximum boost of 1.7 bar gave as much as 800 bhp, although it normally ran at 1.5 bar, which produced 750 bhp.

One lightweight rally car, based on a 911SC, using a 230-bhp engine, was built as an experiment that went no further because of an agreement with Audi—which made their 924 and 944 models—that the two marques would not compete with each other in international rallies. Audi's new four-wheel-drive Quattro was rapidly becoming dominant, even on tarmac, so the

Inter-cooled engine bay of the Memminger Group B 930 pictured during a pit stop in the 1984 Silverstone Six-Hour race.

The 911SC remained a popular rally car for private entrants into the 1980s—this example was driven by Christophe Spiliotis into 11th place in the 1985 Rally D'Antibes.

Porsche project remained still-born at this point.

In the United States, endurance races were run under International Motor Sports' Association—or IMSA—regulations which allowed more highly-modified 935s. The most successful of these was the ultra lightweight full spaceframe JLP3 built for the John Paul team.

For 1982, the Groups 4 and 5 regulations—under which endurance cars ran—were combined with Group 6 for prototype sports racers into two new groups, B and C, with strict controls on fuel consumption. Initial grids were likely to be sparse, so Group 4, 5 and 6 cars were still allowed into some races for a year, providing they ran with 100-litre fuel tanks and refilled only five times every 1,000 kilometres. This meant that the 935s had to run a lower boost or reduce engine capacity, often between 2.6 litres and 3 litres with little more than 650 bhp in race trim.

But once they became obsolete, something had to be produced for 1983-season customers who could not afford the very expensive Group C cars, such as Porsche's 956, and the American edition, the 962, and could not wait until the 959 had been developed. The main problem was that production 911s now weighed too much to be really competitive. It was not worth producing special ultra-lightweight 911s because—with the 959 on the way—there were not enough customers to buy the 200 examples which would have to be built in a year to qualify for Group B. This meant that Porsche had to stick to a virtually standard Turbo.

A handful were developed for private teams along the lines of the original 934. These Group B Turbos had to run in the 5-litre category (a 3.3-litre turbocharged engine being rated as a 5-litre normally-aspirated unit) which had a minimum weight limit of 24.3 cwt. This meant that they could have as much as 2 cwt of ballast in the nose and passenger's footwell for improved balance once the interior had been lightened. The bodywork's profile and platform could not be altered, so the widest wheels and tyres that could fit under the standard arches were used: 245/575 on 9.5J x 16-inch wheels at the front, 300/625 on 11J x 16-inch rear wheels. The suspension was stiffened and lowered, but additional springs were not allowed, so the cars had to stay on torsion bars. However, the brakes could be, and were, uprated to 935 specification. Only limited modifications were allowed to the engine, which had a higher 1 bar boost to give 354 bhp at 6500 rpm with 369 lb/ft of torque at 4500 rpm. Even in this state, though, it needed 935 head gaskets and transmission.

But once it became evident that the normally-aspirated 911SC was going to be replaced by a new model, the Carrera, Porsche were able to exploit a loophole in the Group B regulations. By late 1983, the heavy Quattro was struggling to stay competitive with new lightweight Lancias, especially in tarmac rallies. Audi, therefore, dropped any objections to Porsche building works rally cars for such events. The regulations which made it possible to produce a competitive 911 stipulated that a manufacturer could qualify a model for international competition with a production run of only 20 cars if they were an evolution of an existing machine which had been discontinued. The idea behind this regulation was that it would allow private teams to update existing cars without going to the expense of buying new machinery. But it allowed Porsche to use the 911SC as a basis for their new Group B car as soon as the Carrera had been launched late in 1983. A 911SC-based car was all the more attractive because the dry weight could be reduced to just under 19 cwt in the 3-litre class, against 21.6 cwt for the 3- to 4-litre class in which the 3.2-litre Carrera would have fallen.

The 911RS/SC which resulted had an engine based closely on that of the 1974 Carrera 3.0RS, with Bosch mechanical fuel injection to allow higher revs than with the later electronic systems, forged pistons that raised the compression ratio to 10.3:1, high-lift cams and a nose-mounted oil cooler.

The 3.0RS exhaust system was used with heating for rally car variants

Desert raider . . . a 1985 959 used on the Pharaohs Rally in Egypt was one of the star attractions of the London Racing Car Show.

Porsche's limited edition 953 rally car.

provided by an independent petrol-electric system rather than heat exchangers. The new Carrera's oil-cooled gearbox was used, however, to cope with power outputs in the region of 295 bhp. Peak power was reached at 7000 rpm on the way to a maximum of 7600. Two sets of gear ratios were homologated, the circuit racing versions using a 0.79:1 fifth ratio and the rally cars 0.89:1. A competition clutch and 40 per cent limited-slip differential were standard equipment.

The running gear—with 7J x 16-inch front wheels and 8J x 16-inch rear—was almost pure Turbo, which had been, of course, developed from the 3.0RS. The only real difference could be seen in the use of additional coil springs around the Bilstein shock absorbers, threaded abutment plates being fitted at the front for ride height adjustment.

Weight was saved by using aluminium front wings and doors, plus glass fibre bumpers, engine and boot lids. It compensated for the additional weight of extensive reinforcements to the basic steel hull, including fitting double flitchplates. An interior similar to that of the 3.0RS had thinner-than-standard glass—and there was no underseal, of course.

Works endurance driver Jacky Ickx then brought sufficient sponsorship from the Rothmans tobacco firm—which ran the works 956s and 911SC/RS cars—for Porsche to develop a special line in prototype 911s for the Paris–Dakar desert rallies. The Gruppe B project which would become the 959 had already been announced when Porsche started work on the cars for the 1984 rally, but it needed more development—so only part of its technology could be incorporated. In essence, three cars were built to 1978 Safari specification with modifications to incorporate a simplified version of the 959's four-wheel-drive transmission. A new central tunnel was let into the floorpan with a Porsche 944 propeller shaft linking the two driven axles. At the back a 935-style solid rear axle was connected through a normal Carrera gearbox to an Audi Quattro power take-off in which the central differential was modified with epicyclic gears to give a 30/70 per cent front-to-rear torque split rather than the normal 50/50. This central differential could be locked up, Quattro-style, however, for a 50/50 power split to make the car more stable on fast straight sections. The 944 propeller shaft then ran forward to the transaxle used at the back of the 924 Turbo, in which all the gears except the crown wheel and pinion had been removed. No limited-slip action was incorporated here to minimise steering drag. Conventional double-jointed driveshafts powered the front wheels, which were suspended by double wishbones—the normal MacPherson strut system had been the Achilles heel of the Safari Carreras—although torsion bars were retained as the springing medium. Twin sets of 959-style Bilstein dampers were used at the front with coil springs supplementing Turbo rear suspension because 911s traditionally came down from desert jumps on their tails. Stiffer-than-standard anti-roll bars were used with suspension movement increased from 7 inches to

8.7 inches and ground clearance raised to 11 ins partly by means of 205-section Dunlop sand tyres. Power was provided by a 3.2-litre Carrera engine with its compression ratio lowered to 9:1 so that it could run on low-octane fuel. In this form the power output was 225 bhp at 5800 rpm with 203 lb/ft of torque at 4700 rpm.

The body was strengthened along the lines of the Safari cars with a 10 mm thick carbon fibre undertray. Two fuel tanks were fitted—of 26 gallons capacity in the front and 33 behind the front seats. Wherever possible, weight was saved elsewhere, using items like hollow rear driveshafts, Kevlar body panels, and plastic side windows. Despite the 130 lb lost to the four-wheel-drive system, these cars weighed only 24.3 cwt dry.

The three Paris–Dakar cars that followed in 1985 were far more like the 959 in construction although they retained the tried and tested Carrera engine—slightly uprated to produce 230 bhp at 6000 rpm with 206 lb/ft of torque at 5000 rpm—and 1984 four-wheel-drive system which had been good enough to win. But they now used the PSK clutch in place of the epicyclic gear, which also allowed the torque split to be varied in stages rather than from just 30/70 to 50/50. Dual shock absorbers were now used each side at the back with double wishbone suspension and a bodyshell of very similar construction to the 959. A steel floor was retained but now even the roof was made from Kevlar, so that the overall weight could be reduced to 23.5 cwt.

By 1986, the 959 was sufficiently advanced to run in Safari form—with undershield and 11.7 ins of ground clearance—for the Paris–Dakar. Dunlop sand tyres of 205/70/16 section front and 225/70/16 section rear were used with an engine detuned to 400 bhp with reprogrammed management system so that it could run on poor fuel—from similar tanking to the earlier four-wheel-drive 911s. The suspension sensors were were also modified for desert conditions.

The 959 was then developed into the 961 to run at Le Mans as a prototype racing car. In this case the overall height was lowered by 0.5 ins—rather than raised by 8 ins in the case of the off-road rally car—and widened by 2 ins. The CD drag figure rose to 0.35, which could be justified by the greater downforce and the grip of the 17-inch wheels and Dunlop tyres used on the 956 and 962 Group C cars. Weight was reduced by 6.8 cwt to 22.6 cwt by gutting the interior of all its luxury equipment, and using thinner plastic body panels. At the same time, the engine was tuned to produce 640 bhp at 7800 rpm for the Le Mans 24-hour race by raising the boost level from 0.8 bar to 1.25 and modifying the management system accordingly; as much as 680 bhp could be liberated for ‘sprint’ events of up to 1000 kilometres. The suspension and drive sensors were also reprogrammed at the same time. Although the engine was similar to that used in the 956 and 962, the 959’s duplex chain cam driver was retained rather than the noisy gear drives of the Group C cars. The crown wheel gearing and a competition

The Porsche 961 used at Le Mans in 1987 had wider bodywork than the normal 959 . . . and extensive modifications to the basic structure under the skin.

clutch was used with a 935-style solid rear axle, the six-speed gearbox being used as standard. Normal 959 calipers were used, but the brake discs were uprated to 956/962 specification and the stronger Paris–Dakar 959 hub carriers substituted.

Then, late in 1987, Porsche started a series of 20 desert rally cars for private customers, in a similar manner to the earlier exercise with the 911SC/RS. In essence, these cars bore a close resemblance to the 1984 Paris–Dakar cars, using similar bodywork. Early examples were fitted with a standard Carrera engine, although a turbocharged unit was listed as an option. A five-speed gearbox was used with the permanent four-wheel-drive in the 1985 Paris-Dakar PSK clutch specification. Overall weight of this model, called the 953, was 24 cwt. In these forms the Porsche 911 could be seen to have a continuing future in top-line competition even after the controversial banning of Group B rally cars from international events following accidents involving spectators.

# The 911 in Competition

The Porsche 911 in competition has adopted a character rather like that of a chameleon. It has proved it can be easily adapted to everything from international GT racing to club driving tests and racing across fields in autocross to the savagery of top international rallying. It was in rallying that this extraordinarily tough machine first made its name in competition—works development engineers Herbert Linge (driving) and Peter Falk (navigating) finished fifth in the Monte Carlo with a mildly modified 911 in January 1965. This excellent performance in then what was the world's most important rally was, however, overshadowed by a fantastic drive into second place by Eugen Bohringer and Rolf Wuthernich in a Porsche 904 GTS better suited to road racing than rallying. Only thirty-five cars out of 237 starters finished that year, such was the ferocity of blizzards in the Massif Centrale and the Alps near Monaco. The first five places fell to cars in the GT class although only the 911 could be considered a real grand tourer. The winner was Timo Makinen in a Mini-Cooper S, with Pat Moss third in a SAAB and Peter Harper fourth in a Sunbeam Tiger.

The 904 continued as Porsche's mainstay in GT rally classes and racing until the Porche 911S had been developed, because the basic 911 was too slow to stand a chance of winning against more specialised machinery. Porsche continued to develop the 911, though, in the conditions in which it was going to compete. Bohringer and Wuthernich used the first production coupé, for instance to reconnoitre the Alpine rally in July 1965 before competing in a 904.

Porsche contested few rallies in 1966 with even fewer cars, but managed to finish first and second in Group 3 of the European Rally Championship! Slightly modified, the 911s proved to be equally at home in the snows of Monte Carlo, the dirt of the Flowers and on the tarmac of the Coupe des Alpes with little consistent opposition. No doubt winner Gunther Klass and second-placed Wuthernich could have amassed many more points than they did had not a broken throttle cable (an old Porsche weakness) in the Geneva Rally, and a broken drive shaft (which soon received attention on the production lines), in the Austrian Alpine Rally, cost them two class wins. Generally, however, the 911 was handicapped out of the overall placings because it was a Group 3 car, and even then the Group 2 Mini-Cooper Ss, Lotus Cortinas and Lancia Fulvias were faster.

Against less demanding opposition, the 911 did well with Eberhard Mahle winning the GT class in the European Hill Climb Championship and

One of the earliest competition successes by the 911 was achieved at Le Mans in 1966 when erstwhile Aston Martin drivers Franc and Kerguen took a 210 bhp 906-powered car to fourteenth place overall and a win in the two-litre GT class with 906 sports racing cars occupying fourth, fifth, sixth and seventh places. The 911 is seen here leading the 3.3-litre Ferrari 275GTB driven by Piers Courage and Roy Pike into eighth place overall.

Gunther Klass and Rolf Wuthernich drove the sole works 911 in the 1966 Alpine Rally and were agonisingly robbed of a Coupe des Alpes for a penalty-free run by an accident with an errant cyclist in Digne. The police took only five minutes to clear them of any blame but the time wasted also dropped them to sixth place overall. However Klass went on to win the European GT Rally Championship in his 911.

Jerry Titus taking time off from editing *Sports Car Graphic* to walk away with the winner's trophy in the Sports Car Club of America's Class D production car championship. At Le Mans, Kerguen and 'Franc' profited from other people's misfortunes to finish fourteenth and win their class in a standard 911 with only one other GT car, a 3.3-litre Ferrari 275 GTB in front of them.

Everything changed when the 911S was homologated for the 1967 season. Suddenly the 911 became far more competitive in S form and Porsche had the good fortune to acquire the services of one of the fastest, most spectacular and versatile drivers in the world, when Englishman Vic Elford quit Fords in a state of disillusionment at the seemingly never-ending problems with Lotus Cortinas in rallying. Elford, who had started his competition career as a navigator and then moved into the driving seat in international rallying and circuit racing, won the Lyons-Charbonnières, Tulip and Geneva rallies with a third place in the Monte Carlo to take the Group 3 title again for Porsche with the 911S. As *Autosport* reported while debating who was the best rally driver of 1967:

> 'There is little doubt that Vic Elford is the most likely candidate for this title, as his driving of the Porsche has set new standards on most of the hill climbs and stages used on Continental rallies.'

In 1967, the organisers of the Monte Carlo Rally imposed restrictions on the number of tyres that could be used to help make the French Citroen team more competitive against the British Mini-Coopers and Porsche 911s, which were much faster but used more tyres. As a result, Vic Elford and David Stone, seen here in their works 911S, lost their lead when they lost grip as the snow came down in the mountains, but they hung on for third place behind Rauno Aaltonen (Mini) and Ove Andersson (Lancia).

This was despite his racing commitments restricting the number of rallies in which he was able to take part! Elford was ably supported by drivers such as the Polish champion Sobieslaw Zasada, who won the Austrian Alpine in a works 911S before buying his own 912 to win Group 1 in the championship. The season was also notable for the emergence in a Porsche of Bjorn Waldegaard, who led the Swedish Rally for most of the way before his Group 2 911's transmission failed.

In circuit racing, Elford, Jochen Neerpasch and Hans Herrmann gave a magnificent display of driving to take the Marathon de la Route in a 911R fitted with Sportomatic transmission to demonstrate the new system's durability. The delay in initial acceleration was unimportant in an event lasting 84 hours. A normal 911R also finished third at Mugello behind Porsche 910 racing sports cars with Elford and Gijs van Lennep at the wheel before Rico Steinemann, Jo Siffert, Dieter Spoerry and Charles Vogele broke 16 international speed records at Monza, covering more than 12,500 miles at 130 mph in six days. This was in October 1967, and next month Elford and his regular rally co-driver and navigator, David Stone, took a 911R to third place in the Corsica Rally. Afterwards, Elford gave the Press a demonstration of how to drive a Porsche when he took Manfred Jantke, then managing director of the German magazine *auto motor und sport,* out. Jantke found Elford's handling of the 911R nothing short of astounding. He reported:

> 'In the most audacious rally style, he threw the back end out, and in tight turns it wasn't unusual for him to counter-steer to full lock to keep the car going more or less in the direction of travel. Even at drift angles that you'd normally call a half spin he didn't let go, but battled on, steering madly and tromping the gas. Once again we found confirmation that the rally experts are the acrobats among racing drivers.'

Elford drove in all manner of events, beating Brian Melia's Lotus Cortina by 0.2 seconds to win the first of the Rallycross television spectaculars at Lydden in January 1967, and this was despite being handicapped by too-high road gearing in his semi-works S-specification 911, registered GVB 911D. This car, which was entered by the British Porsche agents, AFN, thrilled crowds in circuit racing, too.

The following month, at Daytona, two 911Ss, driven by Ryan and Bencher and Drolsom and Williamson were the models of consistency to take ninth and tenth places overall in the 24 hour race and win the GT category. Bob Kirby annd Alan Johnson repeated the trick with a 911S to take ninth place and a class win in the Sebring 12 in April.

May was also good for the 911S, as Helmutt Kelleners and Jurgen Neuhaus won their class by less than a minute from Sepp Greger and Multe Huth in another 911S in the Nurburgring 1000 kilometre race. They were

Finns Pauli Toivonen and Martti Tiukkanen (number 116 in the Monte Carlo Rally) took second place to Elford in the Monte Carlo Rally in 1968 with their 911T before going on to win the San Remo Rally in the same car (seen storming an Italian mountain pass). This was the first of a series of wins that was to take them to a record number of major victories in one rally season and clinch the world championship for Porsche.

Americans Jim McDaniel and Glen Sullivan lost time with a broken rocker arm in their 911R during the 1968 Daytona 24-hour race but continued after repairs to take fourteenth place and fourth in class behind three Alfa Romeo T33 prototype sports racers. Elford, Neerpasch, Stommelen, Siffert and Herrmann won the race in a Porsche 907 sports racing prototype.

placed eleventh and twelfth overall. Journalist Bernard Cahier and ski champion Jean-Claude Killy profited from fellow 911S drivers Buchet and Garant's misfortune to take seventh place and a GT class win in the Targa Florio before Jean-Pierre Gaban and 'Pedro' were narrowly beaten to a class win at Spa by Roger Enever and Alec Poole's works MGB following carburettor trouble. They returned to Spa in July and struck more trouble, this time from the 911S's electrics, but hung on to win the 24 hour production race for the first time for Porsche, with an Autodelta Alfa Romeo GTA second.

In the mountains, Toni Fischhaber took the European Group 3 Championship again for Porsche with fellow 911S driver Huth second and Werner Rufenacht's Lotus Elan third. Hans-Peter Nyffeler took third place in the Group 2 category behind Ignazio Giunti's winning Alfa Romeo GTA.

The 911 even won a saloon car race in 1967! Zasada took his private coupé to South America for the 2000-mile Argentine road race, an incredibly tough event over all manner of surfaces. Zasada led from start to finish on all five stages, with a locally-built Torino second, a Chevrolet third, Torinos fourth, fifth and sixth, and a Lancia Fulvia driven by Cacho Fangio, the next European car home, in seventh place.

The 911 really came of age, however, in European rallying in 1968 when the 911ST arrived and immediately began dominating most events in which it was entered. Bjorn Waldegaard won the Swedish Rally from Tom Trana's SAAB with Vic Elford taking the Monte Carlo Rally from team-mate Pauli Toivonen. Toivonen went on to win the driver's championship by dint of his consistency in winning the San Remo, East German, West German, Geneva, Danube and Spanish rallies with a third place on the Acropolis, in Elford's absence. The British star was tied up for most of 1968 in Grands Prix and long-distance sports car racing, but returned to rallying at the end of the year. Mechanical troubles eliminated him from the RAC but he was still highly-placed.

Zasada backed Toivonen well with second places on the East and West German rallies and another second on the Acropolis. He took second place in the driver's championship and gave Porsche a fourth place in the European Constructor's Championship. Despite finishing in only one event, Elford was fifth!

He also managed to squeeze in the first three events of the British saloon car championship into which the 911 had somehow been qualified, before

Vic Elford leads the Snetterton 500-kilometre race in April 1968 in Bill Bradley's 911S with Frank Gardner in an ex-Team Lotus Cortina in hot pursuit. Elford led for the the first twenty-one laps until his engine, based on a 906 unit, broke a rocker after Gardner's Cortina had expired with overheating. John Ewer and Syd Fox came through to win in a 4.7-litre Ford Mustang from 911Ss driven by Erwin Kremer and Terry Hunter.

more important races took his attention. Elford won the two-litre class at the Race of Champions meeting with Bill Bradley's 210 bhp 911, followed by the Silverstone round in this Group 5 championship. It was considered a pity that the Bradley team did not compete in more of these races, which were rapidly being dominated by Fords of varying sizes and shapes. The only time that any Continental Porsche 911 opposition appeared was when Toine Hezemans from Holland took second in class in the Brands Hatch Motor Show 200-mile race.

On the Continent, however, 911s competed everywhere with Greger teaming up with Huth to win the Group 3 class in the Nurburgring 1000 kilometres in May, and crossing the line as the second GT car home in eighteenth place overall, behind Mike Salmon and David Piper in a Ford GT40—4.7 litres of Group 4 car nearly beaten by only 2 litres of Group 3!

Dieter Glemser and Kelleners mopped up the Group 3 class in their 911T in the Monza 1000 kilometres in the same month with eighth place

Dickie Stoop was one of Porsche's staunchest supporters in British sports car racing. He is pictured here at Brands Hatch early in 1968 with his 911S, registered YOU4, the number having been retained from the 904 GTS pictured (inset) in the Tourist Trophy at Goodwood in 1964.

Bjorn Waldegaard and Lars Helmer are pictured here winning the 1969 Monte Carlo Rally in their works 911T with 21,554 penalty points accrued. Gérard Larrousse was second officially in another works 911T with 21,831 penalties, although most people considered that Harry Kallstrom's Lancia Fulvia (21,691 points) was really second. Kallstrom's Lancia was a much-modified Group Six car, however, whereas the Porsches were Group 3 cars. Thus Kallstrom was officially the winner of the 'Rallye Mediterranee' for Group 6 cars run over the same course at the same time. The reason for this confusing situation was that the sport's ruling body, the FIA, had deemed that European Championship rallies should be run only for cars from Groups 1, 2 and 3.

overall in a race won by a GT40. Still in May, the Swiss team of Claude Haldi and Greub produced an excellent drive to take eighth place in the Targa Florio, won by Elford's Porsche 907 sports racing car.

Porsche 911Ts were the only GT cars to finish at Le Mans in June, coming in at twelfth place overall for class winners Gaban and Vanderschrieck and thirteenth for Laurent and Ogier. Glemser and Kelleners continued in their successful way by bringing home their 911T as the first Group 3 car in the Spa 1000 kilometres in eleventh place overall. Kelleners teamed up with Erwin Kremer and Willy Kauhsen for another win for Porsche in the Spa 24 Hour production car race with three other 911s in the first ten places and a 4.7-litre Ford Mustang second.

But what really mattered to the Porsche sales department was a second win in the Marathon de la Route with the officially-new model 911Es which were in fact lightweight 911Ss, running with Boge self-levelling struts. One car driven by Linge, Glemser and Kauhsen won from a second works '911E'

Waldegaard and Helmer used a 911L prepared in Stuttgart to win the Monte. On the Swedish Rally soon after they won again using a locally-prepared 911T. Many spectators thought the power of the Porsche would be an embarrassment on such slippery surfaces as encountered in Sweden, but the young Waldegaard handled the car at high speed as though he was accustomed to driving on sandpaper, cornering at angles which would have been thought impossible to those who were not used to snow rallying.

driven by Herbert Schuller, Bernhard Blank and Gunther Steckkonig, the third works car having been eliminated by trouble with the fuel injection pump.

The 911s were equally successful in America with Peter Gregg and Bob Everett winning the GT class while taking eighth place overall in the Watkins Glen Six-Hour, after Gregg had partnered Axelsson to win the GT class with ninth place overall in the Daytona 24 Hour race. Johnson and Kirby won their class at Sebring in seventh place overall, with only one other GT car, a seven-litre Chevrolet Corvette Stingray in front of them. Earlier, seven out of the first ten places in a TransAm race at the same meeting had been taken by 911s, with Everett's winning.

The next year, 1969, was a mixed one for Porsche in international rallying. They started with the new fuel injection 911 but, despite these cars taking first and second places on the Monte Carlo Rally (for Waldegaard and Gérard Larrousse) the drivers complained that these longer wheelbase cars were not so controllable as the earlier short wheelbase machines. It is significant that Waldegaard won the Swedish Rally that followed with an earlier 911T running on carburettors, as they were also dissatisfied with the fuel injection's reliability. Another source of complaint from the rally drivers was that the new 911 was heavier than their older 911Ts. However, Toivonen won the Acropolis Rally with a 1969-model 911 with Zasada winning the Polish Rally to give Porsche second place in the European Constructor's Championship, only two points behind Ford. Waldegaard and Zasada finished joint fourth in the drivers' championship with Zasada finishing in sixth place in the non championship but very prestigious East African Safari after running second for much of the event.

Porsche ran into problems over finance for their sporting programme in 1969, with their 917 sports racing project costing so much that they had to cut back dramatically on rally participation. Nevertheless, Larrousse won the Tour de France in a 911R fitted with a 911S injection engine after a special four-cam unit from the sports racing cars had blown up in the Lyons-Charbonnières Rally. This engine also proved unreliable in the Corsica Rally later in the year and was written off for rally work because it lacked power below about 5000 rpm. When it was running well however, it made the 911R go like no other GT car and later the engine was developed into an eight cylinder to power the fantastic 908 sports racing car.

Meanwhile the 911 went from strength to strength in GT racing with Neuhaus and Karl Frohlich taking eighteenth place overall in the Nurburgring 1000 kilometres and winning the Group 3 class from five other 911Ts and a 911S. Soon after at Le Mans, the Belgians Gaban and Yves Deprez won Group 3 with tenth place overall from a veritable phalanx of other 911s.

Bruce Jennings, Herb Wetson and Tony Adamowicz even moved up to

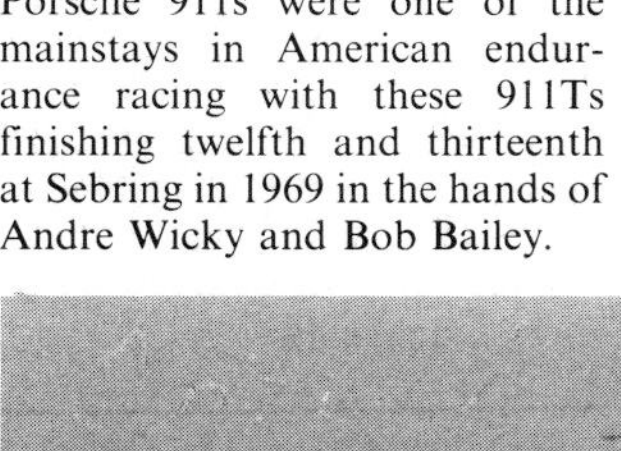

Porsche 911s were one of the mainstays in American endurance racing with these 911Ts finishing twelfth and thirteenth at Sebring in 1969 in the hands of Andre Wicky and Bob Bailey.

*Left:* Porsche 911s provided plenty of excitement as they battled for GT honour among themselves in 1969. Only three minutes separated the first three cars in the 2-litre GT category after six hours and 1000 kilometres at the Nurburgring. The class winners, Newhaus and Frohlic, are seen here on their way to fourteenth place overall.

*Below:* Florida Porsche distributor Peter Gregg rapidly became a force to be reckoned with in American GT racing driving a 911S. He is pictured here in mid-season in 1969.

*Right:* The works continued to use the long-wheelbase 911L rally cars in 1969 despite the drivers' preference for the lighter and more nimble short-wheelbase 911Ts. To make up for the extra weight of the 911L, their engines were taken beyond 200 bhp and sometimes proved fragile. Waldegaard's car, pictured here, had to retire in the Acropolis Rally with a broken piston.

*Below:* Gérard Larrousse and Maurice Gelin's ultra lightweight 911R storms to one of its numerous circuit wins which secured overall victory in the 1969 Tour de France.

fourth place overall while winning their class at Daytona as faster cars fell by the wayside. Other notable results for 911 drivers included Evardino Ostini's tenth place in the Targa Florio (with the inevitable GT class win) and the class win and thirteenth place overall for Larrousse and Rudi Lins in the Spa 1000 kilometres.

The European Touring Car Challenge did not go quite so well, however. Porsche, who had beaten BMW by half a point in 1968, could not afford to field a works team for 1969 and wilted in the face of a determined onslaught from their Bavarian rivals, who turbocharged their 2002 saloon.

Porsche, who still had their money tied up in the 917 project, had to rely on private entrants to defend their honour. Van Lennep and Hezemans were the most successful in this sphere, finishing fourth in the top division in the championship with Georg Loos in the next fastest 911, the ex-Kelleners car that was also driven by Rolf Stommelen.

Four 911s took part in the British Saloon Car Championship, but the only one to contest more than one round was the ex-AFN car, GVB 911D, driven by Nick Faure, and he couldn't raise enough sponsorship to do the whole series.

The East African Safari was included in a new International Rally Championship in 1970, and Porsche, after a very low-key 1969 season decided to go all out to win this new title. Now that they had the back broken of the 917 project, they turned to the 911 again, producing a new 2.3-litre

One of the most successful 911 drivers in North America in the late 1960s and early 1970s was Canadian Jacques Duval pictured here leading the second-placed Porsche 917 driven by Jo Siffert and Brian Redman in the 1970 Daytona Twenty-Four Hour race. Duval retired with transmission trouble leaving a 911S driven by Gary Wright, Bill Bean and Ralph Meaney to win the 2-litre GT category.

Even cars as fast as full-race 911s provided a 'mobile chicane' for such monsters as the Porsche 917 and Ferrari 512 sports racing cars. A 911 driven by Nehl and Perry is seen being overtaken by Elford and van Lennep's 917K at Daytona in 1970. Soon after a tyre blew when Elford's Martini-sponsored car was doing 200 mph on the American track's banking. He hit a retaining wall and the car was almost totally destroyed as it spun down the banking. Elford escaped unhurt, having been strapped into its immensely strong centre section. Mark Donohue, hard on his tail in a Ferrari 512M, slowed and Perry's 911 veered into his near-side. The Porsche crumpled as it rolled over and over but Perry escaped with only slight injuries.

911S Group 4 special with wide wheels and 235 bhp against the narrow wheels and 180/190 bhp of the earlier rally cars.

Three of the new cars were entered for the Monte Carlo Rally for Waldegaard, Larrousse and Ake Andersson. For once, the weather favoured these high-powered, lightweight machines, and despite trouble with ice on some tests, they held three of the first four places before the start of the final stage. It was then that Waldegaard seemingly threw caution to the winds and used racing tyres when everybody else played safe on studs. But driving like a man possessed, Waldegaard simply roared away from the field with Larrousse narrowly beating Nicolas's Alpine for second place.

These Group 4 cars were too wild for the icy Swedish Rally, so Waldegaard used an older 911 rally car to keep up his winning sequence and make it a hat trick in his national event. An administrative mix-up cost Porsche their entries in the Italian Rally, leaving victory to the Alpine team. Zasada borrowed a works car for the Safari and despite driving at a restrained pace to make sure he finished, was leading when he holed his

More than half the field for the 1971 Le Mans Twenty-four Hour race was made up of Porsches of all shapes and sizes (the other half being mostly Ferraris). In the event, in which the tenth-placed 2.4-litre 911S of Kremer, Koob and Huber is seen leading the Lola T212 of Edwards and Enever and the thirteenth-placed 2.4-litre 911S of Cheneviere and Waldegaard, only three Ferraris finished, the other ten cars to complete the race being Porsches. Marko and van Lennep won in a 917K with Touroul and Anselme winning the GT class with their sixth-placed 911S.

sump! Waldegaard made up for this lack of points by winning the Austrian Alpine Rally in one of the older-specification cars.

It was back to the 235 bhp wide wheelers for the Acropolis, but the sustained high revs needed for this event proved to be too much for the con rods, so Porsche picked up no points. They were still leading the Alpine team narrowly, however, which made the final event, the RAC Rally, a cliffhanger. All looked lost for Porsche when Waldegaard and Andersson broke their transmissions. This left the Alpines in the lead, but they broke down and Larrousse crept up into sixth place to take the title for Porsche by two points!

By 1970, however, interest in GT racing was on the wane as touring car events gained in popularity. Unfortunately Porsche could not homologate a lightweight version of the 2.2-litre car into Group 2 in time, so they had to concentrate on the 911S in Group 4 trim. In this form, the 911 continued to enjoy success in GT racing, although it was caught between two classes, the 2-litre for the older cars and the 2.5-litre for the new ones. Frohlich and Toivonen managed to beat Kremer and Gunther Huber by 0.4 seconds for fourteenth place and a class win in the Nurburgring 1000 kilometres with a 2.3-litre car, whereas Scheretti and Zerbini led in a squadron of 2-litre 911s by taking twentieth place overall and a class win in the Monza 1000 kilometres. Haldi and Chenevière did likewise for sixteenth place overall in the Spa 1000 kilometres. And the 911 found a new competitor at Le Mans, with a mid-engined Porsche 914/6 pipping Kremer and Koob's 2.2-litre 911S for sixth place.

Porsche concentrated the works effort in rallying and GT racing on the 914/6 for 1971 in an attempt to boost sales of this new 2-litre sports car. The works rally drivers complained bitterly but had to drive the new car, Waldegaard being especially displeased at being able to finish only third in a 914 in the Monte Carlo Rally whereas he felt that he might have completed a hat trick of wins with the more powerful 2.4-litre 911S. The works did prepare three of these cars for the Safari, though, for Zasada, Waldegaard and Andersson. Waldegard and Andersson were eliminated, but Zasada was still in with a chance of winning when an obscure electrical fault dropped him to fifth place at the end. As if to emphasise his point, Waldegaard took second place in the RAC Rally with a 911S late in the year.

Once more, private entrants kept the 911 flag flying. They even saved Porsche's honour in the Targa Florio when Bernard Chenevière and Peter Keller, and Pucci and Schmid finished fourth and sixth with the 2.4-litre 911Ss as the Alfa Romeo team ground the Porsche Group 6 prototypes into the dust.

Then Kremer and Huber in a 911S managed to beat their Group 4 opposition from Ettmuller and Sealer in a 914 for twelfth place overall and a class win in the Monza 1000 kilometres to show that the 911 was still the best! In similar fashion, Kremer and Neuhaus, followed by Haldi and Keller,

The Group 4 cars which competed in 1972 were the last 911s to run without rear spoilers. This is one of several 2.5-litre Italian entries in the Targa Florio. One of the best known of these cars was run by tuner Ennio Bonomelli, although he had to give the Sicilian classic a miss in 1972 when the local mafioso 'confiscated' his car before the race following a dispute over a restaurant bill . . . and they returned it only after the race was over!

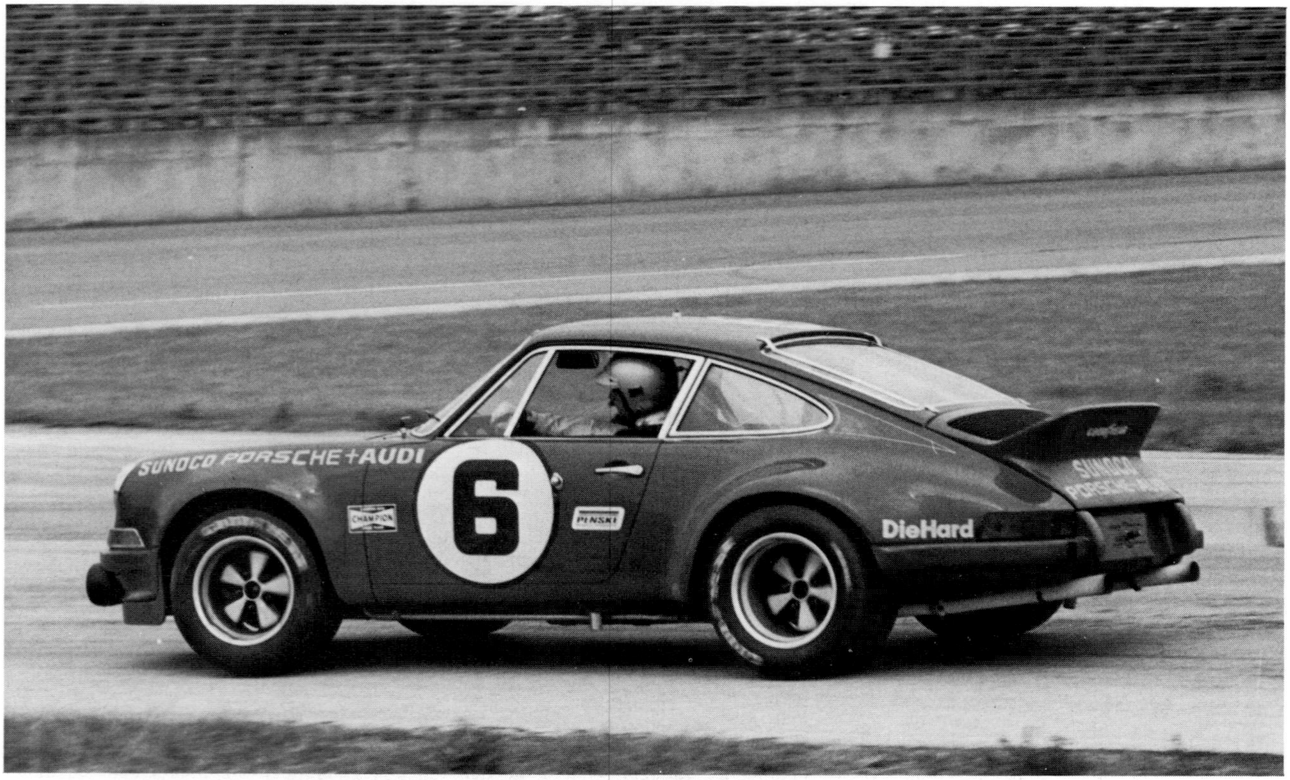
SUNOCO PORSCHE+AUDI
6
CHAMPION
PENSKE
DieHard

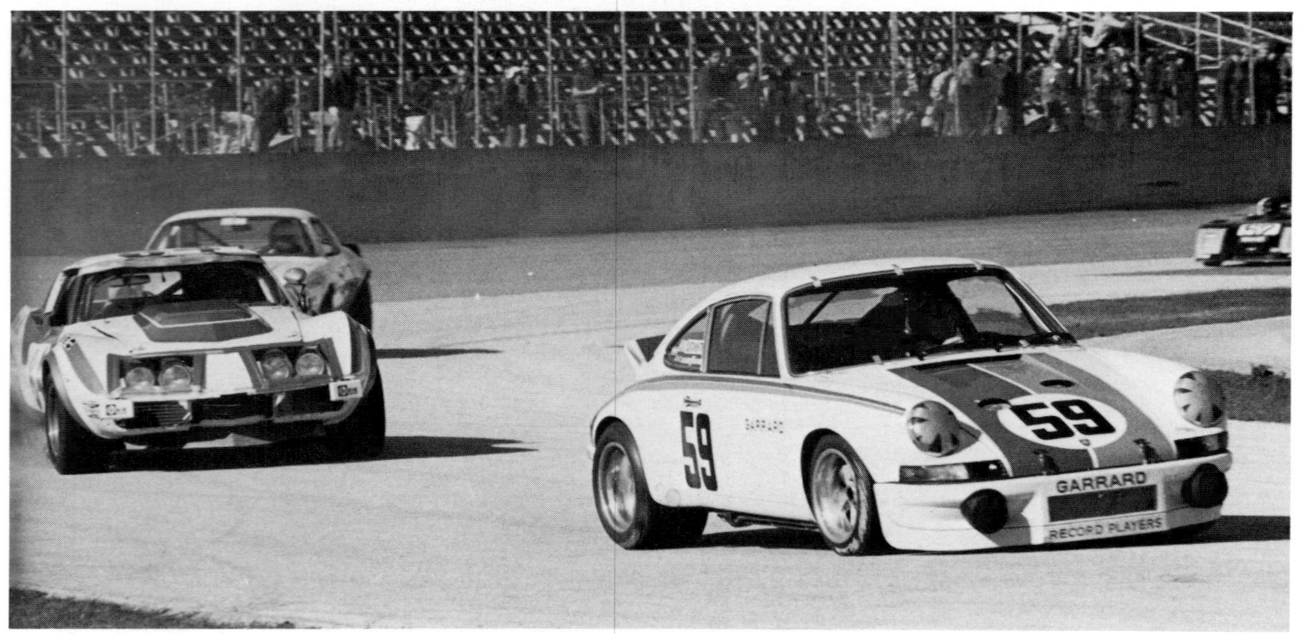

59
GARRARD
RECORD PLAYERS

*Facing page:* Mark Donohue and George Follmer fought a bitter battle with fellow Can-Am drivers Peter Gregg and Hurley Haywood in a similar 2.8-litre Carrera RSR at Daytona in 1973 before their car (number six) blew up, leaving the rival RSR (number fifty-nine) to win.

vanquished the 914 opposition for twelfth and thirteenth places overall and a Group 4 win in the Nurburgring 1000 kilometres.

No less than seven 911s of one form or another were among the thirteen finishers at Le Mans in 1971. A 911S was best placed, in sixth position, driven by Toivonen and Anselme with what was described as a 911E in eighth place in the hands of Rene Mazzia and Jurgen Barth. This car was, in fact, a slightly longer stroked version of the 911S, with 2410 cc against 2381 cc. Four other 911Ss filled the remaining places.

Kremer and Huber kept up the pressure for the 911 camp by winning the GT class in the Spa 1000 kilometres with Schickentanz and Kersten winning their class in the Austrian 1000 kilometres.

From 1972 rallying had to take a back seat in Porsche competition involvement with the factory's money being tied up initially in the 917 project for CanAm racing. However, Waldegaard and Larrousse continued to compete when they could afford it with private 911Ss, with some success, and Zasada battled on with a semi-works 911S. Waldegaard nearly won the Swedish Rally again but found that the sheer power of his 2.4-litre engine was too much for racing tyres on icy patches and lost to a SAAB. In similar fashion, Larrousse finished second in the Monte Carlo Rally on tyres worn out by the power. But Zasada 'borrowed' another Safari special to take

Rapid pitwork played its part in helping the 3.0-litre Carrera RSR prototype driven by Gijs van Lennep and Herbert Muller (pictured in the car) to fifth place in the 1973 Nurburgring 1000-kilometre race.

Clemens Schickentanz had a great season, winning the European GT championship with Claude Ballot-Lena in a Kremer Carrera in 1973.

A picture which sums up Porsche's domination of European GT racing in the mid-1970s. John Fitzpatrick is seen leading the massed ranks of Carrera RSRs at the rarely-used Montlhery circuit in May 1973. Fitzpatrick led the Grand Prix de Paris there until he 'had a moment' when the gearlever knob came off in his hand, letting Ballot-Lena (second in the picture) through to win from Schickentanz (third in the picture). Fitzpatrick recovered to snatch third place from Bonomelli (fourth, partly obscured).

Porsche entered two cars in the 1973 East African Safari, but despite meticulous preparation, both Sobieslaw Zasada (pictured here) and Bjorn Waldegaard retired with mechanical problems.

second place in East Africa and give Porsche a clear lead in the world rally championship. He might have won had he had the service facilities of the winning Ford team. After that it was left to the might of Lancia, Fiat and Ford to dispute the championship, although Zasada did manage to take second place in the race for the drivers' title.

This season was also significant for the emergence of the British driver John Fitzpatrick in a 911. Fitzpatrick had driven a 911 in competition before (a very quick car owned by Ben Pon at the Nurburgring in 1967), and had frequently starred in Minis, Anglias and Escorts in saloon car racing, but until then had not established himself in GT racing. However, Erwin Kremer remembered his performances in the Pon 911 and the Escorts and invited him to join his Porsche team. Fitzpatrick went on to win the Porsche Cup, a $50000 award for the most successful private Porsche driver, and the European GT Trophy with Kremer's 911S in 1972.

One of Fitzpatrick's most outstanding performances in 1972 was taking Kremer's 2.5-litre 911S to ninth place and a class win in the Nurburgring

1000 kilometres race, narrowly beating a rival 911S driven by Steckkonig and Schmid, who overhauled Kremer's car every time the owner was at the wheel, only to fall back again when Fitzpatrick took over!

Another outstanding performance by the 2.5-litre 911S was fourth place and a GT win in the Targa Florio for Pica and Gottifredi. This was the highest-placed Porsche because the sports racers were concentrating on CanAm racing.

In America, Gregg and Hurley Haywood teamed up to take seventh place in the rearranged Daytona Six-Hour event and to win the GT class by a huge margin before going on to beat Bob Beasley's 2.5-litre 911S in the Camel GT challenge.

The racing fortunes of the 911 took a dramatic turn in 1973 after Porsche's new chief, Dr Ernst Fuhrmann decided that the cost of the turbocharged 917 project had got out of hand and that in future the company would concentrate on competitions involving cars closer to production models. The result was the Carrera RSR which had first appeared in

One of the chief rivals for the Carrera RS in the mid-1970s was the de Tomaso Pantera. Examples driven by Nick Faure (Carrera) and Chris Meek (Pantera, pictured here) raced neck and neck throughout the 1973 season with Faure taking the over £3000 class in the British STP Prodsports championship from Meek. Initially Faure was supported by Porsche's British concessionaires, and later by Count Giovanni de Stephano. The main problem encountered during the season was with inadequacy of the road tyres demanded by the series regulations.

highly-experimental form at the Osterreichring in the middle of the 1972 season. This 2.7-litre Group 5 prototype was driven to tenth place—headed only by all-out sports racers—by Waldegaard and Steckkonig, a veteran Porsche development engineer.

The Carrera RSR that was developed from this car had its first victory in the hands of Gregg and Haywood at Daytona in 1973. Although the previous year's six-hour duration had proved popular, the organisers decided to revert to twenty-four hours. They also offered little starting money, so most of the sports racing prototypes stayed away. The four cars that did start, broke down, leaving two 2.8-litre Carrera RSRs to fight it out. Gregg and Haywood in the Brumos-sponsored car engaged in a bitter battle with Mark Donohue (Porsche's brilliant 917 pilot) and George Follmer in a Penske car before the Penske Porsche blew up. Five other assorted 2.5-litre and 2-litre 911s finished in the first ten places.

The 2.8-litre Carrera RSRs had to run as Group 5 prototypes at Daytona as homologation into Group 4 did not become effective until March. After that the 2.8-litre cars went from strength to strength and the works ran two Carrera RSRs under Martini sponsorship. Herbert Muller and Gijs van Lennep in one of the Martini cars, Fitzpatrick and Peter Keller in a 2.8-litre RSR (Kremer's latest acquisition), and Bernard Chenevière and Peter Zbinden in a Swiss-entered RSR, took ninth, tenth and eleventh places and won the GT class in the Dijon 1000 kilometres race. Follmer and Kauhsen pipped team mates Muller and van Lennep for seventh place and a Group 4 win in the Vallelunga Six Hour. After that the Muller and van Lennep car was developed even more extensively, receiving a 3-litre engine and running in Group 5 form, while the second Martini car stayed mostly in

Bjorn Waldegaard is pictured hurling his Carrera RS through the mud of the East African Safari in 1974 to take second place behind the Colt Lancer of Joginder Singh after losing the lead when he had trouble with the rear suspension's trailing arms.

Group 4 trim. Muller and van Lennep took the Group 5 car to fifth place in the Spa 1000 kilometres with Follmer and Reinhold Joest winning the GT class in the Martini Group 4 car after Fitzpatrick had first broken down on the first lap, then taken over with Clemens Schickentanz in his Group 4 Carrera RSR for a thrilling duel with Follmer. Unfortunately, Fitzpatrick's second engine gave up late in the race!

Muller and van Lennep went on to take fourth place in the Nurburgring 1000 kilometres with the Group 5 car with Keller and Neuhaus winning the GT class in the Kremer Group 4 car in the absence of Follmer (crashed) and Fitzpatrick (who could not get out of a Ford works drive). In fact, Fitzpatrick nearly caught Muller and van Lennep while finishing sixth with the Group 2 Capri RS 3-litre!

Carrera RSRs of all varieties made up most of the field at Le Mans in 1973 with the Muller and van Lennep Group 5 car taking fourth place behind two Matras and a Ferrari prototype, Kremer, Keller and Schickentanz coming within ten miles of winning the GT class from Elford and Claude Ballot-Lena in a 4.4-litre Ferrari Daytona while collecting eighth place. They had the consolation of winning the Thermal Efficiency Index, however.

Both works Carreras had to run in the prototype class in the Monza 1000 kilometres because of rear suspension modifications and eventually eliminated themselves with piston trouble, leaving Schickentanz and Kremer to win the GT class in eighth place after Fitzpatrick in a second Kremer Carrera lost time with distributor trouble.

However, Muller and van Lennep outlasted all the other prototypes to win the last of the great open road races, the Targa Florio, with Leo Kinnunen and Haldi third and three other Carrera RSRs in the first ten, including Borri and Barone who finished seventh and won the GT class. Schickentanz crowned a great season by sharing the European GT championship with Ballot-Lena, whose defection to Ferrari at Le Mans from Porsche was only temporary.

Porsche's works rally efforts were confined to the Safari in which they entered two Carrera RSs for Waldegaard and Zasada, backed by a private entry for 1959 and 1960 winner, Bill Fritschy. Gear selection problems delayed the cars intially with Waldegaard and Zasada hauling themselves back into contention for the lead only for Zasada to overturn twice and then lose three gears before retiring and Waldegaard to survive numerous suspension changes before being eliminated near the end when he lost his oil cooler and subsequently his oil pressure.

Torrential rain, even worse than that normally experienced on the Safari, hopelessly bogged down many competitors in 1974, with Waldegaard using the Carrera's enormous traction to its maximum advantage to lead the rally until near the end when once again suspension trouble delayed him, allowing Joginder Singh's Mitsubishi Colt to relegate him to second place.

**Plate One** One of the first two-pedal Porsches, a 1968 911L Sportomatic.

**Plate Two** Jean-Pierre Hanrioud driving his 911S into thirteenth place in the 1967 Monte Carlo Rally.

**Plate Three** Classic of classics: the 1973 2.7-litre Carrera RS.

**Plate Four** Bjorn Waldegaard storming to fourth place in the 1978 East African Safari Rally with a special 911 SC-engined Carrera.

**Plate Five** Bjorn Waldegaard using all his skill to win the 1968 Swedish Rally in his 911T.

**Plate Six** A 935 driven at Le Mans by Jean-Louis Schlesser in 1979.

**Plate Seven** A 2.8-litre Porsche 935 shared by Bob Akin, Rob McFarlin and Roy Woods at Le Mans 1979.

YJH 122T

**Plate Nine** A popular modern road car: the 1976 Carrera 3.

**Plate Eight** *left* The ultimate development of the 911 in the 1970s: The 930 3.3-litre Turbo during performance testing.

**Plate Ten** The 911 Turbo—or 930—that caused a sensation when it was introduced in 1975.

Shell
MARTINI
s1
BILSTEIN
BOSCH
Shell
SCHMITTHELM

Shell

l'huile hautes performances
FERODO FERODO
BP BP BP BP
BP BP BP BP
MARTINI
Dick Barbour Racing
HAWAIIAN TROPIC
70
70
ROLF STOMMELEN
IMSA
BP
BP BP BP
BOSCH
GOODYEAR
SACHS

**Plate Eleven** *previous page* The most extraordinary of the early 935s, the special-bodied 'Moby Dick'.

**Plate Twelve** *above left* Porsche perfectionism at its best: a view of the production line at the factory in 1968.

**Plate Thirteen** *below left* The focus of much attention at Le Mans in 1979: the 935 driven into second place by American film star Paul Newman with Rolf Stommelen and Dick Barbour.

**Plate Fourteen** The 2.7-litre 911 that *Motor Sport* used for their road test in 1974.

**Plate Fifteen** First of the long-wheelbase 911s, a 1968 911E.

**Plate Sixteen** Bjorn Waldegaard driving his 2.7-litre Carrera in the European Rallycross championship at Lydden in 1974.

**Plate Seventeen** The popular Porsche Carrera RS on the 1977 Donegal Rally.

**Plate Eighteen** Manfred Schurti and Helmuth Koinigg driving a Turbo RSR into sixth place in the 1974 Nurburgring 750 kilometre race.

**Plate Nineteen** Porsche 911s have proved to be one of the most popular racing cars in America. Peter Gregg's early example is seen competing in the 1969 Watkins Glen Six-Hour race won by a Porsche 908.

**Plate Twenty** Josh Sadler competing at Silverstone in his 911.

**Plate Twenty-One** Three Porsche 911s lined up for a stage in the 1969 Tour de France.

**Plate Twenty-Two** What more impressive rear end to a car than that of a 930?

**Plate Twenty-Three** Supercar of the Seventies: the Porsche Carrera 3 Sport.

One of the outstanding Porsche drivers in British events has been Irishman Ronnie McCartney, pictured here on his way to fourteenth place in the 1975 RAC Rally in his Carrera RS, normally better suited to tarmac events than those run on a loose surface. At one point early in the rally, McCartney was in ninth place overall, but punctures and a couple of alarming moments in Wales led to his easing his pace. 'At one point in the Lake District, he was short of a bolt for the rear suspension and borrowed one off a spectating Irishman in another Porsche, saying airily that he was sure that it would get him to the boat OK,' reported *Autosport*.

Modsports racing—or events for certain sports cars which can be extensively modified within certain limitations—have long been a popular feature of British motor racing. These races are far more for enjoyment than for publicity, attracting few major sponsors. Over the years the most competitive cars have been Jaguar E types in the larger classes and Lotus Elans and MG Midgets in the smaller classes, plus one outrageously fast fibreglass-bodied Jaguar XK120. All was running happily until the advent of two Carrera RSR-specification cars driven by Nuck Faure and John Cooper in 1975. These sophisticated German machines pulverised the amateur fields, leaving everything standing except the XK120 and the odd Lotus. John Cooper—pictured here—enjoyed the most success in his car, a 2.8-litre based on a 1973 Carrera, which was still winning years later in the hands of Tony Wingrove.

Sandro Munari came third in a Lancia Stratos at the start of a great run that was to take the Italian car to the world rally championship—if only Porsche could have afforded to have backed the Carrera in this form of motor sport. Their only other rally involvement in this fuel crisis year was in private hands, with Irishmen Cahal Curley and Ronnie McCartney driving outstandingly well in Carrera RSR which their countrymen considered to be 'just big Imps', a reference presumed to be to the popular rear-engined Hillman Imp rally car!

GEORG LOOS
GOODYEAR
77
Shell
GOODYEAR
Shell
77

TEBERNUM
81
Shell
TEBERNUM
81

*Facing page:* Chief protagonists in European GT racing in 1975 were John Fitzpatrick (Carrera RSR number seventy-seven) and Hartwig Bertrams in car number eighty-one. The Loos team won most races, but Bertrams took the European GT title on consistency.

Porsche's involvement with GT and prototype racing was concentrated wholeheartedly on the 911 when fuel consumption restrictions outlawed the turbocharged 917 from CanAm racing. Porsche took third place in the World Sports Car Championship (behind ultra-light Matra and Gulf prototypes), with the Turbo RSR in 1974, largely by dint of magnificent driving by Muller and van Lennep. They shared the lighter of the two Turbo RSRs, only failing to finish in one of the nine championship races despite repeated gearbox trouble. They scored two excellent second places at Watkins Glen and Le Mans, with the last five hours of the French event spent with only two gears. They had similar trouble at Spa and Paul Ricard but each time managed to keep the car going to the end to take third and seventh places, plus a sixth place at the Nurburgring. A second, heavier, Turbo RSR was driven at some events by Manfred Schurti and Helmuth Koinigg.

Privately-entered 3-litre Carrera RSRs abounded with four leading cars split between two German teams run by Loos and Kremer. Amazingly they shared the same top driver—Fitzpatrick—who won the European GT championship and the Porsche Cup by taking first places in the Group 4 classes at Monza, Spa, the Nurburgring and Kyalami with George Loos' cars after spending mid-season with Kremer! Fitzpatrick was later to recount in *Motor Sport:*

> 'When it came to sharing [a car] Georg [Loos] was incredibly slow, which I had half expected anyway, but it was so upsetting for him that we had terrible problems.'

So Fitzpatrick quit in mid-season and went back to Kremer, who was backing Keller for the championship. Disputes resulted and Fitzpatrick said:

> 'I went back to Loos, and never had the same problems with Georg again: I think he actually respected me more for walking out on him, because people simply don't do that do Georg Loos.'

During the battle for supremacy betwen these two teams—with few other cars getting a look in in this branch of racing—drivers such as Keller, Arturo Merzario, Tim Schenken, Jody Scheckter, Kauhsen, Elford and Stommelen thrilled the crowds with extremely close racing. Schenken and Stommelen won the GT class at Paul Ricard and then shared their Loos car with Fitzpatrick at Kyalami. In America Gregg and Haywood won the Watkins Glen Six Hour GT class and went on to take the Camel GT and the TransAm championship—a great year for the Carrera RSR.

These 3-litre cars continued to make up the bulk of the fields in long-distance sports car racing in 1975, picking up twenty points for the World Championship of Makes in the Daytona event in January. This happened when the American organisers saw fit to do without the European

Jacky Ickx and Jochen Mass led the Daytona Twenty-Four Hour race in 1977 until they lost an hour through damage, caused by an accident when a tyre failed, being repaired. Even then they hauled themselves back into second place before another burst tyre caused their works 935 to crash again. Porsche still won, however, thanks to a two-year-old Carrera RSR driven by Haywood, Graves and Helmick.

prototypes, classifying some of their Camel GT series cars as prototypes to retain World Championship status. Gregg and Haywood were the winners here before Gregg went on to take the Camel series from Haywood and Al Holbert, racing a long-tailed RSR 3-litre in two events before this development was excluded as not being within the spirit of the rules. The chief opposition to the all-conquering Carreras came from works BMWs, plus Chevrolet Monzas and Corvettes.

Back in the Porsche camp, the factory engineers suddenly found themselves with another year in which to develop their turbocharged racers when the CSI delayed implementation of the changes of rules which would have started a new 'Silhouette' World Championship of Makes in 1975. These new regulations, announced two years earlier, which split international sports car racing into two championships, for Group 6 prototypes, and for Group 5 cars which outwardly resembled machines of which more than 400 had been made in two years, were not now to come into force until 1976. This gave other manufacturers time to catch up and make fields more competitive and attractive. Porsche, however, turned this to their advantage by spending 1975 developing a new and even better Group 5 Turbo for 1976, and so leaving their customers to race the existing Carrera RSRs.

Loos concentrated on the GT classes with his Group 4 Carrera RSRs, the most severe opposition coming from a team of similar cars run by the German Porsche dealers Tebernum. Kremer also ran RSRs in most of the

Sideways as ever, John Greasley corners his Rallycross 911 at Lydden in 1978.

Vic Preston Jnr and John Lyall hammer their Carrera RS to second place in the 1978 East African Safari rally and very nearly a win when the first placed Peugeot driven by Jean-Pierre Nicolas collided with a spectator's car near the finish in Nairobi.

Josh Sadler powers to the top at Wiscombe in 1979 on his way to the British Hill Climb championship in his Carrera special.

European GT championship events. With drivers such as Fitzpatrick, Schenken, Hezemans and Manfred Schurti, it was usually the Loos team which came out on top on overall standings, although consistent individual performances by Hartwig Bertrams in the Tebernum team resulted in him winning the European GT championship. The Porsche Cup was as keenly contested as ever, falling that year to Haldi, who picked up points in rallies as well as circuit racing. Fitzpatrick and Schenken, who were second and third, stuck to racing.

So far as individual results in GT racing were concerned, Schurti, Fitzpatrick and Hezemans won at Mugello and Monza; Fitzpatrick and Hezemans at Dijon; Haldi and Bernard Beguin at Spa; Bertrams and Reine Wisell at Pergusa; Kelleners, Hans Heyer and Bob Wollek at the Nurburgring; Haywood and Hagestad in the Watkins Glen Six-Hour and Fitzpatrick, van Lennep, Hezemans, Schurti and Loos at Le Mans. This classic race was relegated to non-championship status in 1975 because of special fuel consumption restrictions imposed by the organisers. Nevertheless, the Carrera RSR drivers were out in force, with no less than seven finishing in formation behind the fifth-placed car of Fitzpatrick and company! Buried in the also rans was an absolutely standard road-going Turbo driven by Haldi, Zbinden and Beguin which ran faultlessly apart from wearing out its front brakes.

When the new Silhouette formula started at last in the 1976 it was dominated by the Porsche 935 and the 3.5-litre BMWs. Hardly anything else got a look in, but the Porsches and BMWs were so fast and spectacular, and raced in such large numbers that there were few complaints.

Porsche built a run of twenty-five 934s for sale to respectably fast teams to make up the fields. Only three of these cars, run by Loos, made any impression but they were head and shoulders above the other Group 4 cars—which ran with Group 5—and later in the season some were converted part way to 935 specification with big wings at the back, less ballast, and 19-inch rear wheels.

Jochen Mass and Jacky Ickx set the 935 on its winning trail at Mugello in March with 935s, 934s and a Carrera RSR making up the first six places; two BMWs penetrated the Porsche panza at Vallelunga but Mass and Ickx still won; then Fitzpatrick and Tom Walkinshaw in a BMW beat Wollek and Heyer's 935 at Silverstone when the leading 935 lost it clutch. The next round at the Nurburgring was a disaster when the 935 broke its distributor: Dieter Quester and Albrecht Krebs won in a BMW from Hezemans and Schenken's 934/5. Things looked bad for Porsche when the works 935 bent a valve while leading so that BMWs driven by Quester and Gunnar Nilsson, Fitzpatrick and Walkinshaw finished first and second at the Osterreichring. However, the Porsches were back on winning form for Watkins Glen when 935s finished in the first three places with Stommelen and Schurti leading from

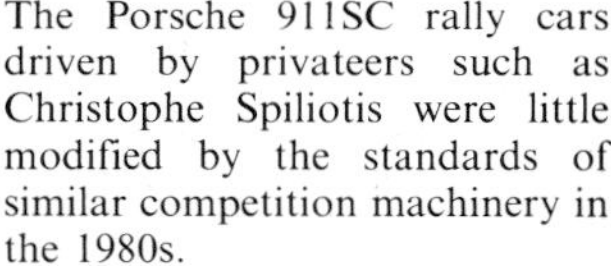

The Porsche 911SC rally cars driven by privateers such as Christophe Spiliotis were little modified by the standards of similar competition machinery in the 1980s.

Kinnunen, Hezemans and Egon Evertz and Ickx and Mass. Porsche clinched the championship when Ickx and Mass won at Dijon in a walkover with the highest-placed BMW in sixth position after Ronnie Peterson's works car had blown up.

After the thrilling duel of 1976, the 1977 World Championship of Makes turned out to be a relatively dull affair with Porsche dominating it by winning at Daytona with a Carrera RSR driven by Haywood, John Graves and Dave Helmick after Mass's 935 hit tyre problems; Stommelen and Schurti winning at Mugello in a 935; Mass and Ickx mopping up at Silverstone with their 935; Hezemans, Schenken and Stommelen performing in similar fashion at the Nurburgring; Ickx and Mass winning again at Watkins Glen; Ludwig Heimrath and Paul Muller interjecting with a 934 at Mosport after the works 935 had piston trouble; Ickx and Mass winning yet again at Brands Hatch before Fitzpatrick returned to the Kremer fold after an excursion with Jaguars to win at Hockenheim with Wollek in a 935. Ickx won in the German Grand Prix supporting event at Hockenheim with the 2-litre 935.

Le Mans remained a race outside the World Championship with Porsche feeling thankful to win it with their 936 prototype (which bore a close resemblance to a 917 with a Turbo RSR engine), and Ballot-Lena and Jean-Pierre Jarier third in a 935. No less than twenty-nine Porsches started, with nine surviving of the twenty finishers. The highest-placed 934 was in seventh position and a Carrera RSR in tenth place.

In rallying, French girl Michele Mouton won the European Ladies' Championship in a Carrera.

Porsche continued unchallenged other than by BMW—whose cars had a litre less and no turbochargers—in 1978 in the World Championship of Makes, so it was hardly surprising that they won. The factory contested only two events with their works cars, winning once; the Loos team won four times and Kremer three times, all with 935/77As. Stommelen, Hezemans and Gregg won at Daytona; Fitzpatrick, Hezemans and Heyer at Mugello; Wollek and Pescarolo at Dijon; Ickx and Mass at Silverstone in the run up to Le Mans with Moby Dick; Klaus Ludwig, Heyer and Hezemans at the Nurburgring; Wollek and Pescarolo at Misano; Fitzpatrick, Hezemans and Gregg at Watkins Glen; and Wollek and Pescarolo at Vallelunga. Most of the places were taken by similar cars except for the odd excursion by a BMW 320i and some Carrera RSRs at Daytona.

At Le Mans, Moby Dick, driven by Stommelen and Schurti, collided with a backmarker and suffered cylinder head trouble but still managed eighth place with the best-placed production 935 in fifth position driven by Brian Redman and Dick Barbour with Anny-Charlotte Verney, Xavier Lapeyre and Frank Servanin winning Group 4 with their twelfth-place Carrera RSR.

*Facing page:* Barry Robinson—pictured here using narrow rims in wet weather at Brands Hatch in 1980—was one of the most successful Carrera RSR mod-sports drivers.

The 935—seen here leading two Mazdas at Sebring—continued in varying forms to be a consistent front-runner in IMSA racing until it was superceded by Porsche's far more expensive 962 sports racing car.

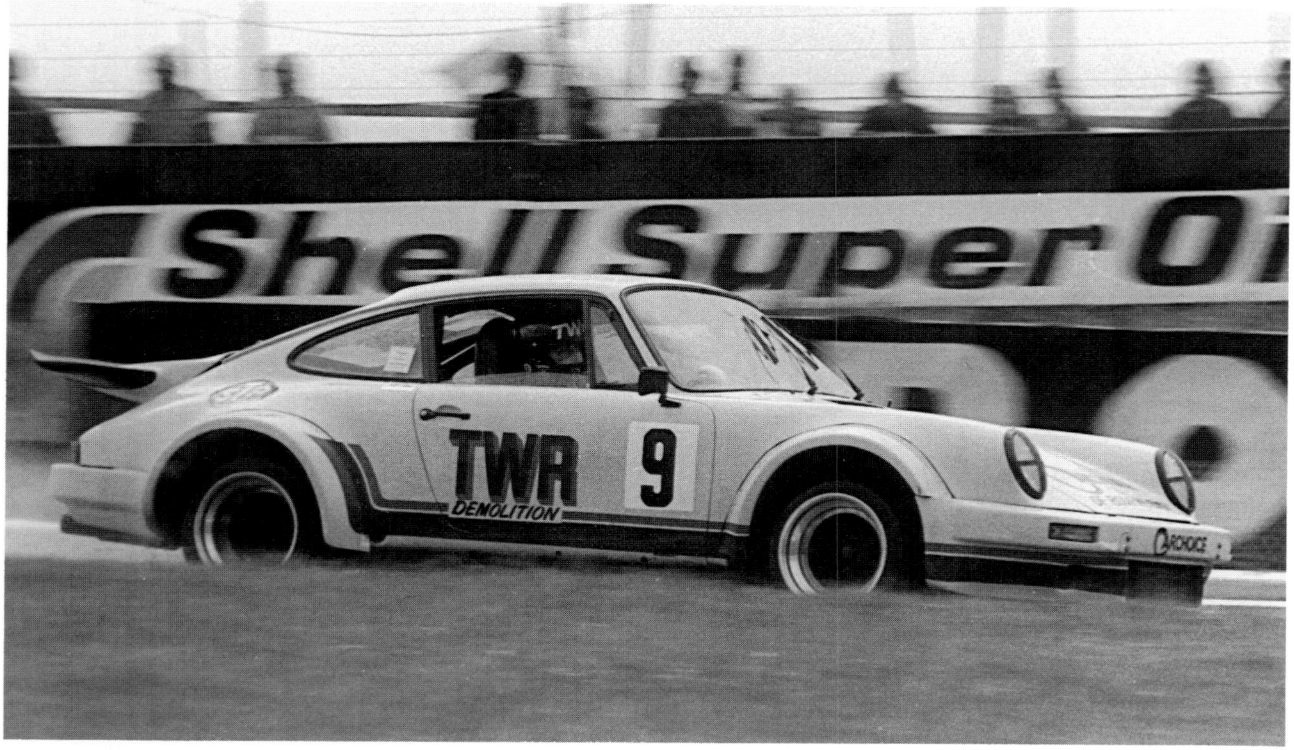

47
MIKE MEYER RACING
66
PDC
82
Western Airlines
mazda
BILSTEIN
GOOD YEAR
CIBIE
RED LINE OIL

The Carreras continued to do well in rallying with Frenchman Jean-Pierre Nicolas winning the Monte Carlo Rally and Vic Preston Junior and Waldegaard finishing second and fourth in the East African Safari.

By 1979 interest was so low in the World Championship of Makes—there was only one possible champion, Porsche—that Le Mans became the most important event for sports and GT cars, with the Kremer 935 K3 winning at a canter for Ludwig and the American brothers Bill and Don Whittington after the Group 6 cars eliminated themselves. Second was fifty-four-year-old film star Paul Newman in another 935 shared with Stommelen and Barbour with the rest of the field dominated by 935s or 934s. In the world championship series, Group 6 prototypes were again raced with the Group 5 cars to make up the fields with the result that Porsche 935s won only at Daytona (Danny Ongais, Ted Field and Haywood), Mugello (Fitzpatrick, Schurti and Wollek), Silverstone (Fitzpatrick, Wollek and Heyer), the Nurburgring (Fitzpatrick, Wollek and Schurti) and Watkins Glen (Ludwig and the Whittingtons) with porsche prototypes winning elsewhere other than at Vallelunga which was annexed by the Italian Osella.

The K3 of Dudley Wood and Barry Robinson was one of the star attractions when the British Thundersports series started in 1983 until it had to give way to lighter and more specialised machinery.

As modsports declined in the 1980s, Carrera RSRs found a new home in the Inter-Marque Challenge, racing against teams of Jaguars, ACs and Aston Martins. Paul Edwards's RSR is pictured here taking third place in a round of the challenge at Brands Hatch in May 1983.

Meanwhile redundant 935s became star attractions on the Giro D'Italia, a six-day tour of Italy made up of 16 rally stages and seven circuit races. Slick racing tyres were legal on Italian roads, so these 935s ran with few modifications, chiefly only to raise the suspension, road and rally ratios being varied by fitting 19-inch or 16-inch rear wheels! They faced stiff opposition, however, from works Lancia Beta Monte Carlos and Renault's new 5 Turbo rally car. But when the Lancias were disqualified for technical infringements, the 935 of Giampiero Moretti/Schon and Radnell won, supported by Facetti and Finotto in an ex-Wollek car, the Almeras brothers in a 935 and a 934 and Marianne Hoepfner's lightweight 911SC.

Private owners continued to campaign 911s in international rallies as the factory concentrated on the 924. Beguin won the French championship, and Franz Wittmann the Austrian with 911SCs as Haldi took the Swiss title with a 934. Major placings were taken by 911SC drivers Nicolas, sixth in the Monte Carlo Rally, and Pierre-Louis Moreau, third in the Tour de Corse. In Britain, Barry Robinson won the STP modsports title with his RSR.

Various 935s continued to dominate the United States's International Motor Sports' Association (IMSA) endurance racing, the K3 of Fibrotic and Barbour leading in seven others at Sebring as 935s made up the backbone of endurance racing elsewhere. But Porsche lost the world manufacturers' championship to Lancia as the Italian Beta Monte Carlos turned out to be

As late as 1984, 935s were contesting international endurance races in the hope of winning the thinly-populated IMSA GTX category. But sponsorship was hard to find, an unfortunate fact confirmed by the largely-unadorned bodywork of this K3. As a result the standards of preparation fell, this example, driven by Jan Lundgardh and Richard Down, non-starting in the Silverstone Six Hours because the team lacked the high ratios needed for the fast grand prix circuit.

Porsche 911s of every variety continued to star in Rallycross in the 1980s partly because of their immense power and superb traction, and partly because they were very strong. John Greasley is pictured here in typical opposite-lock action at Lydden Hill with his 3.5-litre normally-aspirated car.

Head for heights . . . Denis Atkinson crosses the finishing line flat out in a heat of the British Rallycross Grand Prix at Brands Hatch in 1984.

Rolf Nilsson leads a heat of the 1983 Rallycross Grand Prix with his home-built four-wheel-drive Porsche 911 from eventual winner Ollie Arnesson's Audi Quattro, pictured in third place.

lighter and better-handling. All the 935 pilots could do was see who could turn the boost pressure highest without blowing their engine. In the Brands Hatch six-hour, the K3 of Dudley Wood, John Cooper and Peter Lovett took fifth place, leading in five other 911s as Lancia won. And when Lancia failed, Group 6 prototypes built by constructor-drivers took their place, Alan de Cadenet winning at Monza and Silverstone with the 935s of Pescarolo and Barth second at Monza, and third at Silverstone in the hands of Jean Paul and Redman. Then Jean Rondeau won the Le Mans 24-hour race as the K3 of Fitzpatrick, Redman and Barbour became the highest-placed of 15 935s in fifth position.

The Group B Turbos could not match the purpose-built BMW M1s for speed at the fast Silverstone grand prix circuit during the 1983 Six Hours, but they provided plenty of close racing for Heinz Kuhn-Weiss and Georg Memminger in the leading car and works development driver Gunther Stekkonig, paired with Bernd Schiller, following.

Wood's K3 was allowed into one British modsports series, run by the BRSCC, but ran only occasionally and the title in Class A was won by Paul Edwards's Carrera RSR from Robinson's similar car and Adrian Yates-Smith's 911. Robinson took the STP championship, however, with the big class being dominated by the Carreras of Edwards, Yates-Smith, Tony Wingrove and Wood.

In the Giro D'Italia, the 935s of Moretti and the Almeras brothers provided most of the spectacle but failed and left only the 911SC of Pantaeoni, Meloni and Tedeschini in third place chasing the Beta Monte

Carlos. But on the tarmac of the Tour de Corse, the 911SC of Jean-Luc Therier beat off intense opposition from the Renault 5 Turbos to win from Walter Rohrl in his world championship Fiat 131, Alain Coppier's 911SC taking third place.

In America, Redman won the IMSA GT title with a 935 and Lola T600 prototype. The Jean Paul team suffered from a lack of reliability with their JLP3, although they managed to finish runners-up after turning to a Lola. Visitors included Moretti with his 935. Porsche also benefited when the TransAm championship rules were rewritten to encourage more standard machinery, resulting in John Bauer taking the title with his ex-IROC Carrera. His chief opposition came from Gregg Pickett's Camaro and Monte Shelton's 911SC. Meanwhile, in Britain, John Clark joined John Greasley as the main 911 contestant in Rallycross.

Lancia won the manufacturers' title again in 1981, but only by 2 points, as the 935s found a new lease of life. Now they had more power, although aerodynamics remained largely the same as the K4 stayed in the German

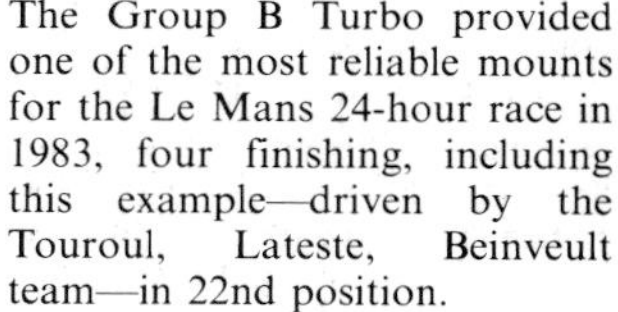

The Group B Turbo provided one of the most reliable mounts for the Le Mans 24-hour race in 1983, four finishing, including this example—driven by the Touroul, Lateste, Beinveult team—in 22nd position.

The Frenchman Robert Laurent—pictured on the way to sixth position in the 1985 Rally D'Antibes—used a 911SC to become one of the most formidable privateers in European rallies.

national championship. Again 935s provided the backbone of endurance racing fields, Bob Garretson's K3 making him champion driver after a victory at Daytona (with Redman and Bobby Rahal), and several placings, similar cars winning at Sebring (Haywood, Holbert and Bruce Leven), Monza (Edgar Doren, Jurgen Lassig and Gerhard Holup), Riverside (Fitzpatrick and Jim Busby), Silverstone (Harald Grohs, Rohrl and Dieter Schornstein) and Mosport and Elkhart Lake (Grohs and Stommelen). Jacky Ickx and Derek Bell won Le Mans in a Porsche 936/81 prototype with Woods, Cooper and Claude Bourgoignie fourth in their K3.

Therier nearly won the Tour de Corse in his 911SC before being sidelined by punctures, fellow Porsche driver Jean-Pierre Ballet taking fourth place behind Bernard Darniche's Stratos. Beguin also took second position in the 24 hours of Ypres with his 911SC, the rally being won by Andruet's Ferrari 308GTB.

In production car racing, the TransAm rules were constantly rewritten as factory teams from Chevrolet, Ford and Datsun returned. Bauer's Porsche suffered, initially, from a 200 lb weight penalty, later reduced to 100lb, which meant that he could finish only fourth behind Eppie Weitzes's Chevrolet Corvette. But, in British production sports car racing, Tony Lanfranchi won Class A and took second in the CAV championship with his 911SC. John Lock also won the Garelli sports car series with his Carrera RS.

And in rallycross, Greasley was joined by fellow 911 drivers, Rob Gibson, John Cavendish, Peter Brown and Colin Parry-Williams in the ex-Yates-Smith car, now fitted with a 3.5-litre long-stroke engine. Sadler used a similar unit to take the Guyson/BARC hillclimb championship in his Carrera RS after close opposition from Roland Jones's 3-litre Carrera.

Confusion reigned supreme in 1982 during the World Endurance Championship with the controlling body, the French-dominated FIA, making up new rules as it went along, some of them retrospective. At one point, when Porsche had been declared championship winners, points won by the home-prepared—rather than factory-built—Group B Turbo of Georg Memminger and Fritz Muller were deducted to allow the French Rondeau team to take the title. The FIA explained that they had changed their mind about awarding points to Group B cars because the Memminger/Muller car was too slow and they did not wish to encourage such machines. But the new Porsche 956s snatched the drivers' championship for Jacky Ickx from Lancia as 935 variants continued to make up a significant proportion of the mixed fields of Groups 4, 5, 6, B, C and IMSA cars. The most consistent 935

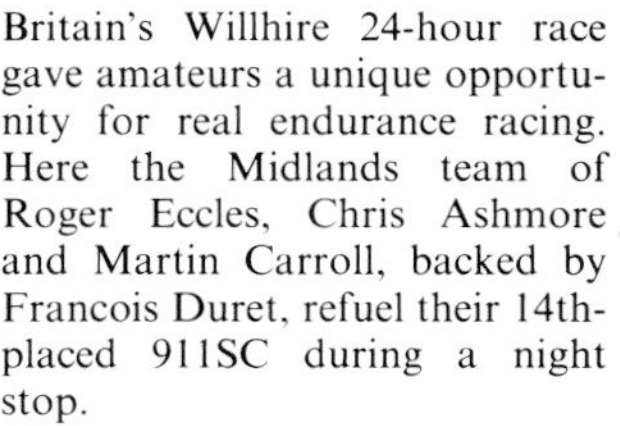

Britain's Willhire 24-hour race gave amateurs a unique opportunity for real endurance racing. Here the Midlands team of Roger Eccles, Chris Ashmore and Martin Carroll, backed by Francois Duret, refuel their 14th-placed 911SC during a night stop.

Bill Taylor became one of the front-runners in the Porsche production Car Challenge with his ex-James Hunt Carrera RS, winning numerous races—and the Willhire 24-hour race.

performer was Moretti, returning to Europe from IMSA racing with an ex-Joest Moby Dick 2.6-litre spaceframe 935. But Fitzpatrick and David Hobbs were more successful overall in a K4 of similar appearance, taking fourth place at Le Mans (behind three brand-new 956s), and third at Brands Hatch. Field and Stommelen also managed a second at Monza with their K3. It is also worth noting that consistent performers Richard Cleare and Tony Dron annexed the Group 4 category at Le Mans and 13th overall with their six-year-old 934.

The FIA and IMSA could not agree on common rules so the American teams could enter events only which included classes for their categories. John Paul junior won the IMSA GT title with a combination of his JLP3 and a Lola T600, while his father, John Paul senior, took the GTO title with a 935 in fields dominated by these cars. The 911 suffered further when Porsche switched their support to the 924 in TransAm racing, a move followed by Lanfranchi in British production sports car racing after early season events with his AFN-sponsored 911SC.

In rallying, Therier took third place with his 911SC in the Monte Carlo behind works entries from Opel and Audi, with Guy Frequelin fourth in another 911SC. Consistent performances, however, gave Belgian Marc Duez—fifth on his home event, the 24 hours of Ypres—fifth place overall in the European championship with his 911SC. Sweden's Rolf Nilsson also won the first Rallycross Grand Prix at Brands Hatch with a Carrera RSR.

Sadler, meantime, battled on with his 3.5-litre Carrera in the RAC Haynes leaders' hill climb championship despite severe competition from Andy Simm's modsports Morgan and John Lowe in another 911. And the 911 became a historic car when Sadler's partner, Steve Carr, with Peter Valentine, took sixth place in the RAC Golden 50 Rally with their 1964 model.

The spaceframe 935s were still competitive on fast IMSA circuits in 1983 allowing Bob Akin to win the GTP class at Sebring, taking fourth place overall behind prototypes, with John O'Steen's similar car fifth. Fitzpatrick also took fourth place at Miami with his K4, with the K3s of Don Whittington and Wollek in sixth and ninth places. Wayne Baker also won the GTO championship with a spaceframe 935 converted into IMSA 934 specification with a 2.8-litre single-turbo engine and modified bodywork. In fact this car went so well that it won outright at Sebring from the K3s of Akin, O'Steen and Whittington!

The Wood and Robinson K3 also made early appearances in the new British Thundersports series for endurance racers, taking fifth and sixth positions before more specialised lightweight machinery took over.

But in Group B classes the 930 became the most popular option although it was not so powerful as the BMW M1. John Cooper, Paul Smith and David Ovey's car ran with great precision to win its class at Le Mans, and 11th overall, from the Memminger/Muller/Kuhn-Weiss car. In seven events, the Cooper car, run by Charles Ivey, was only out of the placings once.

In British production sports car racing, Colin Blower took over the ex-Lanfranchi 911SC to win the large class, running AFN's winning 928S close in the Willhire 24-hour race at Snetterton until having to settle for third overall after being delayed by a broken constant velocity joint. A new star emerged in the 750 Motor Club's sports car championship as Bill Taylor won with his Carrera RS.

Belgian Patrick Snyers became the top 911SC driver in international rallies, taking second place in Madeira, although he was not allowed to score points for the European championship because it had been homologated under Group 4 rather than the new Group B.

Nilsson—who by now like most of his fellow Porsche off-road drivers had converted to home-made four-wheel-drive systems similar to those of the works Paris-Dakar cars—managed second place in the British Rallycross Grand Prix with his RSR behind Ollie Arnesson's Audi Quattro with Seppo Nittimaki third in an awe-inspiring 935, struggling to put down 750 bhp on mud! Gibson also took second place in Division Two of the British championship with his normally-aspirated two-wheel-drive 3-litre 911 as Greasley scored the odd win with his similar 3.5-litre car.

The Porsche Production Car Challenge produced superbly-close racing from full grids—as demonstrated here at Snetterton in 1985.

As the Porsche 956 dominated endurance racing, the four-wheel-drive 911s became the star attraction in the world's premier off-road rally, the Paris-Dakar. The serious action in this 6,500-mile event started in Algeria and continued over appalling roads at high speed through Niger, Upper Volta, the Ivory Coast, Guinea and Senegal, taking in much of the Sahara desert. Porsche team leader Ickx was one of the early casualties, losing four hours with punctures, fuel pump and electrical trouble, but fought back to sixth place behind the winning 911 of Rene Metge and Dominique Lemoyne, with Roland Kussmaul giving Porsche the team award in 26th place. Throughout the event, the Porsches' chief opposition had come from highly developed Range Rovers, one of which—driven by Patrick Zaniroli—was second . . . Saeed Al Hajri enjoyed similar success in the Middle East Rally Championship with another four-wheel-drive 911.

The 911SC/RS also took Porsche back to the forefront of normal rallying, Henri Toivonen enjoying a commanding lead in the European championship (while Audi concentrated on international events) until he injured his back during a crash when driving a Lancia in the world championship. He was then relegated to second place by Carlo Capone's Lancia 037. Belgians Snyers and Robert Droogman took ninth and twelfth place in the European title race.

The odd lightweight 935 was still in evidence in the IMSA series until Porsche customers could take delivery of new 962s, and continued to appear in European events with Group B Turbos. But the pace had moved on so much that they were now also-rans, and easily beaten by the BMW M1s, which had been rehomologated into Group B from the old Group 4. The best showing for these cars was at Le Mans where the 930 of Haldi, Jean Knucker and Altefried Heger took 16th place from the following 911SC of Raymond Touroul, Valentin Bertapelle and Thiery Perrier and the 930 of Jean-Marie and Jacques Almeras and Tom Winlas.

Taylor's veteran Carrera RS dominated the British prodsports series, however, winning the championship and its top event, the Willhire 24-hour race, by a substantial margin. Taylor, partnered by Edwards, Robinson and Lock, had so much time in hand in the all-day event at Snetterton that they could even stop to clean the car just before the end. He also went on to win Class D in the new Porsche Challenge for road-going production cars, with George Evan's Carrera RS winning Class C, Simon Thomas's 911E Class B and Steve Kevlin's 924 Class A. Although this series started only as a

Long-time Porsche exponent Josh Sadler used a 2.4-litre 911S to win his class in the 1985 Porsche Production Car Challenge—and take part in the 750 Motor Club's Road-Going Sports Cars series. He is pictured leading a Caterham Seven in a 750MC event at Brands Hatch.

non-championship event, it became so popular in its first year that two separate races had to be organised at most meetings to accommodate all the cars.

Nittimaki remained the most successful Porsche driver in the European Rallycross championship, taking second place with his 935 to Martin Schanche's lighter 650-bhp four-wheel-drive Xtrac Escort with Nilsson fourth in his RSR and Matti Alamaki's 935 fifth. Gibson took fourth place in the British championship with his 911, with similar cars driven by Greasley, Denis Atkinson and Dave Wallis in the top ten.

Suspension trouble delayed Metge and Ickx with their 959s on the 1985 Paris-Dakar, and when they fought back more suspension trouble for Ickx and a broken oil line for Metge put out both Porsches . . . but they vowed they would be back. The 911SC/RS cars that enjoyed Rothmans backing competed only in selected events – rather than any one championship—with the result that Beguin and Billy Coleman took third and fourth places in the

Nick Faure—pictured at Silverstone in 1986—continued to be front-runner in the Porsche Production Car Challenge with a tyre-smoking Turbo.

Modified Porsches were allowed in British relay racing, including this 959-lookalike driven to great effect by Michael Phillips and Richard Chilton at Oulton Park in 1986.

Tour de Corse behind Jean Ragnotti's Renault Maxi 5 Turbo and Al Hajri fifth on the Acropolis—the first world championship points for a Middle East driver. Droogmans, in a Belga-sponsored 911SC/RS also took third on the Ypres from the inevitable Ragnotti and Britain's Roger Clark, co-driven by Ian Grindrod, achieved a supremely-smooth 11th position on the very slippery stages of the RAC Rally with his SC/RS.

Alamaki became the leading Porsche Rallycross driver, taking the European title with wins in France, Finland, Belgium and Holland although he had to be content with second place in the British Rallycross Grand Prix behind John Welch's Xtrac with Nittimaki's similar 911 third.

Pressure from major manufacturers led to the Willhire 24-hour race being run for saloon cars only, leaving Taylor to concentrate on the booming Porsche Production Car Challenge, now with sponsorship from Giroflex. He narrowly beat Nick Faure's Turbo—by one point—in his Carrera RS for the title in the new Class A (for cars of more than 208 bhp), Sadler's 2.4S winning Class B (179–208 bhp) from Keith Ashby's 911SC, Edwards winning the overall title and Class C (141–178 bhp) with Michael Pickup's 944 second in class, Kevlin again taking the new Class D (up to 140 bhp) with his 924 from Graham Leask's similar car. Porsche 911s also dominated the 750 Motor Club's sports car series, the over-2500-cc class being won by Craig Simmiss's Carrera 3 from Richard Chilton's RS, with the 2.4S cars of Jeff York and Merv Sherlock first and third in the 1801–2500 cc class. In other club events,

such as the Intermarque series for modified cars, and relay racing, 911s remained the most popular cars.

By the beginning of 1986, the 959 was well on its way to achieving lasting fame in Group B as Metge dominated the Paris-Dakar, ably supported by Ickx in second place. But spectator deaths and spectacular crashes by these extraordinarily fast cars led to Group B being banned for international events on the road from the end of the year. As a result, it was not worth developing the 959 for conventional rallies and Rothmans continued with the old SC/RS in some events. But Metge made an excellent debut in the 961 at Le Mans, taking it to seventh place with Ballot-Lena. More significant was the fact that every other finisher, including the winning Porsche 962, bore hardly any resemblance to a road car . . . it was sad then that Canadian Kees Nierop crashed the 961, shared with Metge and Haldi, while it was running strongly, 12th of 18 survivors at Le Mans the following year.

But the 911 remained one of the supreme production racing cars, with Edwards again taking the Giroflex title in Britain after going down to Class D with a 911T (from Dave Lentell's similar car in class). Taylor again won Class A with his Carrera RS from Chris Millard's 3-litre 930, Ashley taking the Class B title with the ex-Sadler 2.4S from Keith Russell's Carrera 3, with Tony Maryon's 2.7S winning Class C from Esfandiar Oskoni's 2.7L and Kevin Morfett's 2.4E. Then with Pirelli sponsorship, this series fell to Class C winner Mike Jordan with his 2.4E in 1987, Dron taking Class A with a Carrera RS, as Edwards won Class B with a 2.4S and Mike Pickup Class D with a 2.4T.

Group B Turbos continue to provide excellent racing for amateur enthusiasts like John Piper, pictured at Donington in 1986.

# The Road-Testers' Reports

Testing a Porsche on the road had always been one of the highlights of a motoring journalist's year. The performance has invariably been so good that few have had anything bad to say about the 911 series, apart from the general dislike of the Sportomatic gearbox that was not necessarily shared by the people who owned the cars. Even the handling of the early 911s, which had been improved by development, came in for praise from many writers, showing that it was far more acceptable in the mid-1960s than it would have been today. The French journalist, Bernard Cahier, was one of the first to test a 911—a pre-production example assembled to exacting standards by highly-skilled fitters—for the American monthly magazine, *Sports Car Graphic*, in January 1965. He was full of praise for it, saying that he found the car 'smoother, more refined and more comfortable than any Porsche built before. The five-speed gearbox is first-class, and once you are used to the shifting mechanism, there is no problem about making fast shifts from first to second gear.

'The 911 is a high performance car but, because of the refinements which have gone into its fabrication, you have very little feeling of speed or great acceleration although you can actually go very quickly indeed!

'With three turns from lock to lock, the rack and pinion steering is quick and feels wonderful. This steering is direct, precise and free of road reaction, the way steering should be. With the earlier 901 prototype [which Cahier had driven in the summer of 1964] this steering was too direct but now a *"juste milieu"* has been found, and shows that enough testing cannot be done before a new car goes into regular production.

'The handling of the 911 is truly superb, and although you're dealing with a rear-engined car, with engine located behind the axle, this handling is very much on the neutral side, with light oversteering only appearing under severe conditions. The 911 gives you a perfect feeling of safety at all times, in the dry or the wet, and even with strong lateral winds (the black point of rear-engined cars). I really didn't find any handling vices in the 911, and for such a comfortable riding car, I was surprised to see how little lean this car has under fast, hard treatment on curvy roads.

'The brakes were powerful and efficient, with relatively low pedal pressure required . . . these brakes require a certain amount of practice,

'Smoother, more refined and more comfortable than any Porsche built before', was how Bernhard Cahier described his pre-production 911 in *Sports Car Graphic*.

particularly in the wet, but as I said, they are very efficient and among the best you can have for a fast car.'

Then followed his criticisms:

'The throttle pedal was surprisingly stiff for such a refined car, particularly when you want to accelerate flat out. Because of the nature of the carburettors used (two triple Solex) in order to get optimum performance from them you must use the throttle pedal all the way down on the floor. It's all right I guess, but a person used to driving lightly and in style will not necessarily appreciate this special throttle feature of the 911. The way it is now, and until corrections are made, you have to hit the throttle hard or your carburettors won't open completely, and the carburation will not be right at times, especially when you accelerate quickly up through the gears.'

He also complained about the noise, having been brought up, like so many Porsche enthusiasts on the aggressive, rasping sound of one of the earlier four-cylinder four overhead cam racing engines fitted to the Type 356 Carrera and other competition Porsches. Cahier said:

'When you fire up the engine for the first time, you are immediately surprised by the sound. It is no longer the famous Porsche sound, but the one of a very familiar flat-six air-cooled engine, named the Chevrolet Corvair! The Porsche purist will be shocked to hear this but I am afraid it is the truth! There's nothing wrong, mind you, about the sound of a Corvair engine, but I am sure you will understand what I mean, and feel what our Porsche friends are feeling!'

Porsche people are nothing if not traditionalists.

Cahier went on to record performance figures of 130 mph flat out, with a standing quarter mile of 16.5 seconds and 0-60 mph in 8.4 seconds. Hansjorg Bendel tested a 911 two months later for the American monthly magazine *Road & Track* and although he wound it up to 132 mph with an identical standing quarter mile time of 16.5 seconds, he could manage only 9.0 seconds for the 0-60 mph time. His comments and appreciations were similar to those of Cahier (except that he considered the ride to be on the harsh side) although he had this to say about the sound effects:

> 'Even with all windows closed, wind noise at higher speeds is considerable. As soon as any window is opened, the noise is definitely objectionable. In spite of obvious care taken to insulate passengers from engine noise (there are even silencers in the warm air ducts!) the engine and, in particular, the cooling fan remain much too audible. At the end of a day's driving, it takes some time before the hum in the ears subsides and one can only hope that development work will proceed to further improve soundproofing.'

In the same month, March 1965, another European-based journalist, Jerry Sloniger, tested a 911 for the British monthly publication, *small CAR*. The original policy of this magazine, which had started with the title *small car and mini owner incorporating Sporting Driver,* and had been conceived around the time of the Suez petrol crisis, was to confine its coverage to cars of less than two litres. But as the energy crisis lifted in the 1960s, they searched frantically for an excuse to test exotic machinery. As a result, the Porsche 911 came as a godsend to them with its tremendous performance from only 1991 cc.

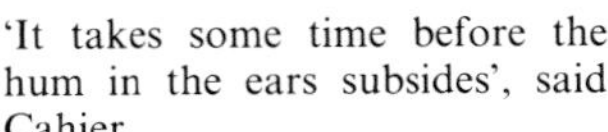
'It takes some time before the hum in the ears subsides', said Cahier.

The early 911 instrument panel described by Jerry Sloniger in *small CAR*.

'The 911 remains a two-seater with occasional rear seats which any true Porsche owner knows let down for bulky luggage', said Sloniger.

The weather when Sloniger tested the 911 was too icy to record maximum speed figures, but he did manage a 0-60 mph time of 8.7 seconds and estimated the fuel consumption at 20-25 mpg in strange contrast to his colleague on *Road & Track* who reckoned it out at 14-19 mpg.

Sloniger echoed the sentiments of Cahier and Bendel, and then—as a Porsche enthusiast of long standing—made some significant comments:

'You can now change a sparkplug without being an asbestos octopus [a reference to the earlier four overhead-cam Carrera] . . . the torque is so good that the five-speed gearbox is a little redundant, though great fun. You *feel* racier with a five and reverse . . .

'Once you've settled into your seat, with all the various adjustments made, you begin to see where some of the money went. The car looks richer for its price than the 356 to my taste, with leather and wood to hold up those five large round black dials with their luminous faces. The tachometer takes pride of place dead centre, with the slightly smaller speedometer to its right and a clock to the right of that (on the left-hand-drive model). On the other side the dial shows fuel level and oil level as well: no dipsticks for 911 owners.

'Knobs are held to the minimum and put within reach, while both high beam blinker (the Germans call it a light-horn, which is logical at these overtaking speeds) and turn indicators as well as the high/dip control repose in one wand at your fingertips. The other wand controls the three wiper speeds (!) as well as the washer. Pass a truck and get your screen drenched—you can sort that one out without ever taking your stringbacks from the matt black-spoked wheel. The washer feeds through four big jets, too.

'This is the sort of thinking which makes a Porsche worth its money to about forty-five people each production day. I'd rate the two piston-type stays to hold the front lid in any position, or the rubber flap around the fuel filler neck to protect your paint from careless attendants, in the same top-bracket luxury class . . .

'The 911 remains a two-seater with occasional rear seats which any true Porsche owner knows are let down for bulky luggage. You can just about get two adults in there, but they'd better be damn friendly. The luggage problem itself has been mightily improved—because there is so much room for it.'

Sloniger then went on to be thoroughly prophetic. He said:

'I wouldn't think a decade and a half would be anywhere near like the maximum lifespan of a 911. More like the minimum.'

The American monthly magazine, *Car and Driver,* were equally enthusiastic about the Porsche 911 when they tested it in Germany in April 1965. They proclaimed that it was 'the Porsche to end all Porsches—or, rather, to start a whole new generation of Porsches.'

They then went on to make some significant comments on its pricing. They did not feel it was the best car that Porsche could have made, and pointed out that they could have put their flat-eight grand prix engine, on which the 911's engine was based, into production.

'That would have put the 911 into the Ferrari-Corvette-Jaguar performance bracket. It would also have raised the price considerably,

'Form soberly follows function,' said *Car and Driver* of their early 911.

and Porsche was understandably nervous about entering the No-Man's-Land market for $9000 GT cars. On price alone, it would have been beyond the reach of anybody but the Very Rich, and the V.R. are noted for such capricious perversity as perferring a $14,000 car to a $9000 car simply because it costs $5000 *more*. The four-cam flat-eight also would have had the same kind of maintenance and reliability problems the Carrera engine had . . .

'At $6490 on the East Coast (or $5275 in Stuttgart), the 911 isn't what you'd call cheap—but then, quality never is. Porsche's kind of quality cannot be had for less, viz Ferrari 330GT ($14000) or Mercedes-Benz 230SL ($8000). It's of more than ordinary interest that the 911 costs a whopping thousand dollars *less* than the Carrera 2 it replaces. A Porsche is either worth it to the prospective buyer or it isn't; he can't justify the price tag by the way the body tucks under at the rear or by the way the steering wheel fits in his hands or the way the engine settles in for a drive through a rain-filled afternoon. But let's see what he gets for his money . . .

'The ads tell you a Porsche is "fun" to drive. Fun? A Mini-Minor is fun to drive because it can't be taken seriously; everything about it is incongruous—it defies all known laws of nature . . . and marketing . . . and gets away with it. The Porsche—*any* Porsche—is no fun at all: Germans aren't much given to frivolity. Porsches are designed by drivers, for drivers, to be driven very matter-of-factly from Point A to Point B in maximum comfort, speed and safety. Form soberly follows function, and the cockpit of a Porsche is laid out to achieve just that end. The controls and instruments are efficiently positioned, and this economy of effort and motion is why Porsches aren't tiring to drive. But *fun?* Porsches are for *driving.*'

For the record, *Car and Driver* really tried hard with their testing: they recorded a 0–60 mph time of 7.0 seconds—a figure that remained unequalled with the early 911. They estimated the top speed at 138 mph and returned 16–24 mpg.

Their standing quarter mile time of 15.6 seconds was equalled, however, by the doyen of British motoring journalists, Denis Jenkinson in the monthly *Motor Sport,* who had a 911 for 'a glorious week' in February 1966. He said it was one of the best cars he had ever driven, expressing equal enthusiasm to the other testers over items such as the gearbox and steering, before going on to say:

'The most outstanding attribute of a Porsche is the remarkable one-piece feel of the whole structure, for no matter what sort of surface you are on, or what speed you are travelling at, you never get the feeling that anything other than the suspension is moving. There is no

The *Motor* road testers Roger Bell and Michael Bowler put GVB 911D through its paces at the Motor Industry Research Association's proving ground near Nuneaton . . . and Vic Elford tries it out on the track.

kick-back through the steering wheel, no movement of the doors, seats or body structure, and you never get the feeling that something is going to fall off. In short, the whole car has a feeling that it is indestructible . . .

'Truly outstanding about the Porsche 911 are the ride characteristics, which smooth out road surfaces in a most impressive manner and put the car in the same category as Citroen and Rover 2000. It is the sort of level ride that all family saloons should have, but very few achieve, and Porsche have it in a pure GT car. Along a local test road which had a bumpy and wavy surface, where 60 mph–65 mph is good going in most cars, the Porsche was quite happy at 85 mph–90 mph. One of the secrets of good suspension is shock absorbers, and the telescopic shockers on the Porsche have progessively-acting rubber buffers inside them . . .

'The harder you drive it the more it seems to come alive, and you can almost hear it chuckling to itself as you really begin to use it the way Dr Porsche meant it to be used. No matter what you do it never seems to become embarrassed, like many so-called GT cars, and I imagine it would be terrific on a journey through rugged mountain country. Above all else it is a car that makes it very clear that it enjoys being driven hard and fast, and it is with you all the way through thick and thin; an incredibly safe car that you know you can trust.'

The equally-respected John Bolster on the rival British magazine, the weekly *Autosport,* managed to record identical times to Jenkinson a month later with the same car! He took the 911, registered FGX 911C, to Belgium for his performance figures, recording a 15.6-second standing quarter mile, with a 0–60 mph time of 8.7 seconds and 131 mph maximum with 200 rpm in hand before he ran out of road. But it was the gearbox that he loved best, saying:

'Enjoyment, that's the word! Imagine a gearbox as light as thistledown, with five ideally spaced ratios! Imagine changing down at 117 mph and again at 92 mph! Excuse me while I drool.'

The British weekly magazine *Motor* eventually managed to test the Porsche concessionaires' demonstrator, a 911 registered GVB 911D, in December 1966, recording 8.3 seconds for 0–60 mph, 16.1 seconds for the standing quarter mile and 130 mph flat out. They were as impressed as the other testers with most aspects of the car, but had some significant comments to make about the handling, seats and heating:

'One might almost criticise the handling on the grounds that it is too neutral—the car can be pushed up to its very high cornering speeds without a clear indication to the driver of what will happen when it finally lets go. On dry roads this doesn't matter very much—it is most stable accelerating round a corner, when it maintains a very mild

*Motor* also subjected another early 911 to snowy roads soon after in 1967 and it passed their test with flying colours.

> understeer, but the limits are so high that few people will reach them on public roads. On slippery surfaces the German Dunlop SP high speed tyres still grip tenaciously but the back end will break away if you use too much throttle in a low gear, or if you corner too fast on a trailing throttle—a moderate amount of power gives the best results. If you want to drive near the ragged edge you must remain alert because the usual early warning symptoms of roll, tyre squeal and attitude change are almost absent . . .
>
> 'The adjustable-rake seats are rather firm and unyielding and nearly everyone who drove the car a short distance complained of aches and pains. Curiously enough, however, those who drove it a very long distance became more and more comfortable and after a couple of days' acclimatization found that they could occupy them for 40 miles at a stretch without moving or fidgeting. Possibly the Porsche seat designers know best and the human frame needs time to adapt to the shape which suits it . . .
>
> 'Perhaps the biggest disadvantage of air-cooled engines is the difficulty of producing a first-class heating system. Air is blown into the interior by the engine cooling fan and heated by passing round the exhaust manifolds . . . the hot air supply fluctuates in temperature with engine output and needs frequent adjustment by means of a rather sensitive lever mounted on the floor just ahead of the gear lever; this lever is difficult to reach when safety belts are worn. We found that the demisting was not good in wet weather and the cold air supply inadequate in warm climates in spite of the built-in air extractor slots above the rear window.'

*CAR* magazine (which had succeeded *small CAR* as a further abbreviation of the title with a no-holds-barred policy on what they covered) were first off the mark with a test of the mouth-watering 911S in October 1966, commenting that 'the gearing seemed just a touch too high for the straights involved, so this coward never quite saw 140 on the clock—but even in drizzling wet the car felt entirely safe at 125 on braced-tread German Dunlops. This strikes us as proper engineering: the kind of safety that keeps average drivers out of trouble.'

The British weekly magazine, *Autocar,* disagreed when they tested an identical car in the same month. They said:

> 'The 911S is not a car for the novice and even the experienced fast driver must slow down when the road turns wet. Initially there is stable understeer on corners but power oversteer can be brought in with the right foot to any required degree. The driver needs to know the car well and what he is about.
>
> 'In the dry, the adhesion is little short of phenomenal and one can

The 911S 'can really be hammered in rally style', said *Autocar*.

hurtle through twisty lanes almost touching the brakes simply by snatching the right one of the five gears for each turn that appears.

'In the wet, the power available is too much even for the excellent German Dunlop SP tyres, and the wheels spin all too easily in first and second gears. One needs to feed the throttles open carefully and progressively to prevent the tail twitching about and to treat the polished surfaces in town with considerable discretion.'

In a very thorough and highly-impressive road test, *Autocar* praised the 911S's performance, light controls, steering and ride. They had this to say of the engine:

> 'When accelerating through the gears, two definite steps in the torque curve can be felt. The catalogue peak comes at 5200 rpm, but before that at about 3000 rpm the engine takes a deep breath and literally surges up to the next step, where the extra punch feels like an additional pair of cylinders being switched in. This kick in the back leaves passengers unaccustomed to it slightly winded, and it is sudden enough to cause momentary wheelspin on wet surfaces, even in third.
>
> 'Once familiar with the car, one keeps the rev counter needle within this punchy band of 3000 rpm to 7000 rpm with the aid of the superb five-speed gearbox when driving fast.'

*Autocar* extracted 137 mph from the 911S with a 0–60 mph time of 8 seconds and fuel consumption of 15.7 mpg, despite the car having done only 2900 miles. They said they were willing to agree with Dr Porsche's claim of more than 140 mph after a longer breaking-in period.

Of the steering, they said: 'It is outstandingly light and very high geared'; of the brakes: 'Exceptionally light . . . they can really be hammered in rally style driving without any signs of distress'; and of the seating, 'comfortable . . .' although clambering out of the back 'is an ungraceful business for both sexes.'

*Car and Driver* loved the 911S, oversteer and all. They said in January 1967:

> 'Sure understeer is safe—great for the masses—but oversteer makes driving fun . . . if you're expert enough to handle it. Fanciers of the marque yearned for the good old days when they used to *wischen* their Speedsters through the turns, tails all hung out, arms sawing away like mad on the steering wheel. Porsche is making a car for these drivers again . . . *Gott im Himmel! Ubersteuer!* We'll hang out our tails on the Siegfried Line.'

They went on to explain that in their zeal to obtain a 911S for a road test, they had to settle for one 'right off the boat'. It hadn't been prepared, but they still managed a 0–60 mph time of 6.5 seconds and a standing quarter mile time of 15.2 seconds, but reckoned they could have taken 1 second off the 0–60 mph time alone with careful preparation. They also saw no reason to disagree with the factory claim of 140 mph maximum speed.

*Car and Driver* went on to say how they considered that rims of an extra

*Road & Track* considered that the 911S's wheels were rather over-styled.

one-inch width would improve the 911S's handling immeasurably, even though they did like the oversteer. Their rival, *Sports Car Graphic,* disagreed, however. Editor Jerry Titus said when he tested a 911S a month later:

> 'It's doubtful if anything could be improved by going wider. The SPs, in this application, are an excellent all-weather tyre and the rumble often experienced with a braced-tread design has been completely dampened out. They are, however, the limiting factor in cornering power, sliding well before the g-load gets to be anything the chassis can't cope with.'

They recorded performance figures of 7.5 seconds for the 0–60 mph time, 15.7 seconds for the standing quarter mile and 132 mph flat out, saying that the car might have been a bit faster had it not had sparking plug problems.

Leo Levine, writing in the American monthly magazine *Motor Trend* in January 1967, considered that the 911S was too good. Where, he asked, are you going to drive it at 140 mph? 'What's more, since its two-litre engine lacks the bullish acceleration of the larger-capacity V8-engined cars, you can't even soothe your psyche by beating Mustangs in the grand prix of the traffic lights. It's obvious that the 911S's future lies in being a competition car . . . will anyone pay $7000 for a two-litre car that will go 140 if you get it out into the Nevada desert? Between the competition-minded and the status-seekers, there's going to be a waiting list a mile long.' He saw no reason to dispute the factory performance figures of 6.9 seconds from 0–60 mph, 15.3 seconds for the standing quarter mile and 140 mph flat out.

*Road & Track* managed to extract 141 mph from their road test 911S in April 1967, despite problems with the ignition cut-out; they said that with more revs than the 6800 it allowed, they could have improved on their 0–60 mph time of 8.1 seconds (the standing quarter took 15.7 seconds). In their opinion, the 911S maintained all the great qualities of the 911 and added a few more of its own. They liked the revised suspension settings which promoted oversteer, although they admitted that 'you'd better know what you're doing in the last phase.'

They subjected the new brakes to a fade test which they passed with flying colours. Their only criticisms were centred on the gearchange pattern (they thought that fifth should be over on its own and out of the normal H pattern), and the wheels, which they considered a little overstyled.

John Bolster had one of the first road tests in a 911 Sportomatic for *Autosport* after visiting the Nurburgring in August 1967. Despite being a self-confessed manual car addict, he liked the Sportomatic, saying:

> 'I am fond of driving slowly through beautiful scenery and this I did, sometimes changing gear a good deal and at other times letting the

torque converter do all the work. On the open road I let her have her head and, although there was too much traffic to allow the maximum speeds to be timed, it was possible to verify that this Porsche is almost as fast as the normal version.'

Porsche were particularly anxious to promote sales of the Sportomatic, so nearly all road tests of the A-series cars that followed the early O series, were of Sportomatic versions; however Bolster managed to capture an A-series 911S for *Autosport* in April 1968. He was as pleased as anybody else had been with the 911S, saying:

'Being selfish, I wanted the road to myself, and so I directed my wheels to the Autoroute du Nord just at that magic hour when all Frenchmen stop for lunch. The car really rockets up to 115 mph, and then the overdrive top is engaged, after which 120 mph becomes a very easy cruising speed. By keeping the accelerator on the floor, 130 mph is reached quite quickly but it takes several kilometres to top 136 mph. I did not actually attain the claimed 140 mph, but if I had bothered to use extra high tyre pressures it would probably have been forthcoming.'

He then had an interesting point to make about the 911S's fuel consumption:

'So pronounced is the preference of the 911S for high revs that it shows remarkable fuel economy when driven near its maximum speeds. In contrast, it is relatively heavy on petrol at low speeds for a car of only two litres capacity.'

The figures he recorded were 17 to 22 mpg, with acceleration times of 7.8 seconds for 0–60 mph and 15.5 seconds for the standing quarter mile, which would indicate that his 911S was, indeed, happier at high revs.

*Car and Driver* also did a mini-test on an A-series 911L Targa in June 1968 which was a marvel of concise assessment. They said:

'The Porsche 911 is the real McCoy. It is what the whole Grand Touring car concept is all about. Its excellent over-the-road performance comes from a strong engine and a compact body, a micrometrically accurate all-independent suspension system, powerful four-wheel disc brakes, and a superb transmission. Driving the car is not only hugely enjoyable, it's also hugely comfortable. The ride is smooth, the controls are where they should be for maximum control, and there is an enormous amount of room for two people.

'Probably the one feature that has attracted so many enthusiasts—and kept their loyalty for year after year—is the workmanship. The body is as solid as a cement caisson, the hardware and switches are not only well-made but intelligently designed, the seats are like something out of one of those high-priced modern furniture showrooms. The whole car is the ultimate expression of the Bauhaus school, a living definition of Mies van der Rohe's dictum: "Form follows function".'

They rated the throttle response as excellent; the noise insulation as good; the gear linkage as very good; the synchromesh as excellent; the steering effort as good; the steering response as excellent; the handling predictability as very good; the evasive manoeuvrability as excellent; the brakes' directional stability as excellent and the fade resistance in the same class; the ease of entry and exit from the front as good, the driving position as excellent, as was the front seating comfort; but they found the rear seats unacceptable.

*Road & Track* did a first-class job on their road test of a 911 Sportomatic in February 1968. After complaining about the Porsche air injection system which was introduced hurriedly to meet new American smog regulations and caused the car to backfire, they said:

'It's the *Sportomatische Getriebe* that's the most intriguing item for 1968 . . . in our acceleration tests, we found that the best technique was to engage first gear, let the clutch in (by taking the hand off the stick), "jack-up" the engine against the converter while holding the brakes, and release the brakes to start. Dropping the clutch (by taking hand off the lever) got a bit of wheelspin, but not better acceleration times.

'What the Sportomatic does, then is to reduce the amount of shifting necessary for everyday driving, especially in traffic. The 911's torque peak is way up at 4200 rpm, which with a manual box means one thing: shifting and lots of it. But with the Sportomatic it's possible to stay in fourth gear down to ridiculous speeds like 20 mph and still accelerate smartly away with traffic. The 911 engine likes revs, and the converter lets it rev.

'It also gives noise . . . American engines are so quiet and overpowered these days that it's no problem with them anymore, but the 911 becomes excessively noisy with Sportomatic. To put it bluntly, it sounds very much like a GM city bus when moving away from rest! Maximum converter efficiency is 96.5 per cent, so the loss is small at cruising speeds . . .

'Out on the winding mountain road it's disconcerting when a shift down to either third or second brings the engine up to about the same speed! We also discovered that the clutch isn't always rapid enough in its engagement; though it's supposed to engage with more energy at higher revs we found ourselves beating it occasionally when driving hard.

'The road test results show the transmission's effects on maximum speed, acceleration and fuel economy. Though we've never tested a four-speed 911 before we can compare it with our original 911 five-speed test. Top speed is down from 132 mph to 117 mph, partly because of converter power loss and partly because of the different gearing. Sportomatic takes 1.6 seconds longer to cover the standing quarter mile and attains a speed of 7 mph less; the 0-60 mph time is up from 9 seconds to 10.3 seconds. Fuel economy is surprisingly good with Sportomatic, at 16-19 mpg compared with 15-20 for the manual five-speed. The converter probably keeps the engine working at more efficient combinations of speed and load and partially offsets its own power loss . . .

'What do we conclude about the Sportomatic? Try it for yourself. We have mixed feelings about it—in fact, we kept wishing that it would shift itself around town—but would venture the conclusion that if Porsche could overcome the extra noise it brings it might be a pretty nice proposition.'

*Sports Car Graphic's* first impressions of the 911 Sportomatic, recorded the next month, were similar to those of *Road & Track*. They said:

'Putting an automatic transmission in a Porsche is like artificial insemination: it's no fun anymore. At least that was our first impression. However, after several miles on freeways, in rush-hour traffic, and on a race track, we found it wasn't so bad after all . . .'

Their change of mind came on the Hollywood Freeway one morning. Bob Kovacik wrote:

'As usual, the cars were stacked for miles. After only a few minutes on the freeway, we were surprised to find ourselves surrounded by three other Porsches: one was a Speedster, another a 912, and the third a 911. Somehow their owners sensed something was different about our particular car, even though it was no different in appearance, except for the word Sportomatic in chrome letters below the number 911 on the engine lid. They stared at the car as we jogged, stopped, crawled and coasted with the traffic. We felt guilty, but relaxed, as we watched them shift from first to second and back to first as the traffic stopped and started, stopped and started.'

*Sports Car Graphic* recorded similar performance figures to those of *Road & Track* and also tried the 911 Sportomatic in Drive only to return 13.3 seconds for 0–60 mph, 16.8 seconds for the standing quarter mile and an estimated top speed of 120 mph with 15–19 mpg in their test in the same month, but they didn't really like the car. They said:

'Just give us an automatic transmission—Porsche thought—and we'll have an everyman's car, everyman who can afford over $6300 that is.

'Well, it doesn't work. Not only is Sportomatic a funny name, but the transmission is a funny transmission—though there is little humour in the added $280 tacked on because they've taken away the clutch. The whole thing put you in mind of Detroit's bizarre efforts at clutchless shifting that died a merciful death in the middle Fifties. The great unlamented Gyromatic, for instance. If the Gyromatic didn't put Chrysler Corporation out of business, it hurt—and hurt badly; and we're sad to see Porsche repeat the experiment.'

They went on to criticise the sensitivity of the change mechanism, but after praising the other attributes of the car apart from the gearbox, had to admit that it was a good idea from the marketing point of view:

'Brace yourself, world: there's a whole new breed of Porsche-lovers on tap thanks to the Sportomatic.'

*CAR* magazine concentrated more on the qualities of their 911L generally than its Sportomatic transmission in their test in April 1968. They started by commenting on its price—£3260, midway between the £2676 and £4120 extremes in the current Porsche range—pointing out that it was cheaper in Germany or the United States, and saying that the same sort of investment would produce ninety dozen bottles of Chateau Lafite wine of an excellent vintage, a small chateau in a remote part of France, a very respectable yacht, a racehorse, or a good holiday twice a year for longer than the car might last. They thought it strange that the 911L should be such a utilitarian machine, but explained that you were paying for the vast amount of design and development work that went into the car.

They had no difficulty in adapting to clutchless gear changing, but the brakes caught them out, locking up at the front twice with near accidents on wet roads. This was blamed on the German Dunlop SP tyres, which offered excellent dry-road grip. The lighting and windscreen wiping caused problems which limited speed, as well. After recording good performance figures of 0–60 mph in 10.6 seconds and 123 mph flat out, they warned:

'We do not hesitate to give the Porsche top marks for predictability under ideal conditions, but by the same token we feel bound to urge that something be done about the serious breakdown in these qualities when the weather is less favourable. Until someting is done it would be wrong to regard this model as the peer of the truly grand tourers. At the same time, however, despite the detail shortcomings we have named, it does retain an almost unique appeal to the man who doesn't drive quite as quickly.'

*Motor Trend's* road test of the Sportomatic was interesting in that it examined the car from the point of view of the people at which it was aimed—the middle-class Americans who fancied a sporting car but still wanted to keep some of the home comforts associated with their family sedans. Unfortunately, *Motor Trend* did not come down favourably on the side of the Sportomatic gearbox, despite the rest of their road test, which extolled Porsche virtues in a similar manner to that of other journals. *Motor Trend* took performance figures using the full range of gears from L to D, returning 10.7 seconds for the critical 0–60 mph; D only, which gave 13.3 seconds from rest; D3, 16.1 seconds and D4 which yielded 19.7 seconds with a standing quarter mile in 17.7 seconds, using L, D and D3, thus showing clearly to the average American executive that it was better to take off from the traffic lights using all the gears rather than just to do it the lazy way. Then their missionary zeal spilled over when they described their feeling about the gearbox. They used a glorious phrase 'wing flapping', to describe the way in which the Sportomatic built up momentum before taking off:

'We'll agree with Porsche that the Sportomatic is easier to shift than a standard gearbox, because you can stay in any one of the forward gears according to driving conditions, never shifting until you stop, reverse, or park. But do Porschophiles *resent* shifting? It is convenient not to

*Below and facing page:* The 911E tested by *Autocar* was one of the first of the B series.

428
Z-4844

428
Z-4844

*Autocar* said they thought that the weight distribution of the 911E Sportomatic—40 per cent front, 60 per cent rear—was similar to that of the 911S they had tested earlier.

shift after prolonged clutching and declutching in traffic, but it's doubtful if an enthusiast could get used to the "wing flapping." And doesn't it take some of the pleasure out of driving such a superb car as the Porsche? The thrill of putting together just the right combination of engine speed, throttle pressure and clutch action to effect the "perfect" shift? It would seem that Porsche would have been the last of those to succumb to Progress. A Corvette with automatic, for sure. Even Jaguar. But Porsche?'

On the other hand, *Motor* disagreed with the general trend of opinion against the Sportomatic option. They went along with the Porsche factory philisophy in their test of a 911L Sportomatic in August 1968, saying:

'Who is the Sportomatic for? Certainly it is the best of the selective automatics we have tried and it doesn't detract at all from the pleasures of fast driving on twisty roads where you can either go up and down through the box, or stick in third and use the torque converter without being much slower. It might have been conceived for the American market, but it's really not automatic enough for them. It's as if Porsche had said: "If you want an automatic, well this is the nearest we're prepared to go without turning our beautiful car into a boulevard special, and I hope it teaches you to use a gearbox properly . . ."

'It fits better as a commuter's car, easy to drive (with two-pedal control), for those who spend a large time motoring in particularly dull conditions, and that's pretty frequent in Britain.'

This excellent test then went on to tell readers how to drive a Sportomatic. *Motor* said:

> 'For upward changes you have to move the lever quite quickly and time the acceleration to avoid a slight clonk as the clutch grips again, but this soon becomes familiar—basically you must keep your foot off the accelerator until the clutch has gripped. On down changes it helps to build the revs up just as in a normal manual change, otherwise the revs drop even more than usual, and there is rather a surge as the clutch forces the engine revs up again. This might sound an overcomplicated technique which is just what you don't want if you have an "automatic mentality", but if you have a Porsche mentality you will quite happily make a little effort to smooth out the changes to an imperceptible level—it certainly works out smoother than most people can manage with a manual and consistently so too . . .
>
> 'If you are driving hard you can easily keep the revs in the best working bands (3500 to 7000 rpm), heel-and-toeing down for the corners being a natural fluent movement. Driven this way, the car behaves just like any other Porsche—superbly . . .
>
> 'On bumpy roads the car is still stable and its wheels stay firmly on the ground. If anything the torque converter has removed the ability to flick the tail with a sudden burst of power, which we only noticed when negotiating a downhill hairpin on a muddy track but, in exchange for this questionable virtue, a torque converter is particularly useful when you are trying to get up the same muddy slope—wheelspin is easier to control . . .
>
> 'Rarely have we been quite so unanimous in our acceptance of a road test car, and rarely, too, have we disagreed so much with some of our contemporaries.'

They then took performance figures (of 3.9 seconds 0-30 mph, 9.8 seconds 0–60 mph, 23.7 seconds 0–100 mph) showing that up to 100 mph, the gearing favoured the Sportomatic against the manual 911L; it was only really the slower getaway from the line that added a second to the 30 mph time and the standing quarter mile (17.1 seconds), and the top speed of 127 mph was only 3 seconds down.

*Motor's* contemporary, *Autocar,* also tested a Sportomatic two months later, but this was one of the first of the B series, a 911E. For this reason, they concentrated on the changes to the new model rather than just on the gearbox. They were unable to work out the benefits of fuel injection over the earlier carburettors in terms of performance or the inevitable power losses associated with the Sportomatic's torque converter. Nevertheless, they considered the 911E to be fast by anybody's standards, returning 9.8 seconds for 0–60 mph, 17 seconds for the standing quarter mile and 130 mph top speed. Fuel consumption was good, averaging 20 mph.

They also took acceleration figures in top gear only with 0–60 mph taking 18.1 seconds and the standing quarter mile 22.2 seconds, adding the rider: 'It's a silly misuse, the gears are there to be used as in any manual car.'

They didn't notice much change in the handling characteristics other than those afforded by the fatter, six-inch, Dunlop SP tyres, noting that the weight distribution (which they recorded as 40 per cent front, 60 per cent rear), was similar to that of the 911S they had tested earlier. The self-levelling suspension fitted to this car did not make much impression in normal driving although *Autocar* said that it had cured much of the high-frequency pitching from which earlier 911s had suffered. The brakes met their approval but the modified ventilation and heating did not. 'It still lags behind cars with water-cooled engines for sheer volume and adjustment.'

John Bolster was quite happy with his 911E Sportomatic when he tested it over rough French roads for *Autosport* in May 1969. He found that the roadholding had improved and that, driven properly, the Sportomatic transmission could be a boon. He wrote:

> 'It has proved unexpectedly popular in Europe, largely owing to increasing traffic congestion. Only an idiot would attempt to compare the Sportomatic with the five-speed box, for they are not competitive

A good example of the oversteer described by Mark Donohue in his *Car and Driver* test.

with each other. The typical sports car driver, with long journeys on the open road in mind, would buy a five-speed Porsche and live happily ever after. The businessman with a lot of city driving to do would find the Sportomatic a much more satisfactory solution, less tiring and requiring the minimum of concentration; yet on fast roads he would discover that the two-pedal car is amenable to the fastest driving, and that the loss of performance entailed is in fact remarkably small . . .

'One should judge the Sportomatic after driving for days rather than for hours, when many unexpected virtues will have been revealed . . . the printing presses were panting for my copy and there I was, in a car that could ridicule the speed limits in any of its upper three gears, sometimes crawling, sometimes standing still. It was a good test of the Sportomatic, and the torque converter was certainly appreciated.'

For the record, Bolster returned the best figures with a 911E Sportomatic, of 9.6 seconds 0–60 mph, 16.9 seconds standing quarter mile, and 133 mph top speed with 18 to 22 mpg. *Road & Track* were most impressed with their four-speed manual 911E, tested in January 1969. It recorded a 0–60 mph time of 8.4 seconds (0.6 seconds faster than their 1965 five-speed 911), and covered the standing quarter mile in 16.0 seconds (0.5 seconds quicker) with 130 mph flat out and 18-plus mpg—all without temperament apart from a full minute's churning needed to start it from cold.

Surprisingly, their weight distribution figures worked out differently

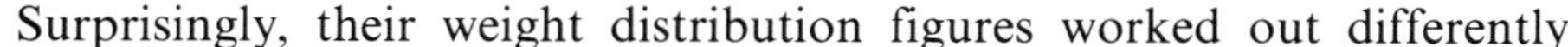

The 'vintage Porsche' floor-pivoted pedals described by *CAR* magazine.

The 911S tested by *Motor Sport* in 1970.

from those of *Autocar* at 44 per cent front and 56 per cent rear—1 per cent more at the front that the previous 911s tested by *Road & Track*. However, the American magazine said that the handling characteristics were not materially different because of the deletion of the front anti-roll bar fitted to the 911 Sportomatic they had tested the previous year. They thought it might have been safer for the average driver to have retained the anti-roll bar, which they noted was still fitted to the current 911S. To sum up, they said:

> 'Even if we feel the 911E is overpriced (at $7240) we have to appreciate its perfection. Anyone who doesn't like the throaty purr of that flat-six hitting 7000 rpm, the precise handling, the sure braking, the solid body structure and the masterful detailing—well, that somebody just doesn't like cars.'

*Car and Driver* really went to town for their B series road tests in March 1969. They hired Mark Donohue, who had been starring in TransAm racing with a Camaro prior to his involvement with Porsche in CanAm events, to test a 911T, a 911E and a 911S. These three cars represented a wide range of Porsche options in that the T model had a Targa top, and the E and S both had the new self-levelling front suspension. Donohue's opinions carried extra weight also because of his reputation for being a good engineer as well as a leading racing driver.

The 911T turned out to be the favourite because of the relaxed manner in which it could be driven as a result of having better torque than the fuel-injected 911E and S. Donohue also thought that its weightier body also eliminated some of the handling problems associated with the more powerful cars. *Car and Driver* went on to say:

> 'What really made the Targa stand out in a group of outstanding cars was the overall balance it exhibited. The two fuel-injection models turned out to be more difficult to handle in traffic situations and were filled with mechanical noises not entirely out of keeping with their more highly-stressed temperaments. But in a reversal of the expected, the roadster turned out to be the much quieter car—a factor much appreciated on long trips . . .
>
> 'The 911T shared an ailment common with the rest of the six-cylinder models—which stems from smog emission adjustments. All the cars continually backfired through the exhaust system on trailing throttle . . .

*Road & Track* found the 2.2-litre 911S's performance shattering.

'Another usual complaint with roadster-style bodies that has been overcome is the lack of visibility when the top is in place. If anything, the Targa—which was equipped with a non-removable glass rear window rather than the more common zip-out type—featured better visibility than in the coupés.'

The 911S made an inspiring noise, but Donohue found the engine 'very peaky' and far less effective than that of the 911E below 5800 rpm. He added:

'Since acceleration is important, whether you're trying to get away from a traffic light, pass or just really make it through that curvy road, I would consider sacrificing the 140 mph top speed—which can't be used in the USA anyway—with a higher numerical axle ratio and, maybe, a closer ratio transmission.'

He was highly impressed with the suspension but disappointed in the performance generally. It was difficult to make a direct comparison with the 911E because it had a problem with one of its rear suspension bushes which affected handling. The three cars had a common fault, however, in Donohue's opinion:

'When you're going deep into a corner, you want to get rid of the initial understeer with the brakes, but as soon as you lift off the throttle all the cars made the transition into oversteer. While this isn't all bad on a race course, I'd like to see it corrected for over-the-road driving. Trailing throttle oversteer definitely isn't what you want when you're coming round a curve and suddenly find someone loafing along in front of you.'

'Almost along among really potent cars, the Porsche retains its sensible size', said John Bolster in *Autosport*.

Predictably, performance figures followed specification with the 911S returning 0–60 mph in 6.5 seconds, with a standing quarter mile in 15.1 seconds, the 911E did 0–60 mph in 7 seconds with a 15.3-second standing quarter mile and the 911T took 7.8 seconds for the 0–60 mph with a standing quarter mile time of 15.8 seconds. Fuel consumption worked out at 19 mpg for the 911S, 23 mpg for the 911E and 25 mpg for the 911T.

*Road & Track's* 911T, tested in June 1969, was a coupé which distinguished itself by not backfiring excessively, although it was a good deal slower than that driven by *Car and Driver*. It recorded 8.8 seconds for 0-60 mph with 16.2 seconds for the standing quarter mile and 122 mph flat out, with 21.3 mpg. Obviously there was a difference in its preparation.

*CAR* magazine awaited their test of the latest 911E with anxiety in June 1969 following their troubles the previous year. They were gratified to discover that the new B series car they tested—a Targa—felt far safer, chiefly because of its new Michelin XVR tyres and improved weight distribution. There was certainly no repeat of the old front-wheel-locking problem, and they were pleased to note that they didn't suffer from an anticipated increase in wind noise due to the detachable top.

The rest of the car they found to be vintage Porsche as they remembered it, with curiously dead and very light steering, extreme sensitivity to road shock, heavy and non-progressive brakes, floor-pivoted pedals that took some getting used to, and a nervous reaction to side winds, all of which were compensated for by the car's outstanding smoothness and mechanical refinement.

*CAR's* performance figures were the slowest recorded for the 911E with 9.3 seconds for 0–60 mph, 117 mph top speed and 17–21 mpg.

*Motor Sport* were first off the mark with a road test for the 2.2-litre 911,

The 911 tested by *CAR* in 1971 was to a typical British specification although it still bore its German registration plates; it was what amounted to a 911S with a 911E engine and even still had its 911S badge on the back!

The 911E tested by *Motor* in 1971.

an S model, in February 1970. Denis Jenkinson said of the 911S:

> 'All the praise that I bestowed on the 911 four years ago, for its superb steering, roadholding, suspension, cornering powers and so on, still applies but more so, as Porsches have not been standing still for four years . . .'

*Road & Track* were highly impressed with the 911S's performance in their road test the following month, pointing out that it was much easier to drive than the earlier S because of its much-improved torque. Nevertheless, they did not consider it to be the ideal model for the States because it was a car that just asked to be 'red-lined' all the way and that meant that you were at the speed limit in California (where a majority of Porsches had been sold) in second gear alone! In any case, 50 mph was the practical minimum in fifth gear, so that the 911T would be a far better bet for most Americans, notably the ones who did not live in states without open road limits.

There was also the matter of the price, which was nearly $9000 due to the amount of development that had gone into the car's improvements and the upward revaluation of the Deutschmark. But it was such a lovely car, that *Road & Track* said:

> 'Oh, well, look at it this way: you're getting performance in the order of an American supercar without the stigma of low cost.'

It was the performance that they found really shattering: 0–60 mph in 7.3 seconds and a standing quarter mile in 14.9 seconds with a car that had less than 1000 miles on the clock. It was the first Porsche that they had tested which could break the 15-second mark for the standing quarter mile with 144 mph flat out and 15 mpg—which, surprisingly, drew no comment.

They also reported in similar vein to *CAR* magazine on the

improvement in handling effected by the stretched wheelbase and Michelin XVR tyres. 'The 911 has become our standard of how a GT car should handle.' They were also impressed with the extension of Porsche's warranty to twenty-four months or 24,000 miles at a time when many other manufacturers were reducing their guarantees.

Their only objection was to the shift pattern (with first on the left and back) because it favoured fifth gear which was not needed as much as first in America.

*Autocar* tended to reinforce *Road & Track's* opinion in a most searching test of a 911T in the same month. It was a five-speed model as were all those exported to Britain at that time. *Autocar* were grateful for this feature (optional in other markets), because the car did not pull well below 3000 rpm, but with well-spaced ratios, this proved no handicap. Their acceleration figures of 0–60 mph in 8.1 seconds, and a standing quarter mile in 16 seconds, were almost equal to those of the early 911S. A top speed of 129 mph and 17.9 mpg elicited the comment: 'Rather low in relation to the engine displacement, but quite acceptable when one considers the car's vivid performance.'

Ride and handling received top marks, particularly on bad Continental surfaces although Autocar's 911T did not have the self-levelling struts normally fitted to cars with the 'Lux' package of options. Wet road driving still required care, however, and gusty winds caused a lot of yawing, although 'when checking maximum speed in far from ideal conditions, we found that this seemed no worse at 130 mph than at our cruising sped of 90/100 mph.'

On the debit side, the heater still did not meet the standards of the best hot-water systems and the ventilation (despite its extractor vents), seemed rather ineffective. To balance this, the front luggage boot proved deceptively spacious. *Autocar* concluded by saying: 'It cannot be denied that the 911T is expensive, but it has an appeal all of its own. We found that the more we drove it, the more we liked it and appreciated it.'

John Bolster certainly appreciated his 911E when he tested it for *Autosport* in August 1970:

> 'GT cars are getting too big, and those wide monsters can be beaten by small saloons in modern traffic. Almost alone among really potent cars, the Porsche retains it sensible size, even though the engine has gone up to 2.2 litres. Driven in anger, it is almost unbeatable on Continental roads, but it also has improved flexibility, which makes it a very pleasant car for England's restricted conditions . . .
>
> 'On the road, the 911E gains tremendously by its size. The value of its very great performance is almost doubled because the car is narrow and can nip through the smallest gaps. This makes high averages possible with incredibly little effort and journeys always seem to take less time than anticipated.'

Bolster's performance figures were as good as the rest of his comments: 7.6 seconds for 0–60 mph; 14.9 seconds for the standing quarter mile and 137 mph maximum speed with 19 to 23 mpg.

*Road & Track* got their 911T—with Sportomatic transmission—for test in April 1971 and their comments confirmed their previous theory that the 2.2-litre T model, with or without semi-automatic gearchange, was the car for America. Compared with the 911T manual, they gave the following performance figures:

| | *911T Manual* | *911T Sportomatic* |
|---|---|---|
| 0-69 mph: | 8.1 seconds | 9.1 seconds |
| Standing quarter mile: | 16 seconds | 17.2 seconds |
| mpg: | 21 mpg | 19.8 mpg |

They also added a warning about the clutchless gearchange:

> 'The Sportomatic can have a clutch pedal, in the proper use of the term, if you're not prepared. Going around a left-hand turn (in a left-hand-drive car), if you brace yourself with your right foot and splay your knee far enough, it hits the gearshift and the pressure activates the switch, leading to a disengaged (and racing) engine. A baffling phenomenon for a split second and an embarrassment if there's someone in the car.'

Ian Fraser of *CAR* tested a 911T Sportomatic in the same month and extracted a better 0–60 mph time of 8.7 seconds, with a top speed of 128 mph and 21–24 mph. He reminded established readers of the rewarding and the difficult aspects of 911 ownership in such a way that his test, doubtless, provided an education for readers new to the marque. He also raised a new point:

> 'Visibility is both good and bad. There is plenty of glass and an excellent view forward over the bonnet which slopes out of sight so quickly that the driver never really sees it. Catch is that there is no reference point at the front (any more than there is astern), so one has to be mighty careful not to park under the differential of the car ahead. The front quarter panes are fixed and contribute something towards blind spots.'

*Motor* tested a 911E to typical British specification in July 1971. It was essentially a 911S with a 911E engine; in other words, it had the 911S suspension and options such as a rear window wiper because that was the way the average Briton preferred his Porsche. The performance figures were good: 0–60 mph in 7 seconds with a standing quarter mile in 15.4 seconds and 128 mph top speed, although *Motor* saw no reason to dispute the factory claims of 137 mph flat out, explaining that a longer straight would be needed. They said of the suspension:

> 'The ride is a little choppy in town, with some pitch, which can make the headlights upset other road users. But at normal Porsche out-of-town speeds, the ride and damping are everything one expects and the suspension is completely rattle-free however bad the surface.'

*Autocar* were the first specialist magazine to test a 2.4-litre 911, in this case an E in November 1971. They were very impressed with the way in which Porsche had coped with looming regulations on lead-free petrol by improving the performance at the same time as reducing the octane requirement for the engine, saying:

> 'In terms of bottom and mid-range performance, the Porsche is, quite simply, one of the fastest cars we have every tested. The standing start figures are helped a good deal by the fact that there is now enough torque to take the car cleanly off the line. If the clutch is fed in quite sharply at 5000 rpm, full throttle causes enough wheel*slip* (as opposed to traction-defeating *spin*) to mark the tarmac for 50 feet or so, with a suggestion of a judder from the back end, feeling almost like axle tramp. The result is a staggering set of acceleration figures . . .'

It took only 6.4 seconds to reach 60 mph from a standstill with the quarter mile mark passed in 14.4 seconds on the way to a top speed of 139 mph. Fuel consumption had suffered, naturally, at 15.6 mpg overall, but thanks to the new-found ability to run on two-star petrol, this was the equivalent of around 16 mpg on the figures in terms of price.

The *Autocar* test machine also had the revised gearchange pattern, of which they had to say:

> 'Office argument on this point was inconclusive: there have always been backers of either layout on the road test staff. In the test car, the change suffered from rather long movements and a slight vagueness, but the synchromesh could not be beaten even during acceleration runs.'

This car had the five-speed gearbox fitted to most British models, but *CAR's* road test of a 911E, a Targa, was carried out in Germany by Jerry Sloniger on the four-speed machine more popular on the Continent. He had this to say in the February 1972 issue:

> 'There is a five-speed gearbox option, but I can't see the sense of it beyond oneupmanship. Day in and day out the driver with four speeds and fewer motions (of any sort) will cover the ground faster. At no point did the 2.4 feel as though it was falling off the cam.

> 'Actually, the new 2.4 prompted Porsche into building a new gearbox as well. Chief goal was greater durability, particularly in the face of ham-headed owners who have been running over the top of the synchromesh in second gear. The penalty for the alteration is a tougher action with perhaps a minute fraction longer spent between the gears. Movements in their new four-speed are long fore and aft but close across the gate. Try to force the second to third change and you'll go right past into the dead slot above reverse. Proper method is a nudge almost directly forward to allow the lever to find its own proper path.'

Then, in one of the most searching tests ever of a 911, Sloniger said of the handling:

> 'Everyday handling is neutral, though the ultimate accident will still happen tail-first when you exceed the admittedly high limits. Until that point the car tries to push its nose outwards with gentle understeer in fast bends in the preferred attitude. I found the Targa taking habitual 70 mph corners around home at 90 without fuss. On wavy surfaces, however, there is a tendency to skitter, due in part to a very short wheelbase and steering-by-throttle performance level. At least both ends go simultaneously in such side hops with movement of inches which are easy to catch if you don't fight the wheel. Porsche 2.4 driving is an acquired taste. It can be fun with all the torque now offered if you don't have to think what it costs to buy . . .'

He continued on the same theme when commenting on the Targa top:

> 'Whether you want to pay the price of a Targa is something else. At any speed over 80 (why buy a Porsche otherwise?) the padded soft top set up such a wind roar we literally couldn't hear full-lung shouts from the other seat. I could have tested aero-foils in the draughts passing through. Most of this racket was traced to door windows which missed the lid by a quarter of an inch at the top rear corners. Admittedly their top is a true one-woman quick-fit job . . .
>
> 'A topless Targa is hardly louder at 100 than one with lid on and certainly more pleasant for a sunny afternoon's ramble since you get only minor buffeting in the short hairs. Still, give me the coupé with electric sliding roof any time for enjoyable practical Porsche speeds. Also, the Targa lid shifts and squeaks over cobbles at low speeds.'

Sloniger then said that the front seats were superb, but the back seats were a bad joke, the switches couldn't be learned even by a skilled fumbler, and most of the goodies, such as a long-range tank and rear screen wiper were available only as extra-cost options. Next in line for a lambasting were the lights:

'A topless Targa is hardly louder at 100 than one with the lid on', Jerry Sloniger complained in *CAR* magazine.

> 'Lighting is a major flaw. It is high time Porsche figured out a way to design four lamps into the front of a small GT machine. The current two, even with iodine bulbs, are totally inadequate for the car's easily-attained speeds. Whale oil and smoky wicks would have done as well over 100. Also the heater is so dependent on revs that you spend blocks of time twiddling the lever between the seats. Answer: the petrol auxiliary model, yet another extra. For all my carping this remains the nicest Porsche yet, thanks to a balance of high handling parameters, easy progress from that meaty engine and outstanding workmanship—the Targa top apart, that is.'

Sloniger's performance figures with the four-speed 911E were: 0–60 mph 7.3 seconds; 135 mph maximum speed and 16.3 mpg. *Road & Track* gave the impression that the five-speed 911E was a far better buy with their road test of an otherwise identical car in the same month as their equivalent figures were: 0–60 mph 6.6 seconds (with a standing quarter mile in 15.4 seconds); 138 mph and 18.6 mpg. They also welcomed the new gearbox's revised shift pattern as being much better suited to the American market although they realised that the older pattern was better for other countries without the same speed limits. Otherwise they agreed generally with Sloniger.

February 1972 was an absolute bonanza for Porsche fans with *Car and Driver* also publishing a 911 test, this time of variations of all three models. Their 911T was a coupé, their 911S a coupé with sun roof, and 911E another Targa. All were fitted with alloy wheels and a variety of extras, including anti-roll bars. They said:

> 'Knowing that, you would expect handling to be identical, but it wasn't. Part of the difference was because of tyres—the E had Pirellis, the others, Michelins—and part of it due to subtle differences in weight distribution as a result of optional equipment . . .
>
> 'The T was the lightest, it had the most forward weight distribution and we liked it best because it was the most predictable. The E, whose Targa roof probably gives it a fractionally higher centre of gravity, has slightly more steady-state understeer and more vigorous tail wag in transients. Its most conspicuous trick, however, was its three-legged dog stance in turns. Typically, 911s lift the inside front wheel but few to the dizzy heights of this Targa . . .
>
> 'In handling, the S was much like the E. Perhaps a little less understeer and an extra increment of twitch. Like the T, the S was a coupé, but its electric sun roof alters its weight distribution somewhat. There were extra pounds in the roof and the electric motor was back in the engine compartment. If handling is your goal, it's best to stick with the plain coupé.'

Their acceleration figures for the 911E Targa were notably better than

'Typically 911s lift the inside front wheel', said *Car & Driver*.

Rear end of a 911T with Targa top.

those of *Road & Track* and *CAR:* 0–60 mph in 5.8 seconds, a standing quarter mile in 14.3 seconds and 15–18 mpg with an estimated 135 mph top speed. Strangely, their 911S figures (0–60 mph in 6 seconds, standing quarter in 14.4 seconds, with an estimated 140 mph and 14-17 mpg), were inferior to those of the E, while the T was a good deal further behind (0–60 mph in 6.9 seconds, standing quarter in 15.1 seconds, estimated 125 mph and 16–20 mpg), giving the impression that they had an exceptionally fast 911E.

*Autosport* were quickest off the mark with the legendary lightweight Carrera RS 2.7-litre tested in May 1973. It was RGO3L, Nick Faure's back-up car in the STP Prodsports Championship, driven on this occasion by journalist Doug Nye. He said:

> 'On the road, the lightweight Carrera is a wolf in cub's clothing, demon or docile dependent on the driver . . .
>
> 'It's when you find yourself caught out by an unexpectedly tight turn (or to be honest, an unexpectedly fast entry because never before have you come along that short straight so damn fast!) that the car's basic understeer becomes embarrassing . . .
>
> 'In tight hairpins, things can become very tricky, and the rear end traction of the Carrera is so good that it is very difficult to unstick and bring the tail round. The untidy way is to plough into the hairpin, back off, bang on that crisp fuel-injected power which is on instant tap and catch a lurid side-swipe on the way out. I'm told that Nick Faure has the understeer problem all sorted out on the circuit yards before each corner . . .
>
> 'The only real criticism is the baulky gearchange, which could occasionally hang up in neutral at times when you didn't really want that to happen, but I understand that this is typical of new Porsches,

and that they do not reach their optimum until they have 8-10,000 miles on the clock.

'But in tricky situations like this it was really nice to feel your reflexes working faster than any considered though process, and after a few miles the whole business became second nature. You are a part of the Carrera and the Carrera is part of you. It is one of those cars you put on rather than sit in, and it does wonders for the ego as busy roads suddenly become empty.'

Nye managed 144 mph on what straight was available and saw no reason to disagree with the 'conservative' Porsche factory performance figures of 153 mph flat out and 0–60 mph in 5.2 seconds.

*Autocar* tested a 2.7-litre Carrera RS in the same month—the 'heavyweight' Touring model, registered MYX4L, used by Faure to win the first round of the STP championship in March. Despite being 250 lb heavier than the 'lightweight' Carrera RS, this car produced startling performance figures: 149 mph maximum speed, 5.5 seconds for 0–60 mph and 14.1 seconds for the standing quarter mile with an overall fuel consumption of 16.7 mpg. *Autocar* were also full of praise for the civilised way in which this car performed, saying:

'Turn the key and the engine leaps into life with stirring alacrity, almost as if there is no flywheel at all. Throttle response is more like a racing car than a roadgoing one. Press the clutch pedal, which needs a surprisingly-low 30 lb effort, and engage first gear—the gearchange, too, is very light most of the time—and move off. One might expect to use high rpm and lots of clutchslip to get away. Nothing could be farther from the truth. More so than its smaller brothers, the Carrera will potter about contentedly for as long as you like, tick over reliably,

Nick Faure in action with RGO 3L, in company with his constant companion in prodsports racing in 1973, Chris Meek and the de Tomaso Pantera.

and is appreciably more flexible than the others. We have a suspicion that it is also slightly quieter, though only a side-by-side test could decide the point . . .

'Thanks to the increased flexibility, one is not gearchanging all the time on a give-and-take road. Properly used, the thrilling reserves of power make overtaking wonderfully quick and safe, one is on the wrong side of the road for the shortest possible time.

'Another major reason for the readiness with which one uses the performance is found in the superb way the car puts down all the power on the road. No wasteful attention-getting wheelspin and attendant slewing; it simply *goes*—and how. Leaving a slow corner is one of the greatest and most satisfying pleasures of Carrera driving. You can "put the boot in" that little bit earlier on the exit, the car rocketing up the straight with the back wheels apparently glued to the road. Obviously, one has to respect the risk of breaking away at the back end in such circumstances in the wet, but it is still remarkable how little twitch there is and how much acceleration—provided you don't abruptly alter your right foot.'

*Road & Track* really went to town with a track test of the two fastest Porsche 911s that could be driven on the road in August 1973, a 911S and a Carrera RSR, although it had to be admitted that the RSR was not only illegal for road use in the United States, but it would have been rather unhappy in such a situation, to put it mildly. It served to demonstrate, however, the radical difference between a road racing car and a road machine. The 911S was in the most advanced state of tune for such a machine

A Carrera RSR as tested by *Road & Track*.

but proved to be slightly slower than the *Road & Track* 1972 911E up to 60 mph and for the standing quarter mile. It was faster above above 100 mph but that was purely academic for the American market by that time. The times recorded by the 911S were 7.8 seconds for 0–60 mph, 16.3 seconds for the standing quarter mile, 142 mph flat out and 12.5 mpg. These acceleration figures were roughly one second slower than the 1972 911E, but the 0–100 mph time of 19.1 seconds was virtually the same as that for the 911E (18.9 seconds), and acceleration after that was considerably better. The RSR was in a completely different league, however, with a 5.6-second 0–60 mph time and 13.2 seconds for the standing quarter mile on the way to a 178 mph maximum speed. Fuel consumption suffered, and was reduced to approximately 6 mpg! Lap times on the Ontario racing circuit were 2 minutes 34 seconds for the 911S and 2 minutes 17 seconds for the RSR. Racing driver and Porsche distributor Alan Johnson, who supplied the cars, said:

> 'I took the 911S out first and really felt good in it. It had the Michelin XWXs, which are good tyres. Despite having sway bars front and rear it seemed to have quite a bit of body roll. On freeways or ordinary roads its suspension is a good compromise and I wouldn't want it any stiffer. The 911S behaved fairly predictably and was easy to drive, though the slide points were earlier than the race car's—as I said, it rolls a lot, maybe more around the front. But it was fun to drive and I can't say that about all Porsches on a race course . . . for instance a 911 without bars.'

Of the RSR, Johnson said:

> 'A Porsche that does this well in fast corners usually hasn't been good also in tight, slow corners. It's probably because of the bigger tyre sizes plus the bigger difference between fronts and rears . . . the RSR is stiffer than the 911S, so the difference in acceleration feel isn't as great as the real difference.'

John Bolster found the 911S to be a joy on the road when he tested a 2.7-litre example for *Autosport* in January 1974:

> 'The 1974 Porsche which I have been using recently has an entirely different character. Whereas the previous 911S had a smaller engine, peaking sharply on its torque curve at 5200 rpm, the new 2.7-litre unit peaks at 4000 rpm and comfortably exceeds the maximum torque of the 2.4-litre from 3250 rpm to 5500 rpm. This enormously wide band gives vivid acceleration with a minimum of gearchanging, but the unit retains the pre-revving attribute of all Porsche engines, developing 175 bhp at 5800 rpm. This is sufficient to propel the well-profiled little car at speeds in the region of 140 mph . . .
>
> 'The flexibility of the engine is almost beyond belief. The car can

> potter along at well under 10 mph in fourth gear and then accelerate smoothly away at a touch of the accelerator . . . There are some high-powered monsters which might out-accelerate the Porsche on a dry road with a perfect surface, but on wet, gritty, or bumpy routes, its fantastic traction makes it virtually unbeatable. The sensation of fierce acceleration is terrific and though the engine is so docile at low speeds, it gets on the cam at 4000 rpm and thereafter becomes a ball of fire.'

Bolster's 0–60 mph time of 6.5 seconds and 0–100 mph time of 17 seconds bore him out and he estimated the fuel consumption to be in the region of 20–30 mpg—a valuable feature at the start of the world's energy crisis. *Motor* agreed with his findings even to the extent of recording an identical 0-60 mph time with their Targa version of the 911S in the same month. Their fuel consumption figures worked out at 19.8 mpg.

*Road & Track* tested the range of Porsche 911 coupés available in the United States in January 1974, but were confused by the optional extras fitted: their 911 (which corresponded to the former 911T coupé) had alloy wheels, XWX tyres and front and rear anti-roll bars; their 911S (which was like the European 911E) had Dunlop SP57 tyres and front and rear anti-roll bars; only their Carrera (which amounted to a Carrera RST with 911S engine) was 'standard' with six-inch front wheels and seven-inch rear and Dunlop SS tyres. *Road & Track* said:

> 'What we got in our handling evaluations was a comparison among various tyres, not among the 911 models . . . Around the rather rough Lime Rock race course, we felt most confident in the Carrera. Its wider rear tyres do what you'd expect and what the 911 needs: tame the oversteer. But when we set up a slalom course (700 feet of cones spaced at 100-foot intervals) we found the 911 with its equal-sized Michelin the best. In the braking tests, the Michelins fared as well as the Dunlop Super Sports despite the Carrera's wider rear wheels and tyres, although the less exotic Dunlops did oddly well in the 60 mph stop test. Otherwise the 911 models handled as we expect 911s to handle: crisply, with a lot of road feel in the steering and strong final oversteer. The Carrera did *ride* noticeably more firmly than the other two, presumably because of its tyres since the spring is also the same. It was also more stable in a straight line from 90 mph up, thanks to the rear spoiler and (probably) big rear tyres—easily the most serene 911 we've driven.
>
> 'What about the other 1974 changes? In general we liked the new seats; they give lots of lateral support for hard driving and their high backs don't impede rearward vision . . . the new overcentre spring in the clutch linkage lightens the clutch action . . . those new vents in the dash aren't big enough for blasts of air, but we suppose every little bit helps . . . we liked the new steering wheels . . . but the same old wind leaks at the

front edges of the doors are there . . . it seems incredible to us that in all these years of building this body Porsche has done nothing about this fault. In summation, these 1974 Porsches remain in the very top rank of the world's sports cars.'

They took performance figures for the 911 at 0–60 mph, 7.9 seconds, standing quarter mile, 15.5 seconds, maximum speed 130 mph, and fuel consumption 17.5 mpg with equivalent recordings of 7.5 seconds, 15.5 seconds, 144 mph and 16 mpg for the Carrera. Next month, during a comparison test with other expensive open sports cars, they produced figures of 8.5 seconds, 16.4 seconds, 127 mph and 15.5 mpg with a 911 Targa Sportomatic.

Clive Richardson, deputy editor of the normally very reserved *Motor Sport,* had nothing but praise for the 2.7-litre 911 coupé he drove in July 1974:

'Such is the lot of a motoring journalist that he usually becomes rather blasé about the more expensive cars he drives yet at the same time hyper-critical, perhaps trying to avoid the impression that he might be trying to be too kind to the particular manufacturer. However, every so often the lot of *Motor Sport's* staff includes a car which provokes uninhibited enthusiasm and unavoidable eulogies and more often than not the cause of the pleasure is the Porsche 911 badge on the tail.'

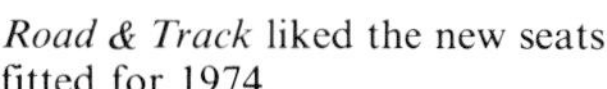

*Road & Track* liked the new seats fitted for 1974.

He explained that the new larger-engined car was 'quite amazingly easy to drive so that even grandmother stepping out of her Minor 1000 wouldn't find herself in too much deep water, indeed would probably love the car. At the end of the scale, few up-and-coming racing drivers would wish to be without one as a road car if they had the chance and the choice . . .

'While standing start stop-watch figures may have suffered fractionally, overall performance would almost certainly be found to have been improved were it possible to do a back-to-back test between the 2.4 911E and the 2.7 911 over a reasonably long and varied stretch of road . . .

'What I found so remarkable about the 911 and the proof of real all-round performance was the way in which I was able to average 70 mph without exceeding 75 mph on winding "B" roads in mid-Wales. More significantly the 2.7-litre engine called for nothing more than fourth and fifth gear to achieve this . . .

'My idea of Utopia would be to have Porsche 911s as the Environmental People's Car.'

In August 1974, *Autocar* took performance figures for the same car as Richardson tried, and tested a 911S 2.7-litre separately. The 911 took 7.8 seconds for 0–60 mph, and 15.8 seconds for the standing quarter mile, with an estimated top speed of 130 mph. Fuel consumption worked out at 23.2 mpg. This confirmed that the 2.7-litre 911 was marginally slower than the earlier equivalent, the exceptionally fast 2.4-litre 911E, but it was much more economical, and, as both journals agreed, much more flexible. The 130 mph maximum speed figure was based on data supplied by the factory, which was almost invariably extremely conservative, because, by German

The 2.7-litre 911 tested by *Motor Sport* in 1974.

law, all cars that left the works had to be capable of their stated performance. The 911S, by comparison, was capable of 142 mph on *Autocar's* figures but its acceleration times were only marginally quicker (6.1 seconds for 0–60 mph, and 15 seconds for the standing quarter mile), giving the impression that the standard 911 was capable of a good deal more than 130 mph. Fuel consumption figures were identical at 23.2 mpg.

The Carrera 3.0-litre homologation special that Paul Frère drove for *Road & Track* in October 1974 managed only half that fuel consumption and only 149 mph, but the rest of its performance was shattering: 0–60 mph in 5.2 seconds and 14 seconds for the standing quarter mile with an average speed of 124 mph for seventy-eight miles of autostrada between Milan and Triun despite being stuck behind a truck for two miles of that! He then went on to comment on the car's price (around twice that of a standard Carrera) and said:

> 'Since last year's lightweight Carrera RS closely matches this car's performance, the driver interested in fast road work rather than racing is surely better off with that model, considering things on a value-for-money basis. Even for the fastest road use the normal production brakes of the 2.7-litre car were fully adequate (the Carrera RS 3.0 had 917 racing brakes) and roadholding was as good as anyone could wish for along with a slightly better ride. At a higher level, which usually can be reached only on a track, handling and roadholding are of course better, but basically like that of all other Porsches. The car understeers, though lifting off at the limit of adhesion will swing the tail out rather sharply. On hairpins there is an increased tendency to push the front end straight because of the limited slip differential, unless you enter the bend fast enough on a trailing throttle and swing the tail round under power. On the Casale track, near Turin, I found that fast bends must still be approached with some power on and that getting the car round fast and safely still calls for a certain amount of delicacy. From experience I know that even with stiffer springs and shocks, lower ride height and racing tyres, a far lesser degree of this delicacy is required; but it is nevertheless required.'

*CAR* magazine were the first to road test a Turbo, in December 1974, two months before production started. Their car was the only right-hand-drive prototype and it came complete with factory driver Nick Faure. Nevertheless, it was an experience that Mel Nichols will never forget:

> 'We move off; the solid torque is noticeable, the engine's incredible willingness to rev unmistakable. But Nick obviously isn't using more than a modest pressure on the throttle and we're still talking cheerily and we don't seem to be accelerating hard; only moving at a pace that feels briskly natural in the car. But glance at the speedo, my friend, and

The Carrera RSR 3.0 tested by Paul Frere for *Road & Track*.

see that already, as we drift easily into mid-range in third, we're doing well over 90 mph. It is unintended, we have merely moved away just as one might do in a surburban street in a family car, using the available torque to bring smooth, steady and sustained performance but certainly not wringing the engine out. That is what the Turbo is like.

'Have I become blasé about such power? Do I adjust too quickly to this sort of performance after experiencing the Countach and the BB? [Lamborghini and Ferrari]. I don't know, but it most certainly isn't a frightening performance, quick and all as it is. You can feel the quick thrust of the power, but it is so smooth and so progressive; not at all like the BMW Turbo which goes tamely until it reaches 4000 rpm when the turbo comes in to thrust the car forward as if a second engine has cut in. There's none of that in the Porsche, no peakiness although you can detect that the pull comes steadily faster after 3000 rpm. There are, however, certain things that must be learnt. From 3000 rpm onwards the turbocharger keeps boosting (roughly speaking) so that even without increased pressure on the throttle the car accelerates. It isn't strong acceleration within the Turbo's capabilities, but it's potent by normal standards. Understanding this self-acceleration and knowing how to adjust to it is the secret of driving the Turbo. You're constantly backing off.'

There were spots where Faure and Nichols did not back off, however, as they managed to extract a speedometer reading of 160 mph . . .

Stephen Wilkinson presented a different picture of the Turbo when he tested it for *Car and Driver* in December 1975. He was just as impressed with the car, but expressed some grave reservations:

'We used to talk grandly of "getting on the cam", which was supposed to make it obvious that your engine had a peaky, high-performance torque curve. But the age of the turbo will change all that. From now on, you'll be "building boost." When you get the Turbo Carrera as it is called in America off the line and put your foot down hard, nothing surprising happens. The car accelerates almost lethargically, just like any 2800-pound, 3.0-litre, low-compression machine should. But when the rpms reach 3000, an incredible sling-shot suddenly launches the car. No production machine ever got on a cam as spectacularly as a turbocharged Porsche Carrera when its blower has spun enough to poke its power through the intake ports.

'This artificial aspiration is good for 13.5-second quarter mile times and 103 mph through the trap (terminal speed at the end of the quarter mile), which are production car figures we haven't seen much of since the late 1960s. You won't get any help from the Turbo Carrera's four-speed gearbox, though, for the first is high enough to take you all the way to 51 mph; third and fourth are both overdrive ratios. If you

An early Turbo as tested by *CAR* magazine.

'can't keep the tyres spinning, the revs at 3000 or 4000 off the line and the blower pumped up, the car will bog down long enough to add at least a second to your elapsed time. And if you're ever going to lose your grace under pressure, you'll do it with a Porsche's gearbox. What seems a precise transmission even under brisk road driving becomes a recalcitrant grauncher during maximum-effort takeoffs when chassis/powertrain binds the linkage bushings and hangs up the lever momentarily between gears . . .

'Porsche handling is a subject of much contention, for the car has long defined excellent handling for many enthusiasts. So to hint otherwise is considered sacrilege. The truth is that what many of these people are talking about might better be called apparent handling—the supple, well-balanced way in which a Porsche eats up the bumps and ripples and camber changes of twisty back roads at brisk speeds, the precise steering and overall responsiveness of the car. Probe the depths of a Porsche's real handling, however—which can only be done on a large skidpan or road with plenty of room for spins and no threat of traffic—and you'll fish up the other side of the coin . . .

'On the track, the Turbo reveals itself as a rocket to be launched with extreme respect. The exhilaration of acceleration when the blower comes in is dangerously-hypnotic, and there are corners of the car's performance envelope that are best left unexplored by any but the professionally-skilled.'

Paul Frére was back in the racing Porsche for *Road & Track* in March 1975, this time one of the Martini 2.1-litre Turbos at Porsche's test track in Weissach. He wrote:

'Compared with the racing Carrera in GT version I drove last year, this one handled infinitely better. Those seventeen-inch rear rims and appropriate tyres have certainly cured any tendency to oversteer, despite the much increased weight bias. Also gone completely was the typical Porsche tendency to react sharply to throttle opening when cornering fast, calling for quick steering corrections: the car would just close its line gently if the throttle was lifted. If you want to be fast, however, this is just the thing not to do with the turbo, because despite everything that has been done to reduce the blower response time you are almost sure to come out of the corner with too little power on tap. If some moderation is required one should always try to reduce the throttle opening gently rather than shut off completely, if only for a small fraction of a second.'

*Autocar* made an interesting comparison between their road-going Turbo tested in September 1975 and the 2.7 Carrera they tried two years earlier:

A Turbo RSR like that tested by Paul Frere.

'Side-by-side comparisons of the Turbo and Carrera accelerations show how the unblown smaller capacity car keeps pace at the beginning, and is left behind each time the Turbo's blower gets down to business. Turbo time is shown first, Carrera in brackets, each preceded by relevant gearchanges in italics: 0-30 mph, 2.8 seconds (2.1); 40, 3.5 ( *1/2* 3.5); 50, *1/2* 4.3 (4.6); 60, 6.1 (5.5); 70, 7.3 ( *2/3,* 7.8); 80, 9.0 (9.6); 90, *2/3,* 11.5 (11.8); 100, 14.5 ( *3/4,* 15.0); 110, 17.4 (17.9); 120, 21.3 (21.9); 130, *3/4,* 28.7 ( *4/5,* 31.5). The Turbo then carries on joyously to record 140 mph from 36.3 seconds from rest, where the Carrera performance falls off, though not that much, as the apparently small difference in maximum speed suggests. The Turbo, on an admittedly very hot day but in virtually still air, did a timid 152.9 mph one way and 153.1 the other—one of the easiest and most secure feeling maximum speed tests we can recall.'

Their standing quarter mile (in the first set of authentic non-factory figures), took 14.7 seconds and fuel consumption worked out at 20.3 mpg on average.

*Autosport's* Grand Prix correspondent, Pete Lyons, got closer than anybody to summing up what a Turbo is like following a drive in one in June 1975. He wrote:

'The engine is howling hard behind you, but the exhaust is so muted by all the turbocharger plumbing that the louder noise is the whistle of air around the canopy—and that's not so loud you can't talk. The car, balanced by the broad rubber-edged *Heckfluegel* on the back lid, tracks almost perfectly steadily with just a trace of a weave. The trees alongside the roadway are smeared into a blurr at the corners of your eyes, and the road itself is vanishing under your heels so rapidly the material seems to sparkle. Your eyes are riveted, all by themselves, as far ahead as they can stare. Your mind, wary about the possible antics of the next knot of traffic ahead, seems very, very alive.

'No wonder European governments are one-by-one making this kind of speed illegal. It's habit forming; once tasted, you hate to give it up. Altogether too nice to be allowed.

'In Germany today there are a few lengths of motorway where, for experimental purposes, a limit has been set at 81 mph. Generally the rest of the nation's system is still unrestricted. The only thing to hold you back is your own common sense—that, and the endless weaving chains of lumbering great lorries and buzzing little family cars and the aggressive groups of big BMWs, Opels and Mercedes steaming along at their relaxed, economical 90 mph cruise. To rush up on milling clusters of these at 155 is to understand with stark suddenness why drivers of 917 coupés used to drop their voices when they spoke of the Mulsanne Straight.

'With a turbocharged 911 on the autobahn, in daylight hours in the

'The car, balanced by the broad rubber-edged *Heckfluegel* on the back lid, tracks almost perfectly', said Pete Lyons in *Autosport*.

more congested areas, you're on the brakes quite as much as the throttle. Except in bursts, 155 is not really a very practical speed. But by the *geist* of the sainted professor, it's nice!'

*Road & Track* carried out a comparison between the 911S and their Turbo Carrera in January 1976, reporting:

> 'The 911S (a forty-nine state version) was appreciably quicker than the California Carrera we tested in June 1975. It got to 60 mph in 7.5 seconds versus 8.2 and covered the quarter mile in 15.8 seconds versus 16.5. The differences are probably attributable to the federal version's 50 lb lower curb weight (California cars have dual thermal reactors and exhaust-gas recirculation) and five extra horsepower because both cars had identical gearing. Fifth-gear response is still marred by a bit of a jerk, snatch and gear rattle below 2500 rpm but otherwise the engine is impressively flexible. It comes on the cam strongly at about 4000 rpm and zooms towards its 6600 rpm red line at a dizzing rate. Driveability was excellent and the forty-nine state car doesn't have the strong dashpot to hold the throttle open during deceleration to reduce hydrocarbon emissions that we disliked so much in the 1975 Carrera.
>
> 'Porsche had a good reason for increasing the displacement of the Turbo engine to 2993 cc. When it's running below 3000 rpm it feels like a low-compression engine. This should come as no surprise . . . off boost the Turbo is less torquey and less responsive than the small S unit; drop to 2000 rpm and it's even more fussy and juddery than the S. But when the tach needle swings past 3000 rpm, look out.'

Two British magazines, *Autocar* and *Autosport,* tested the new three-speed Sportomatic in 1976. *Autocar* pointed out that it was an option that had proved far more popular in America than in Britain, but they quite liked the car. The torque produced by the normally-aspirated 3-litre Carrera engine was good enough to provide more than adequate performance although the semi-automatic gearbox still took the edge off what was available. *Autocar's* test figures were 0–60 mph 7.3 seconds, standing quarter mile, 15.9 seconds, top speed 141 mph and fuel consumption 21 mpg on average. They also commented on the suspension revisions to this I-series car:

> 'These evidence themselves in improved reaction to a mid-corner lift off the accelerator, there being less tendency to move towards terminal oversteer, and like the Turbo, the Carrera 3 can now be rated as a very safe sports car indeed—provided nothing silly is attempted.'

John Bolster was lucky enough to test a Turbo as well as a Sportomatic for *Autosport* in October 1976 following an accident to the manual five-speeder he was to have tested. The Sportomatic was a 911 Targa and proved to be only slightly slower than the Carrera despite its smaller capacity, returning a 0–60 mph time of 7.8 seconds, standing quarter mile of 16.4 seconds and top speed of 131 mph with 21 to 29 mpg. Bolster agreed in general with *Autocar's* comments, adding that the only real criticisms were wind noise above 120 mph ('somewhat overpowering') and:

> 'When there are so many practical features, such as the warmed front screen and external driving mirror, the latter adjustable from inside the car, the electrically-raised windows, and the sterio radio, the omission of an independent ventilation system seems curious . . . it is therefore extraordinary that these luxuriously equipped and beautifully made cars should have no eyeball ventilators, or fresh air ducts separate from the heating system.'

He then went on to comment on the Turbo:

> 'An astonishing feature is the low revs at which full boost is felt and even when driving extremely fast, one need never go up to the red mark on the rev-counter. The acceleration is tremendous, but it is entirely controllable and with those tyres, plus rearward weight distribution, traction can never be broken.'

Bolster's figures were 0–60 mph, 6.0 seconds, standing quarter mile 14.1 seconds and 15 to 25 mpg, with no top speed actually taken because:

> 'As regards the maximum speed, the makers claim 155 mph and this seems very close to the mark. I usually make several timed runs, but on this occasion, with the speedometer just passing the 160 mph mark one of the rear tyres deflated. As the speedometer is only slightly optimistic, I would guess that the claimed maximum of 155 mpg was in the bag, but with just a (slightly illegal?) emergency spare in the boot, further attempts were obviously impossible.
>
> 'The cause of the flat tyre has yet to be established, but I'm almost glad it happened, for nothing else could give greater proof of the incredible stability of the Turbo. The noise and vibration were tremendous but the car never deviated an inch, pulling up without the slightest drama.'

There followed three fascinating tests of special Porsches in the 911 idiom: two with Al Holbert's 934, one of them including a Martini 935 for comparison, and the third with a Kremer-modified 3 litre. The first of these tests, by *Car and Driver* in October 1976, featured the 934 in comparison with a Chevrolet Monza modified by Dekon Engineering. Of the Porsche, Patrick Bedard from *Car and Driver,* said:

> 'Moving away from the mark was . . . laborious for the Porsche. Its

rear weight bias ruled out any chance of spinning the tyres, and since the turbocharger has no effect at low engine speeds, there was no choice but grunting it into motion and waiting for the boost to come up. And the wait is significant. The time to 30 mph is nearly twice as long as the Monza's. Consequently, quarter-mile times are poor by comparison—14.6 seconds and 115.4 mph. But once the boost comes up, the rate of acceleration is nearly as quick as that of the Monza. The time from 60 to 120 mph is 8.2 seconds, only 0.3 seconds off the pace.

'Under braking, the advantage shifts to the other court. The Porsche's rate of deceleration was slightly greater: 1.10 G compared to the Monza's 1.05 G. The rearward weight distribution, long heralded as a feature of mid and rear engined cars, no doubt comes into play here, keeping the Porsche's front tyres from being overloaded as weight transfers forward.'

Holbert, who owned both cars, racing them in American GT events, said he had yet to manage a really satisfactory lap in the Porsche despite the 934 having won in the TransAm series! Holbert said:

> 'I've done a few turns right, but never every turn on the circuit. You have to lead so far in advance with the throttle. You need the power at a certain place in a turn, but to actually have it there, you must order it up well in advance. If you ordered too late, you're slow. Too early and you have to lift it off. Then it's really gone. Even when you do it right, if something comes up to interrupt your plan, like getting caught in traffic, you won't lose just a tenth or two per lap. It will be one or two seconds. So I constantly think about getting on the throttle at exactly the right time, sometimes to the point that I make mistakes going into turns. This lag is contrary to the whole theory of racing car design.
>
> 'I've found that I need a new reference point, and the turbocharger whine seems to supply it. The turbo makes the exhaust quiet—I don't even wore ear plugs—so I can hear the impeller winding up. After listening to it for a while, I'm beginning to know that when it reaches a certain point the power will be along in the next split instant. This makes driving a little easier.'

Performance figures for the 934 were 0–60 mph, 7.4 seconds, standing quarter mile 14.6 seconds, and top speed 162 mph. *Road & Track* returned a similar standing quarter mile time, of 14.2 seconds, with the same car in January 1977 but managed a much better 0–60 mph time of 5.8 seconds with no top speed recorded but a fuel consumption under racing conditions estimated at 4 mpg! For comparison, a normal road-going Turbo returned 15.2 seconds for the standing quarter mile, 6.7 seconds for the 0–60 mph and 17 mpg. The single-turbo Martini 935 tested at the same time was much more spectacular. Its standing quarter mile took only 8.9 seconds, the 0–60 mph an

A 935 of the type tested by *Road & Track*.

incredible 3.3 seconds and the top speed (on factory figures) was 205 mph. Fuel consumption was again estimated at 4 mpg.

In comparison testing at Watkin's Glen, with Jochen Mass at the wheel, the 935 lapped in 1 min 55.25 seconds against Holbert's 934 (2 minutes 2.4 seconds) and his standard Turbo (2 minutes 33.2 seconds). This emphasised the difference between the 934 and the standard Turbo when the power was really on as they were of similar weight and shape. Later *Road & Track's* Ron Wakefield had an opportunity to drive one of the Martini 935s at Weissach. He reported:

> 'The basic exercise with this car is learning the turbo. It comes in almost violently, and a mistake with it could put you off the track. But by the end of my session with the 935 I'm learning to brake late enough so that the brakes are actually working, to get through the turns at something near the cornering limit of 1.4G. The tach is reading 6500 rpm on the long near-straight of the CanAm circuit, which amounts to 170 mph. This is a bit short of the car's maximum of 209 mph, but no driver is likely to reach that on this short, gently bent straight.'

The third test was by *CAR* in March 1977 of an incredible road-going Porsche, built by Kremer for pianist Keith Jarrett. It started life as a basic 1977-model 911 with optional limited slip differential, rear window wiper, five-speed gearbox, special trim, electric sunroof and exterior mirrors, Cibie lights and Recaro seats. Kremer removed the engine and keeping only the original block, crankshaft and connecting rods, took it to 3 litres and increased the power from the standard 165 bhp to 250. They replaced the standard wheels and tyres with 7-inch and 8-inch wheels fitted with Pirelli P7 tyres and covered them with Carrera arches. The front torsion bars and stabiliser remained standard, but the rear torsion bars were replaced with thicker ones, a special rear stabiliser system was fitted with Bilstein shock absorbers all round. A Group 4 racing spoiler almost brushing the ground incorporated both the driving lights and a big-capacity oil cooler. The cost of this lot was equal to that of the car in the first place . . . but the results electrified Mel Nichols, who wrote:

> 'The clutch, from Porsche's own RS racer, came out beautifully, steady as you like, but short and positive in the action, full of feel and without any impression of heaviness. The nose rose but a fraction, the tail barely twitched and with the three pipes blaring their mighty song we tore down the track. When we stopped, the watches said we'd reached 60 mph in 6.0 seconds, and 100 mph in 12.6 seconds. For God's sake, we hadn't been trying! This was just a practice run, the first time the car had been opened up, the first time I'd so much as sat behind its wheel. We lined up again, with a few more rpm for the take-off this time and running each gear out to the full 7300 rpm that Kremer had set as the change-up points, we had 5.5 seconds and 12.1 seconds . . . and there was more . . .
>
> 'It had become apparent that revs on take-off were critical. Too few and the grip of those squat Pirellis was tenacious enough to bog the car down a little; too many and there was needless wheelspin. The right figure, it transpired, was precisely 3300 rpm. Slip the clutch then, and the Porsche was away as clean as a whistle with wheelspin for just a few feet and the engine firmly into its power band to go on revving so strongly. But I kept getting it wrong, thrown by such readily available wheelspin in a Porsche (you can't get it in the Turbo because at the very high revs necessary the clutch slips), fearful that the loss of traction was indeed at the clutch and not twixt tyres and road surface. But then it was just right and we were looking at times of nothing more than 5.0 seconds and 11.6 seconds. Kremer had given my friend the edge he sought over the Turbo . . .'

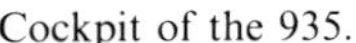

Cockpit of the 935.

The roadholding and handling came in for similar praise with the only drawback to the conversion being the necessity for blanking caps to be fitted to one or two of the three exhaust outlets to keep the noise below legal limits in town. *Motor* tested a car in January 1977 which was similar to Jarrett's machine before Kremer modified it and were equally pleased:

> 'Bearing in mind that the last "mundane" Porsche that we tried (the

911T of 1973) was a bit of an anti-climax after the breathtaking 911S, we were very impressed with the 911 Lux. For £11,500 the 911 Lux offers true Porsche motoring barely diluted from the heady heights of the Carrera 3 which costs £2500 more. It isn't as quick, of course, nor does it hold the road quite so tenaciously, but we doubt that many buyers would notice the difference. The Lux doesn't have the Carrera's thermostatically-controlled heater either, but the heater with its own electric fan introduced in 1975 is far superior to that of the earlier 911s; at long last the car also has fresh air ventilation.'

They considered it to be one of the best supercars with excellent handling and roadholding, a comfortable and quiet disposition, and performance figures of 0–60 mph, 7.2 seconds, standing quarter mile, 15.7 seconds, and an estimated top speed of 135 mph with an average fuel consumption of 21.5 mpg.

*Car and Driver* didn't feel the same way at all about the 911S Targa with Comfort Group fittings tested in March 1977. Don Sherman wrote:

'Perhaps they should call this car the Porsche Brougham—the Soft Porsche. While the exterior projects the regular 911S's flinthard aura of aggressiveness, the inside is soothing balm for the frenzied executive. Porsche, you see, has discovered product planning. And the product planners, in turn have discovered that as Porsche prices went up, a different sort of customer started buying the cars. These new guys gravitated to the Porsche image, but they have enough hassles during the course of their business day and take no pleasure in the kidney-kicking ride and the racer-stark furnishings of the traditional 911S.

'For this kind of man, the product planners have contrived a special set of options . . . the serious stuff can be found in the tyre, shock absorber and torsion-bar departments. All of these suspension pieces have been biased about as far in the Cadillac direction as Porsche dares—and after driving this example, we can say that Porsche dared a lot.'

The handling on its narrow rims came in for severe criticism, having returned to the old trailing throttle oversteer character. The performance, however, at 130 mph top speed (limited by the 'rather soggy HR-rated Uniroyal Rallye 240 tyres'), and 15.5-second standing quarter mile got full marks, as did the new brake servo which 'lessens pedal effort without sacrificing a bit of sensitivity'.

However, *Car and Driver* wound up by saying:

'We think it best that you consider this Soft Porsche to be a marketing experiment—and one which the product planners are sure will work.

The 911SC as tested by *Autocar* in 1977.

Now there are 911S Porsches for riding and 911S Porsches for driving. Let your preference by your guide.'

Mixed feelings were expressed in six tests of the 911SC. The Sport version, registered 911 HUL, tested by *Autocar,* in December 1977, definitely met with their approval:

> 'Porsche have refined a car in the 3.0 Carrera that few can have thought needed any change. Though one might mourn the passing of this very thrilling car, Porsche have produced as its successor, a very civilised, yet still exciting, machine. The addition of P7 tyres to the Sport specification has given a new dimension to the handling and roadholding which are now of the highest standard. It remains one of the most desirable of cars to the enthusiast.'

They found the P7 tyres a problem during performance testing in that they couldn't make them spin while taking off below 4000 rpm, yet at 4500 rpm on blast off the car slithered dramatically on a damp surface. Once they had got it right they hit 60 mph from rest in 6.5 seconds and covered the standing quarter mile in 15.1 seconds. Top speed was computed at 141 mph with a fuel consumption of 17.9 mpg on average. To balance their problems in obtaining ultimate acceleration, they were enchanted with the new-found flexibility of the engine. So far as ride was concerned, they found the tyres 'distinctly lumpy at town speeds' but better when travelling fast. Otherwise, comfort received top marks apart from the thermostatically-controlled heater, which they considered to be an improvement on previous systems, but whose use still needed a lot of practice to perfect.

*Car and Driver's* test of a 911SC Targa without the Sport package stood up to everything that *Autocar* had said and managed better acceleration times of 5.5 seconds for 0–60 mph and 14.8 seconds for the standing quarter mile—obviously, the car was quicker off the mark with its higher profile and narrower tyres. Editor David E. Davis Jnr gave it fullsome praise, concluding:

'There is a hard-to-define "rightness" about this car, inside and out. It's tight, solid and apparently very well put together. It fairly shouts quality. Driving it is an exercise in euphoria, a chance to sample something as different from conventional cars as turbo-props were from piston-driven aircraft. If you've never owned a Porsche, or driven one, you owe yourself the experience . . . especially since there can't be too many years of life in the 911 series. I wouldn't want to grow old without counting a Porsche among my memories, and neither should you.'

*Road & Track* tested a 911SC coupé without the rear spoiler but with the Pirelli tyres in April 1978 and managed a 6.3-second 0–60 mph time with 15.3 seconds for the standing quarter mile, thanks in part to a slightly dusty track that must have helped the initial take-off. They agreed with *Autocar* and *Car and Driver* over the 911SC and added the following comments:

'Though lacking a rear wing . . . the SC is quite stable, even at twice the legal limit [55 mph in America]. Above that speed, however, the car starts to feel a little loose and floaty and a wing would be an asset . . .

'Porsche has really gotten its act together regarding noise. The SC's lack of engine noise makes driving somewhat eerie. Drivers familiar with previous 911s wanted to pass everyone, only to find they were going the legal limit and that driving to the engine sound put them somewhere between 70 and 80 mph. What's more, the dreaded wind noise that has plagued 911s since Day One is gone. Even the noise around the mirrors is subdued. An indication of the car's tightness comes when you slam a door with the windows closed. It usually takes two or three tries because of the air trapped inside the car.'

Clive Richardson returned an identical 0–60 mph time of 6.5 seconds to that recorded by *Autocar* when he tested 911 HUL for *Motor Sport* in May 1978. His comments were in the same vein as those of *Autocar* and he added:

'Any misgivings I might have had about Porsche ruining the legendary braking and sensitivity and performance by fitting a servo (another case of pandering to the US market I suspected) proved to be practically unfounded. True, the sensivity has lost a few per cent, if the non-servoed system is marked at 100 per cent, but the progression remains excellent, the stopping power probably unchanged, though feeling superior because it is achieved so much more effortlessly.

A 911SC with Sport package as tested by Mel Nichols for *CAR*.

"Effortlessly" is really a wrong choice of word, for this is not an over-servoed, lightweight system: heavy braking from high speed demands a sensible amount of muscle power. Taken to the ultimate, the front brakes lock first, but this is not a characteristic which will intrude in normal, fast driving, even in the wet. The servo scores in subtly reducing the effort required in give-and-take motoring, a sensible concession to the increased frequency of brake application demanded by today's denser traffic conditions.'

Mel Nichols, of *CAR*, with the Kremer Porsche still implanted in his mind, was at variance with the other testers after driving a 911SC with Sport package. He wrote:

'Respect, admiration and excitement have been among my feelings for the 911 in each of its ever-changing forms. But so too has reserve. More importantly, all-embracing affection has not; and if, in its absence, I have kidded myself that, like a groom entering a marriage of convenience, it might come with time, I now know that it cannot.'

It was to be one of the best descriptions by any journalist as to why so

The 911SC as tested by John Bolster for *Autosport* in 1979 devoid of rear spoiler.

many people who admire Porsches do not want to own a 911. Nichols continued:

> 'Not even the mighty Pirellis can overcome the inherent liabilities of the Porsche's engine-aft-of-the-rear-axle design. At least, with the SC Sport they can't. Experience with certain of the more firmly set models of the past and certainly with the Kremer Porsche, indicates that a great deal more stability can be achieved; but then Porsche are caught having to provide something approaching the comfort and refinement consistent with today's standards, and those standards have changed a lot in the past few years. So, marvellous as it can be, I am left with the impression that the SC Sport is rather like a terribly well developed hot rod—a car with truly dynamic performance, and beautifully engineered; but a car without the supreme integrity, inherent refinement and sheer breeding that stems from design rather than developmental superiority.'

Nichols also tried a standard SC on its German Dunlop SP Super tyres and found it to be far more 'traditionally Porsche, moving around on the road more with the wheel jiggling lightly from side to side in the hands but not really deviating from its line.' He considered that this showed far more of the car's true character. He added:

> 'But enjoy that character as one might, the SC can, of course, be just as unsettling in adverse conditions as the Sport. A road that dips and

rises as well as curving makes it feel just too insecure for me. I found, for example, that I was not making such good time along a certain piece of road in the south west as I had a few days earlier in both a Lancia Gamma and a Peugeot 604Ti. There, of course, is the rub. The 911 has come a long, long way—but so have ordinary saloon car standards and many of them can handle a wide variety of conditions with more aplomb than the Porsche, and the result can be more sheer speed over a given stretch of road (and certainly with a lot more comfort and quietness) despite the Porsche's far greater straightline speed. Porsche could, no doubt, go on developing the 911 as superbly as they have done in the past—retrograde offshoots like the finless Carrera 3 apart—for a long time yet. But times and conditions are against them; the times and the conditions that have finally put the 911 into perspective for me.'

Nichols's performance figures equated with those of the other British magazines and so, remarkably, did John Bolster's with his test of 911 HUL (now devoid of its rear spoiler) in *Autosport* in January 1979. His 0–60 mph time was 6.4 seconds, the standing quarter mile faster at 14.6 seconds, top speed the same at 140 mph, and fuel consumption almost identical at 17.23 mpg. He commented:

'For long journeys, the 911SC is marvellously effortless and the cornering power is high. In normal driving the machine understeers and few owners will wish to go beyond that stage. A daring driver may eventually hang the tail out, but rapid correction is then imperative for there is eventually a point of no return. In general, the cornering power is so high that one can forget the rear-engined configuration on dry roads. In the wet, it would perhaps be advisable to use a modicum of discretion.'

He then stepped part of the way into the Nichols camp by concluding:

'It has a personality that is all its own and I can understand how people become addicted to the marque, even though I am perhaps not totally convinced myself.'

Total faith was restored in the 911 concept with *Motor's* road test of a 3.3-litre Turbo in May 1979 (*Car and Driver* also tested a 3.3 Turbo in August 1979, but they had engine trouble so it would not be fair to quote from it). *Motor's* performance figures were tremendous: 0–60 mph in 5.3 seconds, a standing quarter mile in 13.4 seconds and 160 flat out with possibly another couple of mph had the exterior mirror been folded flat. *Motor* said:

'The 60 mph figure and the 0–100 mph time of 12.3 seconds breaks new ground, making the Turbo the quickest production car we (and as far as we know, anybody else) has ever tested. The standing quarter mile

PORSCHE
70

S-AY 2808

S-AY 2808

is in 13.4 seconds, passing the post at 104 mph; if this is not quite in the same league as a dragster, it is certainly enough to blow off almost anything else on the public road . . .

'The important increments in a car of this type are 50–70, 60–80, 70–90 and 80–100 mph, for accelerating past other traffic without the need to drop down a gear: the Turbo covers these in 7.2, 6.0, 5.7 and 6.1 seconds, so once you're out of town you can treat it virtually as an automatic.'

They found the fuel consumption 'excellent' at 15.9 mpg; thought the gearbox could do with an extra ratio—'there are times when first gear is too low and second rather too high'; handling among the best in the world; brakes 'astoundingly' good; accommodation, providing it is treated purely as a two-seater, 'very practical'; ride far better than it sounds; driving position excellent; visibility fine providing you don't forget about the rear wheel arches; instruments attractive although it was curious that the speedometer only went up to 150 mph; heating difficult to operate; ventilation somewhat stuffy; noise by no means silent but not too much; finish severe but superb; equipment as comprehensive as you would expect for the price; servicing intervals 'demonstrate Porsche's confidence in their engineering,' and conclusions:

'We said of the three-litre Turbo that "Few, if any, cars have impressed us so much." That's a difficult act to follow, but the 3.3-litre version is an even better car which fully lives up to Porsche's claim that it offers "Racing performance with saloon car comfort".'

Few testers were better qualified than John Miles to compare a Carrera RS with the latest 3.3-litre Turbo for *Autocar* in June 1979—only a few years before he had been driving Grand Prix cars. Miles was one of the first journalists to predict that the RS would become the all-time classic. He wrote:

'Ask me which car I would rather own or take on a long cross country trip and the answer has to be the Carrera . . . although not as quick ultimately, the Carrera is, in practice, far nimbler and every bit as quick on the road. Mid-range acceleration is often slightly better on the Carrera.

'Throttle and acceleration responses are immediate. When the overtaking opportunities come—and they come more often in the 5-inch slimmer Carrera—the throttle releases thrillingly instant urge. This is where the Carrera scores. You find yourself slowing the Carrera while the Turbo is still gathering itself up only to have to slow just as the real benefits of boost build up . . .

'But where the heavy Turbo is rock stable in cross winds, the

*Facing page:* Porsche's testing ground at Weissach was expanded rapidly in 1969 and 1970 when it was proposed that they should take over all engineering and development work for the giant Volkswagen concern. As a result Porsches built since have benefited from these extensive facilities.

lightweight Carrera has a more nervous feel to it. It is almost as if the slightly unnerving steering vagueness about the straight ahead has been intentionally built in to stop the driver fighting an endemic twitchiness . . .

'Perhaps the difference is that typical Porsche handling has been engineered almost out of sight in a sometimes slightly ponderous feeling Turbo whereas the normally-shod lightweight Carrera is taut and sensitive. It responds more precisely to steering and throttle movements (a tightly set up limited differential helped). The Carrera rewards those who are prepared to learn its ways—given time you feel in touch with it—while the Turbo remains remote, perfected, dedicated to making those behind the wheel *look* good . . .

'Give it five years, then have another look. The 2.7-litre lightweight Carrera could just be the ultimate "real" Porsche.'

*Road & Track* then had the opportunity to test one of the new '50-state' 911SC Porsches in May 1980. This had a new three-way catalytic converter that made the exhaust clean enough even for California, but an engine that had sacrificed no power or torque because the compression ratio had been raised to 9.8:1. So the performance remained largely the same as that of the 1978 car tested by *Road & Track,* but the advantage they found was in crisper throttle response, better driveability and improved fuel economy: down to 18.5 mpg from 18. The popular options of electric windows, air conditioning, leather-covered steering wheel, centre console, black window trip and engine compartment light had also become standard equipment.

*Motor* found that the performance of their European 911SC with the uprated engine had improved considerably when they tested it in November 1980. They estimated a top speed of 148 mph for this basic car without the Sport package and recorded 5.7 secs for the 0–60 mph. Mid-range flexibility had also been improved along with fuel consumption, down to 20.4 mpg. Despite a recent price increase the 911SC was still one of the cheapest supercars at £16,732—considerably less than a BMW 635 CSi, Ferrari 308GTB, Jaguar XJS, Mercedes 280SLC, Maserati Merak and De Tomaso Pantera GTS. *Motor* summed up: 'We see this latest Porsche as the best non-Turbo 911 yet, with its stunning performance and and excellent economy together with the previous 911 attributes of superb handling and traction. In fact many of our testers felt that in a number of ways it was superior to the 3.3 Turbo, mainly because its power is more useable and readily available . . . one wonders if there is any limit to the development of this thoroughbred of sports cars.'

Ian Fraser likened a 911SC of the same specification to Rasputin—hard to kill and tricky to handle—when he tested it for *CAR* in December 1980. He appreciated the improved fuel consumption figures of 20 to 22 mpg, but

The ultimate Porsche according to John Miles? Two examples of the Carrera RS sandwich a Turbo in the Porsche Production Car Challenge at Brands Hatch in 1987.

pointed out that it was the range that mattered more. The new fuel-stop frequencies of between 320 miles and 375 could be readily made to coincide with human requirements. Fraser noted, however, that fifth gear was now as tall as the Post Office Tower and pointless in a restricted area. So far as the handling was concerned, he considered it fierce: 'Anyone who does not scare himself at least once in the new 911SC has simply bought the wrong car, or been fooled by the vehicle's obvious qualities . . . having said that, I must also say that the SC is a safe car. Safe because whatever you do in it you do with your eyes wide open . . . I always knew that I was going fast in the SC, not because it felt crude but because it felt fast: 130 mph in the Porsche was as fast if not faster than any 130 mph I have done in anything. Exactly the same at 50, 80, 100: the car reveals all so if you get it wrong there's no blaming intangibles.'

A month later *Autocar* tested the same 911SC. Their findings were similar to those of *Motor* and *CAR* but their comments on the Porsche's

front end were more graphic:

> 'Certainly the 911 is not a car that can be left alone to run straight at high speeds on a windy day or if it is wet *and* windy as much of the test period was. It was under these conditions that we quite simply could not in complete confidence stay with a Citroen CX while running at between 80 and 90 mph on the Brussels-Ostend motorway. While it was knifing through the wind and cutting through water, we were occasionally experiencing some aquaplaning, and yawing 3 ft either side of our chosen track.
>
> 'In near-still conditions and on dry surfaces straight line stability is good up to 130 mph, and adequate beyond, and noticeably improved when the front is weighed down with a full fuel load.
>
> 'Ride quality at low speeds is firm, and just occasionally a little harsh (certainly noisy) when running over broken surfaces. As speeds increase so does the 911SC's ability to absorb poor surfaces, yet blessedly never to the point where one feels the Porsche's solid reassuring feel is removed. A minor quirk was the tendency (also noticed in other 911s) for the lighter front end to react in a livelier manner than the rear over a series of undulations leading to a mild pitching motion (also more evident when low on fuel).'

Patrick Bedard achieved a notable first for *Car and Driver* when he tested the Whittington brothers' Le Mans-winning 3.2-litre K3 at Road Atlanta in March 1980. Its considerable weight was reflected in a 0–60 mph acceleration figure of only 4.9 secs after which it stormed up to 100 mph in 8.2 secs on the way to a maximum speed (at Le Mans) of 219 mph with around 3 mpg. Following warnings not to spin the rear wheels—which would instantly reduce the tyres' grip—Bedard sampled 700 bhp on 1.3 bar which could rise to 800 at 1.5. He said:

> 'The power is amazing, even when shifting at 7,000 rpm—about 1,000 rpm under the usual point and 1,600 under what Don Whittington will take it to when he's really in a hurry. Turbo lag is still a factor, even with a twin turbo that is said to have less than half the delay of a single-turbo set up . . . all braking must be finished before bending into the turn so that the power-building process can be started well before you actually need it. And when you open the throttle, you don't ease it open for a gradual increase in power; you stand right on it to get through the burbling transition as quickly as possible. The turbo alone decides how fast the power will build up, and it bases that decision mostly on engine revs at the moment and how long youve been off the gas. The speed of your right foot is pretty much immaterial.'

Former works driver Paul Frère then had a brief test inPorsche's 935/77

*Facing page: Road & Track* found that the new 50-state SC—pictured here with a 1980-model year European Turbo—had a crisper throttle response, improved fuel consumption and was, simply, more driveable than earlier strangulated 911s.

Motor's 1981-model year 911SC, without Sport package, returned a stunning 5.7-second 0–60 mph time.

The prototype twin turbo 935 as tested by Paul Frere—pictured here leading a single-turbo version into Copse during the 1977 Silverstone Six Hours—rewarded the driver who was prepared to drift it.

2.8-litre twin turbo prototype, reporting in *Motor* in July 1980:

> 'There is never any suggestion of understeer, as many people think there should be with solid drive. This obviously implies that you must drive fast enough to get the car into a drift and transfer enough of its weight on to the outer wheel to make quite sure that it plays the leading role. The torque it exerts around the car's vertical axis will then actually help it around . . .
>
> 'Driving that sort of car is mainly a matter of darting from one corner to the next, but the man who goes quicker around the corner is still the one who's going to win the race. It's not just the speed that can be held on the corners and bends that counts here, but related factors that include how late you can brake and how soon you can start to accelerate out.'

*Car and Driver* had the opportunity to try a Special Equipment Turbo in February 1983 followed by a road-going 935 lookalike in May. The factory car, with steel bodywork and 325 bhp in Federal form proved capable of 160 mph, but the private conversion, by Kremer associate Designer Plastics Automobilbau, topped that by 2 mph thanks to a claimed 370 bhp that needed a 3 psi higher boost setting and considerable quantities of octane-booster. Its glass-fibre panels also kept the weight down and with 205/50VR15 and 285/40VR15 tyres the acceleration improved to 4.6 secs for the 0–60 mph with a standing-quarter-mile in 12.8 secs. *Car and Driver* commented: 'Even these fabulous figures don't convey the car's sheer thrust. The DP935 delivers an incredibly strong shove in the back, and the punch never seems to quit. Even at 120 mph it pulls harder than a Scirocco at 50. Not until well past 140 mph does your breath come back and the acceleration of this juggernaut fall to a familiar level.'

Ian Fraser had mixed feelings when he tested a 911SC Sport Cabriolet for *CAR* in their June 1983 issue, reporting:

> 'Whenever I drive a Porsche 911, I worry. But probably for the wrong reasons. It could be argued that conducting a rear-engined anachronism developing more than 200 bhp is single-handedly cause enough for concern, yet that is not the reason. What furrows the brow to bone depth is trying to establish why its archaic design continues to flourish in the face of modernity . . .
>
> 'The 911 survives and continues to appeal because of its solid old-fashioned values, not despite them. Old-fashioned values dominate the 911. No matter how much the car is changed to update the specification, it has always been so far behind the pacemakers as not to be in contention. It scores because it is establishment, known and recommended by those too inflexible to try anything else . . .

The performance of the K3 as tested by Patrick Bedard was dominated by turbo reaction.

Private versions of the slant-nose 911 vary considerably in appearance—from the British Dage Sport version to the bizarre Almeras Freres conversion from France.

The 911SC cabriolet that worried Ian Fraser . . .

But *Motor* found the 911SC cabriolet to be in the steam catapult class.

'I would have done more open-air driving in the Porsche had the hood been a little quicker to raise and lower. It is not one of those affairs you grab with one hand, slam onto the windscreen rail and secure in a blink of the eye. But then it does actually keep the weather out even in completely appalling conditions, and is free from draughts, rattles and excessive windnoise. The old-fashioned values have failed to some extent in that the roof has no internal lining so that all the vulgar metalwork is exposed to view. The plus-side is that it folds down compactly while a clip-on cover keeps it tidy.

'I am annoyed with myself for liking the Cabriolet . . . what the 911 lacks in the face of more modern designs it apparently makes up for in genuine practicality. Although I never liked the 911 Targa, I think I could tolerate the Cabriolet, at least for one summer of chasing around after lost youth. I doubt if I would catch it, but it might be fun trying.'

*Motor* then tested the same car in June 1983, wasting no time in finding out how fast it would go:

'Although no one in his right mind would attempt to drive the Cabrio flat out with the hood down, it is a perfectly feasible exercise with it up; the hood is so well constructed and efficiently sealed that wind noise, while obtrusive about 100 mph, never becomes intolerable. Not even at 147.3 mph, the speed at which the Porsche lapped Millbrook's high-speed bowl . . . when it comes to sprinting ability, the Cabrio moves into the steam catapult class. Ignoring Porsche's curiously conservative "under 7 secs" claim, and making the best possible use of the traction afforded by its rear-mounted engine and those wide, grippy, P7 tyres, the Cabrio snakes off the line in a plume of tyre smoke to reach 60 mph in just 5.8 secs, 100 mph in 14.2 secs as it passes the quarter-mile post and 120 mph in 23.7 secs. Make no mistake, only the big league supercars are notably quicker . . .

'Quick though the Cabrio is, thirsty it is not. Conducted with unabashed enthusiasm, our test car returned a very creditable 20.1 mpg.'

*Autocar* returned virtually identical figures with the same car in the same month and said:

'Torsional rigidity is very good when running with the hood down. Side windows rattle a little when wound up because they have no guiding channel or support with the roof down, and when encountering a series of bad bumps or potholes you can see the gap between the door and the fascia opening and closing as the door and scuttle shake, but to a perfectly acceptable degree.'

Old time Porsche fan Denis Jenkinson was excited by the Turbo, seen here with John Morrison at the wheel taking off for the title of 'The World's Fastest Car' in 1984.

Group editor Quentin Spurring had the next turn in this car for *Autosport* in July 1983, reporting:

'When I took a 911SC Cabriolet to Le Mans, the single most intriguing aspect of the trip was that, within seconds of being parked, the car was surrounded by admiring people. It was almost uncanny. When I stopped for lunch in a sleepy little French village, people went out of the restaurant to look at my car! After the two now-obligatory laps of Rouen on the way down through the countryside, people appeared from nowhere to gaze at the Cabriolet.'

Meanwhile long-time Porsche fan Denis Jenkinson had been sampling a Turbo on loan to *Motor Sport,* writing in February 1982:

'I got up this morning and did 100 miles round Hampshire before the public woke up. Fantastic. The ultimate tool, and so docile Auntie could go shopping in it. By nine o'clock it was all over, the public had woken up and it was a case of squirting from one traffic jam to another. It was then I realised that *real motoring* is now the province of the very rich (it always was really, though for a fleeting moment it looked as though peasants like you and me were going to be able to do it, but it was false). You keep a Porsche Turbo or something similar like people keep boats. You don't use it to go anywhere, but when the weather is fair you go off for a sail. When the public are in bed, or stirring uneasily, you go off for a 100-mile blast, then put it away and go about your business in a Eurobox or an Execubox in the streams of traffic. An extravagant pastime, but then so is a three-masted schooner, a Spitfire aeroplane or a power boat. *Motoring* has returned to where it started. A pastime for the rich . . .'

*Autocar* were highly impressed with the performance when they tried the same car in April 1983, commenting:

'In far from perfect weather conditions it proved to be the fastest-ever accelerating production car to 120 mph and the fastest over both the standing quarter mile and kilometre. It surged to 30 mph in just 2 secs, got to 60 mph in 5.1 secs and went on to 100, 120 and 140 mph in 12.2, 17.8 and 29.6 secs respectively (Lamborghini Countach LP500S 2.4, 5.6, 12.9, 18.5 and 28 secs). It is only at the very top end that cars like the Countach, the legendary Ferrari Daytona, or perhaps the Aston Vantage, can catch up, and of course in real terms such top end gains are of little value. In the event the 911 Turbo came within a whisker of equalling the Ferrari 512BB's 163 mph and LP500S's 164 mph, by matching (in quite blustery conditions) the manufacturer's claimed 162 mph . . . with so much glorious performance on tap, the 911 Turbo needs a great deal of self-restraint to drive with economy in mind, though, it is utterly docile and fuss-free. With this in mind it was perhaps no surprise to find that for most of the test period the car returned figures in the 15–16 mpg bracket. If the performance potential is considered the overall figure of 16.4 mpg betters all the supercar opposition.'

Naturally *Road & Track* welcomed back the Cabrio when they tested a US version in February 1983 emphasising that around half America's Porsche population could be found in their home state, California—and it was to be assumed that a substantial proportion were open versions in view of the warm and dry climate. They also discovered that the heavier Cabrio was only marginally slower than the coupé, taking 7 secs—against 6.7—from 0–60 mph and 15.5 secs (versus 15.3) for the quarter mile, returning an identical 23.5 mpg. The top speed suffered, however, from the inferior aerodynamics of the cloth hood: 124 mph in the catalyst-equipped car whereas the Californian coupé was capable of 140 mph. They also noted how suspension tuning, wide wheels and meaty tyres had tempered the old tail-wagging habits to such an extent that the 'dreaded, trailing throttle-induced spin (it was once said that most 911s left the road going backwards), there's only a slight kick out of the rear. And that's unusually brief because the rear tyres' large footprints quickly take effect and scrub off most the rear end's lateral movement.' They concluded: 'If it is a sunny, but not uncomfortably hot, day, the top of your 911 Cabrio is down, the road is clear. You motor along, alternating bursts of spirited driving with leisurely cruising. The $1905 leather seats and interior look and smell great, the $795 four-speaker Monterey radio sounds terrific. Take this next turn fast and feel the $1580 16-inch forged alloy wheels and Pirelli P7s (or Goodyear Eagle NCTs) go to work. Who said money can't buy happiness?'

Alternative ways of getting the best out of a Porsche were illustrated in two tests by *Motor Sport*. The first, in April 1982, of the AFN prodsports 911SC raced by Tony Lanfranchi revealed that little had been done to the car other than to reduce the weight from 2558 lb when *Motor* road-tested it in non-Sport guise in 1980 to 2320 lb by removing the carpets, sound-deadening material, rear seats and underseal to help counter the addition of a rear wing, aluminium roll cage and fire extinguisher. Sixteen-inch forged alloy wheels were also used with 205/55 and 225/50 Pirelli P7 tyres and Bilstein, rather than Boge, dampers. These were on their hardest settings with more toe-in and negative camber at the back and the suspension at its lowest ride height. In this form, the 911SC Sport proved capable of lapping the Brands Hatch club circuit, two-up, in 59 secs without drama.

Tony Lanfranchi at the wheel of the 911SC tested by *Motor Sport* in 1982.

Then, in April 1983, Alan Henry had a brief outing in Josh Sadler's 3.5-litre hill-climb car, based on a 1972 911T. The engine capacity had been increased to 3,506 cc by mating a 3.3-litre Turbo bottom end with a special Mahle piston and cylinder kit taking the bore out to 100 mm. Normal 3-litre cylinder heads were used, opened out and gas flowed, with the original valve gear and Carrera RS cams. A RSR injection system was used with an uprated fuel pump and four-pipe exhaust system to give an estimated 270 bhp at the wheels at 6500 rpm with a 'dramatic' amount of torque. A reinforced gearbox casing was used with Carrera RS suspension and four-pot brake calipers. Pirelli P6 tyres were fitted to 8-inch front and 9-inch rear rims for road use, with 9-inch front and 11-inch rear for competition. Henry reported:

> 'The engine will tick over at around 1,000 rpm without showing any inclination towards stalling and will pull from about 2,500 rpm in any gear without shuddering or any other reluctance. Once over 3,000 rpm it really comes into its own, the lack of sound-proofing making life fairly noisy, but not oppressive, within its cockpit. From that point onwards, the rev counter needle simply races round towards 6,000 rpm with the sort of punch that jerks back one's head and keeps one's left hand close to the gearchange ready to snatch the second ratio.'

Sadler quoted its 0–60 time as fractionally under 5 secs and its 0–114 mph best at 12.89 secs, as measured over the first 60 yards at the Prescott hill climb.

*CAR* were well satisfied with the performance of the new Carrera when Georg Kacher tested it in October 1983, commenting that with a 6.1 second 0–60 mph time and 153 mph top speed—official figures—it was little slower than a Turbo and cost only two-thirds as much. He added:

> 'The new effects of the Montronic system become apparent the moment the clutch is released. Throttle response is immaculate at last, even at very low revs. The clutch feels lighter and notably more progressive, and it engages much more smoothly now in first and second gear. This makes driving in heavy traffic so much more effortless and relaxing. The test car pulled better from low revs than the SC, but the 3.2-litre engine does not always spin cleanly at part load, and there are the occasional misfires under trailing throttle when the engine is hot . . .
>
> 'The five-speed gearbox is one of the Porsche's few weak points. The lever movements are rather long, precision of the action is barely average, and more often than not the bottom three gears engage with a certain reluctance.'

*Motor* gave the new Carrera Sport its first comprehensive test in October 1983, recording 151.1 mph on a blustery day at Millbrook with a searing 5.3 secs for the 0–60—an identical time to their last Turbo—and 13.6 secs for the 0–100, only 1.3 secs behind the 930. Fuel consumption was equally impressive, at 21.1 mpg, 3.4 per cent better than the last 911SC, and they summed up:

> 'Little has changed for 1984 except that the Carrera Sport is quicker than ever—back at the top of the junior supercar acceleration league table. The 911 is also remarkably economical for its stunning performance. Still a great driving machine, with rewarding (though tricky *in extremis)* handling, potent brakes, superb ratios, good driving position and turbine-smooth engine. The gearchange could be better, though, and remaining flaws include a hard ride, poor heating and ventilation, and uncertain ergonomics.'

*Autocar* went almost as fast with the same car at Millbrook later in the year, reporting in December.

> 'Like all other 911s we have driven, the Carrera has a nervous feel about it . . . that uneasiness did not reach the levels we experienced with the 911 Turbo, with its even greater rearward weight bias (35/64 compared with the Carrera's 39/61) . . . driven sensibly, the Carrera should not bite back; its excellent grip allows it to be powered through bends at speeds which would leave most competitors standing. One of the most impressive features of the Carrera's engine is its flexibility. The engine pulls well in fourth gear from below 10 mph with very little initial vibration, and runs sweetly and smoothly right up to the 6,200 rpm red line.
>
> 'High-speed cruising is an easy pleasure in the 911 Carrera, since noise levels are low; there is seldom any more than a light murmur from the engine at the rear, and wind noise is virtually absent until speeds in excess of 80 mph are reached (mind you, it gets almost deafeningly loud at 150 mph . . . ). The ride is firm, as you would expect in a sports car, but it does have the disadvantage of passing a lot of road noise and bump-thump through into the passenger compartment.'

Racing driver Tiff Needell thoroughly enjoyed his three days in the same car for *Autosport* in December 1983, writing:

> 'The tremendous acceleration of the 911 is the feature that impressed me most, even though foul conditions left me continually balancing power against wheelspin in both first and second gears! Given its natural habitat—somewhere around the Alps on the way to the Mediterranean—I doubt if there's any problem, but I feel a limited-slip differential is a must for good old England. I presume they are not fitted as standard because they probably make the 911 a bit heavy around the

Alps, adding weight to the steering and worsening the turn-in understeer.

'It's only when the red needle of the rev counter—correctly placed in the middle of the steering wheel—nears 4,000 rpm that things really start to happen. In first gear the smooth and essential rev limiter often chimes in; in ideal conditions the limit of 6,300 rpm and a speed of about 40 mph is reached in some 3 secs, while in the wet, the wheelspin can require the limiter's attention even sooner than that. Now we unfortunately reach another problematic stage in enjoying a 911—we have to change up from first to second. It's a problem that everyone knows about, but nobody cures. Basically, it's a long, stodgy, movement which you finally learn cannot be rushed, and your passenger learns to keep cover, as the close proximity of the seats can cause a clash of elbows during the gearchange.

'Once into second gear—and I began to start in it after a while—the joys of the 911 are unrestrained. Our legal speed limit is reached at the same time as the rev limit in second. Change to third, and the revs drop to 4,400 rpm before launching us up to 95 mph, and a change to fourth.

Alan Henry enjoyed an all-too-brief outing in Josh Sadler's 3.5-litre championship hill climb car.

*CAR* commented that the new Carrera was little a slower than the Turbo and cost only two-thirds as much . . .

At this speed, the engine runs at 4,800 rpm, which coincides exactly with the maximum torque figure and produces some amazing road-car acceleration from 95 mph to 120 mph in 11 secs. Fifth gear is then engaged (slowly) pushing against the gate's spring and a claimed 152 mph is available at around 6,000 rpm. I had a few blasts into the 130s and even then there was still notable acceleration for those who dared!

'In the handling department the Carrera felt very similar to Colin Blower's 911SC [the former Lanfranchi and Porsche Press car] which we drove to third place in this year's Snetterton 24-hour race. That car was on BF Goodrich rubber while the new Carrera was on Pirelli P7s, and I couldn't really say if there was any difference there. Like the SC, the Carrera will understeer when pushed into a corner too fast, understeer more if too much throttle is added too soon, and then burst into glorious power oversteer once the front has decided to stick. This represents the most frustrating characteristic of the car's handling, but even the Sport Equipment uprated dampers have to give a reasonably comfortable ride, and this concession to softness allows the rear to squat and the front to lift, taking weight off the front wheels as the power is first applied. After a while, you learn not to bother with the power until well round a corner, and then the 911 can provide really rewarding high-speed driving in any conditions.'

*Road & Track* were equally impressed with their 200-bhp American-specification Carrera on test in February 1984, recording 20.5 mpg, estimating the top speed at 146 mph and reporting:

'Like every major 911 change that has gone before, this one produces tangible improvements. One is foot-to-the-floor performance. At lower speeds, the Carrera isn't a quantum leap ahead of its predecessor, nor does its need to be. But as momentum gathers, so does steam. With fewer than 400 miles on the odometer, the test car's 6.2 secs for the 0–60 sprint beat the 1983 car by 0.7 secs; by the quarter-mile mark it had gained 0.9 secs on its predecessor and was fully 8 mph faster . . .

'Just as impressive as the surge of high-end power is the Carrera's new-found flexibility. With each enlargement the 911 engine has won low-speed torque, but this time it has reached the point where it can be driven like other cars. It tugs lustily on the tyres from 1,000 rpm in fourth, and even at 40 mph in fifth—wonder of wonders!—there's enough acceleration for virtually any traffic situation on level ground. In fact, the upshift light calls for fifth gear at 40 mph with light throttle. Maximum efficiency *and* strong response are now possible at the same time by using low revs so the Carrera should place less auditory strain on the environment than previous 911s.'

*Car and Driver's* Carrera road test figures in the same month were extraordinary, making you wonder whether they had been testing a European version or one running on an exceptionally rich mixture: 149 mph, 5.3 secs for the 0–60 and 17 mpg. There was no doubt that they liked it, though:

'It is the evil weevil, the rock-solid, steely-eyed grim reaper of sporting cars, the paragon of knife-edged incisiveness and buttoned-down insanity. More than any other factory-fresh passenger car available here today, the Porsche 911 Carrera is the absolute embodiment of clench-jawed, tight-fisted, slit-eyed enthusiasm run amok, a car for making the landscape pass with explosive fluidity. Strange that a car so serious can bring such unadulterated joy, but there you are, sporting an enormous, cheek-splitting leer when you unstrap and step out. You devil, you.'

Editor Steve Cropley thought of the Turbo Special equipment model as a poseur's chariot until he drove it for *CAR* magazine in January 1986, recalling:

'There is nothing like a very high-geared car, which can still go

Like all 911s before it, the new Carrera Sport had a highly-competitive performance.

extremely hard in top, to give you an impression of supreme, limitless, performance. The Turbo SE, stronger even than an ordinary Turbo, is just such a car. The engine will function smoothly in any gear from about 1,400 rpm. From about 2,600 rpm the boost gauge begins to show signs of puff. By 3,000 rpm there is a a definite push in the back and by 3,300 rpm, if the throttle is opened wide, you cannot avoid going extremely hard.

'Beyond 4,000 rpm, if you are in a lower gear, all hell breaks loose. It is as if you're being launched bodily. If first happens to be the gear you're in, there is only time to concentrate on timing your change into second at 6,800 rpm, so that you will not over-rev the engine and come ignominiously up against the rev-limiter. Second is a remarkable gear. That one ratio encompasses the entire performance span of many lesser cars. It is possible (though why you should want to, I can't imagine) to get the Porsche rolling in second. You can still be in second nearly

*Motor* decided that the new Carrera was still a great driving machine.

90 mph later. Into the red, the speedo shows 95 mph, but about 4-5 mph of that you have to allow as speedo error. The car's sheer, thunderous performance has to be experienced to be believed. Forty to 60 mph, 50 to 70, 60 to 80 mph: they are all consumed in 2.5 secs or less. Suddenly you're doing 90, right up against the red, and since there are plenty of places where 90 mph is not a harmonious speed on British non-motorways, you had better think quickly.

'Third gear has a persona of its own. If it is 24-carat performance you want, third's really not much good to you below 3,500 rpm or 70 mph. You need to be in second. But between 70 and 130, the Porsche has effortless, soaring, performance which lifts it beyond even the level of the Italian 12s, since it's so long-legged, so extraordinarily effortless in its self-energised power delivery—and so amazingly quiet. Oh, there *is* engine noise. The flat-six scream is there and welcome. But the silencing effect of the turbo, the lack of rasp or whine from the superbly-strong gearbox, means that the engine is really very refined. On the over-run there might be a hint of vibration as the engine comes down through the 4000s, but only a paid critic would notice it. Anyone else would merely be impatient to slow, just to do it all again. The car's performance is intoxicating. Think, if you can, of the surge from 100 mph to 120 in just over five seconds. It's so fast.

'Top does its best work over 90 mph. Over the ton, really. That's where the car has its seven-league boots on. Never has so much been achieved by one simple squeeze on a road car's accelerator. And if it's cruising you want, this car will steam along showing 145 mph and 5,000 rpm (it's about 138 mph true, actually) with nearly 2,000 rpm left to the red line . . .

'But one thing is critical in this car as a result of the four-speed box. You must cover yourself against falling into vast gulfs between the ratios. Thus, when you're travelling fast it's best to hold on to a lower gear if you can't see over the hill, rather than risk allowing the revs to fall below 3,500 rpm. This is actually quite brisk as long as the engine's turning at over 2,000, yet so great is the rate of acceleration difference between that and when it's at 4,000, that you're interested only in one thing. Thus, in difficult going, you should change down to third below 30. It's a curious routine until you get used to it, but if you adhere to it, your ability to find power and put it down in every situation is awesome.'

*Car and Driver,* however, were left with mixed feelings about the latest US-specification Turbo when they tested it in January 1986. They reported:

'With a searing 0–60 mph run of 4.6 secs and a clocking of 13.1 secs at 105 mph through the quarter mile, the 911 Turbo is most assuredly this season's acceleration ace—providing you're willing to resort to rough, wheel-spinning, drag-race starts.

'Out on the road, though, these numbers pale next to the Turbo's boost-lag arthritis. Even the healthier of our two test cars took forever to spin its turbo up to lift-off speed. Once it was up and running, it was plenty strong, but it just didn't awe us the way the old 930 used to do.

'Then again, there's more to our memories than pure speed. It was also known as one of the trickiest handlers around. Driving one hard was a job for experts. Putting the power on aggressively in a corner would pitch the nose way up, and the 930 would try to run straight over its front tyres. Lift off the gas just a few millimetres in these conditions and the 930 would swing sideways so fast, it would jump-start your heart.

'Not so the new 911 Turbo. On the tortured curves of California's Ortega Highway, it shows real poise. In the last six years it's obviously been taught some manners. Antics that would have spun you out before hardly faze it. The brakes are superb. It's still hard work to drive very, *very* fast, but it's much more forgiving now.

'Comparing this experience with our last 930 outing in 1979, it's clear that things have changed. The 930 was deadly in the curves and awesome on the straights, and the 911 Turbo is mellower in both areas.

'This pass through the time barrier, the 911 Turbo's performance [recording a top speed of 155 mph] just hasn't blown our minds—and we think we know why. Back in 1979, there really wasn't any other car in America that offered the 930's kind of speed. Today, we're in the middle of a horsepower boom. We've got 157 mph 944 Turbos, 154 mph 928s, 151 mph Corvettes, 140 mph Camaros—hell, even Saab is in the 140-plus club these days.'

Meanwhile three of the British magazines had been among specialists testing Roland Kassmaul's four-wheel-drive Paris-Dakar 911 at a Munich off-road site in 1984. John Miles, who had driven the Lotus 63 four-wheel-drive car in Grands Prix 15 years earlier, reported in *Autocar* in May:

'Start up is normal, we leave the collection point, and turn—with the greatest of care—into the first cone-marked corner on a trailing throttle, not thinking much. Suddenly, I'm wide awake. It understeers strongly . . . Once the power is on, you cannot play with it like a two-wheel-drive car, adjusting attitudes with steering and throttle. On gravel, steering efforts are light considering the addition of drive to the front wheels, adding to the feeling that it doesn't want to "point." Backing off the throttle has only a marginal effect on the understeer, none at all in the slow corners—unlike the two-wheel-drive 911 road car! A few minutes later it is going better for us. Add power, and even in first gear the traction is staggering. Getting the car balanced is the bit that comes awkwardly. Confidence and commitment are needed. To brake and turn the wheel as you are coming off the throttle gets the rear to swing a little, just enough. Not once did we experience a big oversteer slide unless the car was upset by bucking and jerking under braking, but then the rear swings out involuntarily, not because the driver wants it.

'Down the straight, full throttle leaves me fully absorbed, trying to keep the car going straight over the hollows. It rides them well enough, but doesn't actually want to run straight naturally. The parameters seem narrow. It's twitchy when you are going quickly, but not twitchy enough at slowish speeds. The right way seems to be to brake, turn, wait for the rear to unsettle, and bang on the power.'

Jeremy Walton estimated the four-wheel-drive 911 was capable of a 6.5-second 0–60 mph time in *Motor* in June, like Roger Bell in *CAR* the following month, who agree with Miles's assessment of the handling. Bell added:

'Even on the loose, the 4 x 4 Porsche leaps into action with little

*Autocar* felt that, driven sensibly, the new Carrera should not bite back.

wheelspin. Despite its high stance, it doesn't feel insecure or roly-poly. Far from it. Poise and ride quality on the rough are amazing. Rubble-strewn, pocked gradients are mere nursery slopes, tackled at blistering pace with much stone hammering from beneath but little disturbance. It is over the yumpy bits, deep depressions and peaky mounds, that the car will fly, and not always horizontally. Get it wrong and you can crash-land with neck-snapping violence as the suspension hits the bump stops—not that it seems to do the car any harm.'

*Motor* then had a rare opportunity to test a Carrera Super Sport coupé in January 1986, which left them with mixed feelings. On the one hand, they recognised it as a 'marvellously entertaining car to drive, arguably the best 911 yet, with significantly-improved handling and grip towards the outer limits' but on the other hand they were disappointed with performance—a top speed down to 144 mph, 0–60 mph time up to 6.1 secs, and average fuel consumption increased to 20 mpg. They added: 'No one who drove the Super Sport needed a stopwatch to tell that it was slower than its predecessor. There was less zap, less eyeball sinking, less viciousness to the kick. Acceleration was brisk, but not brutal. Mind you, we didn't expect quite such good figures [as those of the standard Carrera]. The extra weight of 110 lb was bound to take its toll. So was the greater tyre resistance and wind drag.'

*CAR's* European Editor, Georg Kacher, was not a 911 fan, but could not help being intrigued by the Carrera Club Sport he tested in Otober 1987. He reported:

> 'There is no doubt that the noise is a considerable part of the fascination of a lightweight 911. Take the engine noise: the irregular coughing and bellowing under trailing throttle, the metallurgical singing and jingling when pottering along in high gear with all claws drawn in, the unrestrained hungry roar that accompanies every flat-out acceleration manoeuvre, the deafening thunder which creeps in to your ears like live cottonwool during a full-bore autobahn journey. Or listen to the mechanical noise: the plop-plop of the hard charging suspension fighting the potholes, the hollow drumming of the tyres, the slightly grinding melody of the slow-moving gearlever, the cracking of the brake pedal.
>
> 'In principle, the Club Sport model handles exactly like any other 911, but its actions and reactions in this field, too, are purer, quicker

Tiff Needell found the handling of the new Carrera very similar to the 911 he raced in the Willhire 24-hour race.

and ultimately more communicative. Since all movements appear to be absolutely honest and unfiltered, the search for the limit requires skill and confidence rather than skill and courage. In the final analysis, it is this uncompromising chassis which makes the lightweight 911 a little easier and a lot more rewarding to drive than any other rear-engined Porsche.

'Since tomorrow's 959-style 911 is going to be very expensive and probably not as much fun to drive, I would buy my 911 now. Whether I would—for the same money—prefer the Club Sport to the Carrera is hard to decide. A refrigerated, leather-clad Carrera may be the better everyday business express, but as a collector's item to run and keep as a milestone in the history of the sports car, the lightweight version must be the winner.'

Graham Jones, road test editor of *Autocar,* was especially impressed with the performance of the Carrera Club Sport, recording a similar time to the standard Carrera of 5.6 secs for the 0–60, as the Club Sport surged ahead to 14 secs, for the 0–100 (1.8 secs better), and 20.8 for the 0–120 (3.9 secs better). Top speed was up to 154 mph from 148 with fuel consumption a little better at 19.9 mpg against 19.2.

Finally, the 959 left writers in no doubt that it was the world's best sports car, yet at the same time, with a strange sense of anti-climax. *CAR* magazine's editor-to-be, Gavin Green, did a personal best top speed of 175 mph in one before he had to lift off for two lorries which might have started an overtaking manoeuvre far ahead. He wrote in September 1987:

'The engine wails in the normal flat six tone—although the twin turbos do soften its glorious roar. Hydraulic tappets quieten it further. First, actually known as the G-gear (for *gelande,* or super low) is good only for 35 mph; you can start the car easily in second, which stretches to just over 60 mph. So far, everything is simple: you could almost be driving a Ford Fiesta. The power, at low to medium revs, is not enormous either. Porsche's sequential turbo system allows for one of the identically-sized blowers to operate from low revs, when all the exhaust gas is directed to it allowing it to build revs rapidly. At higher revs, the additional blower is engaged.

'Below 4,500 rpm, a 959 feels fast, but not that much quicker than a normal 911. You can even be excused as you drive smoothly and briskly over the twisting and poorly surfaced roads around Weissach for wondering what all the fuss had been about . . . spin the engine around to 4,500 rpm and you'll find out.

'Suddenly an eruption behind your right shoulder interrupts the muted engine note, and the 959 charges violently forward. That second turbo comes in like an afterburner, and your back, nestling comfortably in the seat, is suddenly gripped by the back rest. Your head is forced rearward, too. The whole beast springs into life like some frenzied animal surging forward with irresistible urgency. Seven-three on the tacho, change into fourth, the needle falls back to just under 5,000 and, after a momentary hesitation for the gearchange, returns to the 7,300 mark, again with impossible-seeming alacrity. Change into fifth, you've passed 125 mph, and are going far too fast for a secondary road, so you back off. Your palms are sweating. Calm yourself before confronting the blast along the autobahn . . .

'When the road ahead is clear, it's time properly to exercise the fastest road car in the world. At 160 mph the red line says go no further, so you grab sixth and still the car thrusts onward. And it's still easy going, still quiet, still accelerating strongly. This car seems to defy the law of physics which impedes Ferrari Testarossas and GTOs and Lamborghini Countachs and Aston Vantages back at 160 and beyond. Every other fast car struggles when grasping at higher velocities, gaining those extra mph slowly. Not this one. This is a performance car on a different plane. At 175 mph the car is still surging ahead relentlessly, still handling its speed with unfussed confidence. You can still converse at that speed. The car remains stable, relatively quiet . . .

'In standing start acceleration tests, the 959 scores an even more emphatic victory over its rivals (if it has any). Helped enormously by its four-wheel-drive, the Porsche can sprint from 0–62 mph in 3.7 secs, 0–100 mph in 8.3 secs and 0–125 mph in 12.8 secs. It covers the standing quarter mile in 11.9 secs. No other supercar even gets close to those times . . .

'The engine's relative quietness reinforces the high speed missile—rather than high speed road car—feel of this machine. It is so unlike any other ever made, in its power and in its roadholding capabilities, that it stops feeling like a car . . .

'Around large radius, fast bends, its guided missile character is particularly evident. The 959 stays flat, its tyres avoid so much as a chirp, it handles neutrally, the steering feels strangely desensitised yet sharp, and the car just goes where it is pointed. What it lacks is feedback . . . to a feeling that this beast is so supreme a machine that Porsche engineers have forgotten one vital ingredient: human involvement.'

Former *CAR* editor Mel Nichols, now editorial director of *Autocar,* had no second thoughts about the 959, however, when he reported in November 1987:

'I started the task of tackling Porsche's fastest-ever road car with a measure of trepidation. Responsibility, I kept telling myself, had to be the order of the day: don't feel compelled to try to run flat-out; don't

'The 959 was the car that rewrote the supercar rules', said Mel Nicholas.

attempt to push this four-wheel-drive paragon of automotive technology near its cornering limits. Just take it as it comes and go as far as you feel able, nothing more.

'But in 12 hours, the 959 had taught me to relax, to know that I could use all 450 bhp *even in the wet*. It taught me that I could open it up on almost any half-decent stretch of road and travel at speeds that would have been unbelievable if they weren't so uneventful. It taught me that I could run beyond the edge of its staggering roadholding and not fear the consequences. It taught me that upsetting its composure or losing its tail was all but impossible. It taught me that all I had to do was to calculate speed and distance as never before and not to run out of road.

'But most of all, as my spirits soared even higher with the increasing realisation that I was driving a car that rewrites the supercar rules, the 959 demonstrated that Porsche has achieved the fantastic goal it set in 1980: the creation of a car that nudges the performance realms of today's racing cars yet which any man or woman with average experience can master within a short learning period.

'Here it was: a car that accelerates from 0–60 mph in 3.7 secs, to 100 mph in 8.5, to 150 in 21.5, runs on to 197 mph but can be driven by you or me and our wives and sisters in comfort and in any weather, anywhere, anytime.'

# Strengths and Weaknesses

The Porsche 911 has become a legend in its lifetime for providing the ultimate rewards in performance, largely due to the magnificent engineering that shows everywhere in its construction. It is also one of the few exotic cars, if not the only one, which is really reliable, largely because of dedicated quality control on the mechanical and electrical side. Sadly, however, the early examples have also earned themselves a reputation for being some of the worst rust buckets of all time. Until 1971, when galvanised floorpans started to appear on most models, there was one thing you could be sure about with a Porsche in a damp climate: it would rust away from the moment you bought it unless really high standards of maintenance and protection were applied. Between 1971 and 1976, more and more galvanised steel panels were used until the whole body was made from this material and the old Porsche fault appears now to have been delayed for many years. Until then, you could count on a 911 being a seven-year car without major body repairs on the average salt-laden European or North American roads. Even seven years could be a long time for a Targa body; it suffers particularly badly from the penetration of water and saline solution because it is not so stiff as the coupé, and flexing opens the seams. On the credit side, Porsche still produce body parts, so it is possible to rebuild a 911, but it is expensive, partly because of the relative strength of the German Deutschmark, and partly because of the short production runs associated with Porsche replacement parts.

The best thing about the front wings from the point of view of corrosion is that they are bolted on. This saves quite a lot of money if they have to be replaced by an expert and makes the job much more practical for the amateur. In a manner that has now become almost traditional with cars designed in the 1950s and 1960s, these wings—especially the mild steel variety produced before 1976–rust in all the places that mud and road debris accumulates. These dirty deposits never really dry out and the moisture contained by the mud corrodes the metal it sticks to, which in the case of the Porsche 911, is at the rear edge of the front wings, around the wheel arch lips, the fuel filler flap box and especially the box section that contains the headlamp units. These boxes can be bought separately or as an entire unit with the wing but, again, they are expensive and it is well worth keeping the inside of the wings free from road debris to prolong their life. The rear wings suffer from similar problems and although they are a little cheaper than the front wings, their replacement usually costs more in total because they are welded on. This means that it takes more labour to replace them and presents

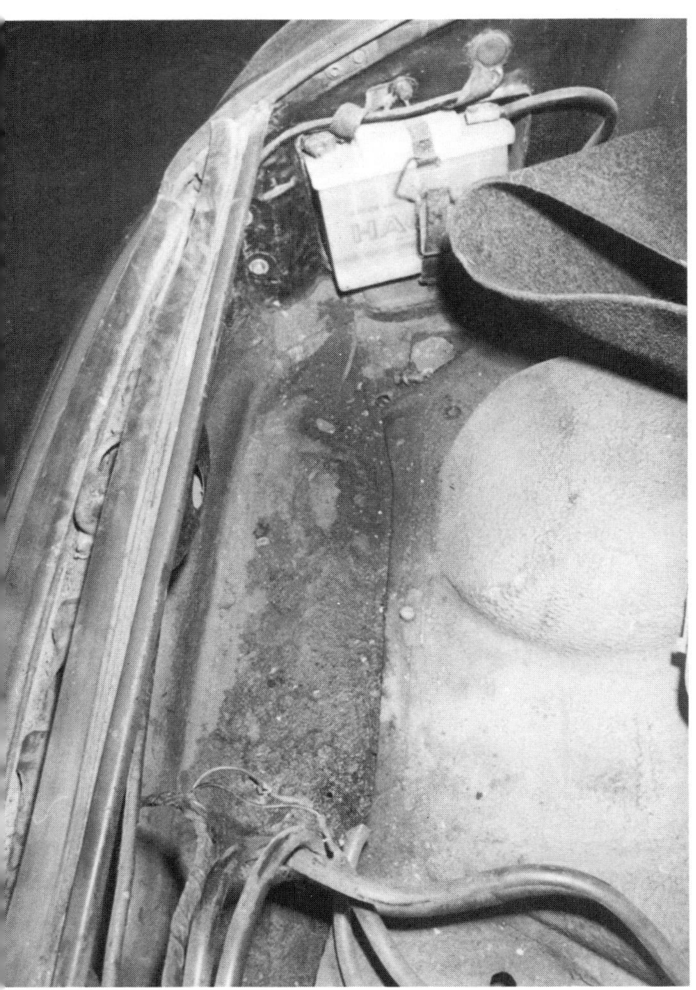

The extreme front of a 911 shell showing the 1969–73 two-battery layout, in this case looking at the right-hand battery. The front of the floor ahead of the petrol tank is prone to corrosion, illustrated in typical form here.

The almost bare underside of a 911 shell. This example is from a 1973 model, but they are all similar. In this case, the right-hand front battery box has been removed with its attendant front inner panel.

a task that is frequently beyond the means and ability of an amateur owner. The rear lamps are housed in similar boxes to those of the headlights and suffer from exactly the same problem: mud collects over the box and it corrodes the surrounding metal. Another corrosive problem that rears its head is at the top of the rear wings at a point where there is a rust trap underneath.

Again, in common with cars built in the same era, the 911 tends to rust around the perimeter with the sills as one of the areas likely to be worst affected. They are very important for the car's strength and are made up of two basic parts, an inner and an outer sill, plus the jacking points. These parts are not too expensive, but a great deal of work is necessary to replace them, so their condition is doubly important from the aspect of the car's strength and value. All parts must be replaced if there is any doubt as to their

The heart of a 911: in this case, a 1977 Targa chassis in the course of being rebuilt as an Autofarm 935-style special.

The 1977 Targa shell mounted in a jig to have its damaged rear corner rebuilt.

The front corner of the 1964–8 O and A series cars is a common corrosion point: the front wing and apron have been removed for repairs to this example's left-hand corner. The inner wing has been plated at the bottom and a new front apron bracket fitted. The front of the wishbone is visible on the right.

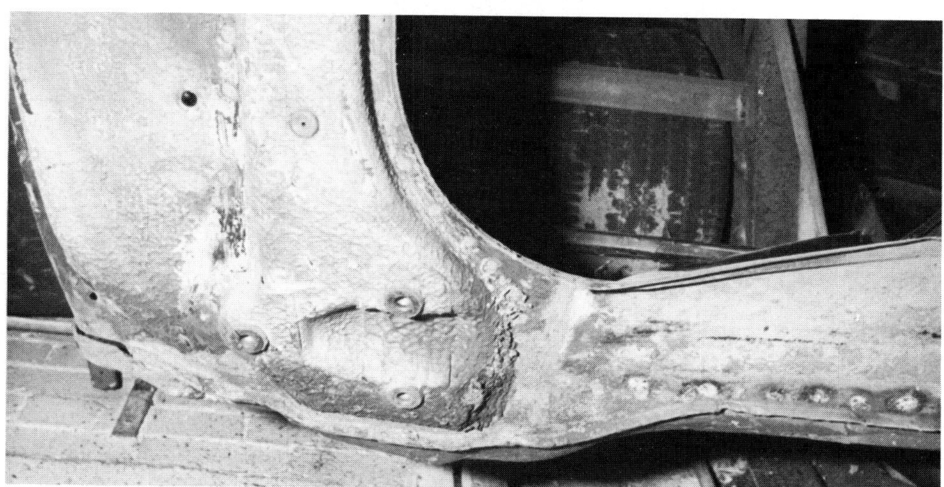

The front crossmember, which provides the front mounting for the wishbones, is prone to rust on O to B series 1964–9 cars with the danger of the entire mounting pulling out. It is pictured here from the right hand underside.

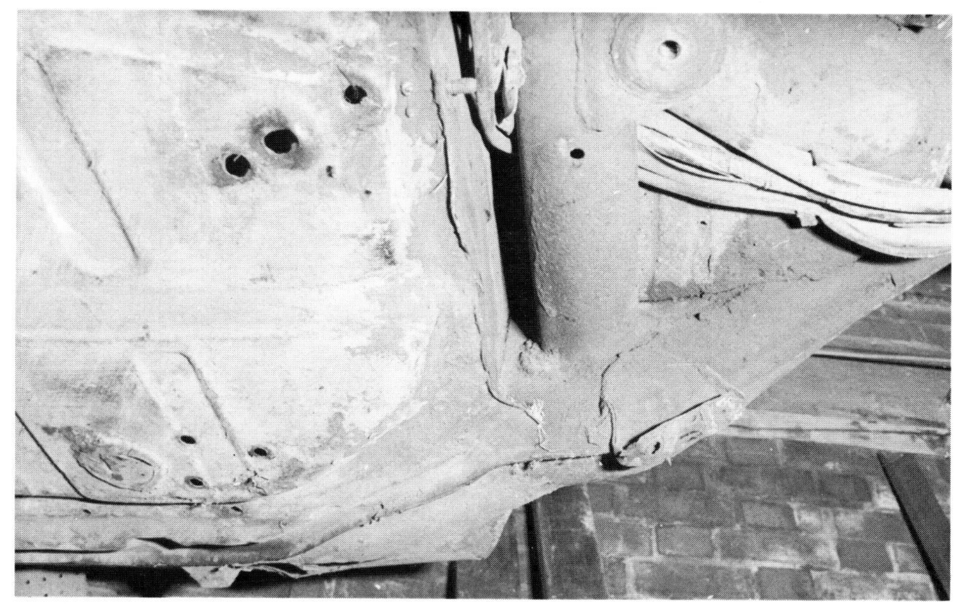

One of the most vital points on a Porsche 911: the rear torsion bar tube, viewed from the underside at the right-hand end. The gearbox mounting point is at the top of the picture with the anti-roll bar bracket at the outer end of the tube. This tube is prone to failure on 1968 and 1969 A and B series cars.

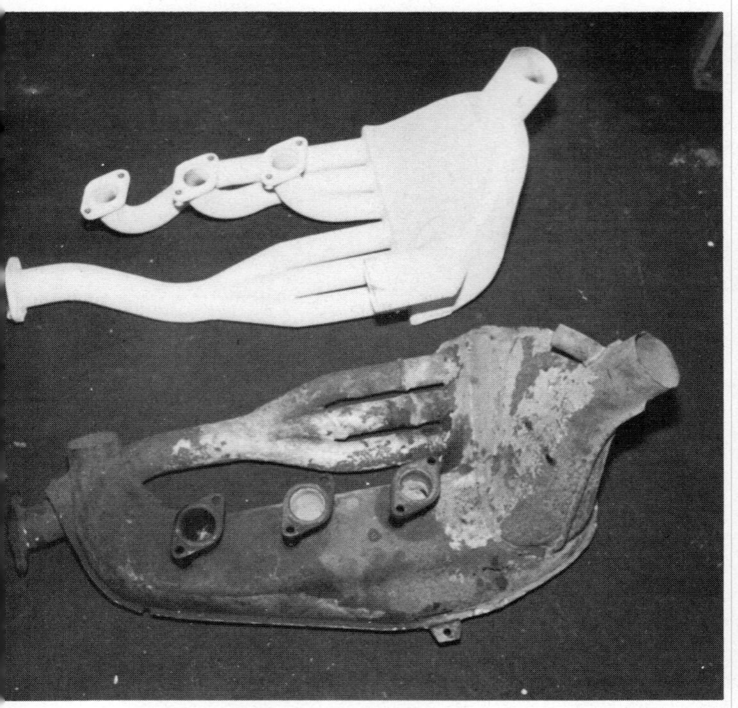

Old and new exhaust heat exchangers. At the top, a new right-hand unit from Autofarm; at the bottom, an original left-hand unit.

A corroded oil tank taken from a 1973 911.

Two types of front MacPherson strut: the top one is a conventional unit and the botton is one of the self-levelling units fitted as standard to the 1969–71 911E.

strength; it is no good simply having new outer sills tacked on to cover up the corrosion inside. Such a repair is purely cosmetic, of little value and will not last long as the corrosion already present will spread like cancer to disfigure the new outer sill or show itself when a jacking point collapses. On the weaker Targa bodyshell, the sheer weight of the engine and transmission can cause the body to sag when the sills are weakened by corrosion. The roof on a coupé does a good job of keeping such a body in shape and has the advantage of being virtually rust-free. Front luggage boot lids do not suffer from much corrosion either, but the doors rust at their bottoms and in their shut faces—again almost all round the perimeter. In severe cases, the door securing catches can fall out in much the same manner as a child's first teeth. The engine lid can rot away along its bottom edge and the rear centre panel which carries the number plate suffers badly from this condition, probably due to its constant exposure to changes of heat around the rear silencer and the ever present threat from mud and road debris. However, the rear quarter panels do not suffer so much as the temperatures surrounding them are more constant.

The floorpan itself is very strong and seems to escape a lot of corrosion except around its outer edge, where plating is often a good repair. Two essential parts of the bodyshell that are prone to corrosion are the front crossmember and the rear torsion bar tube. The crossmember provides the front mount for the wishbones and is especially likely to be rusty on cars made before the C series and is worth checking on any car more than three years old. When it has been sufficiently weakened, the whole mounting pulls out, so its stength is obviously a vital factor for the well-being of the car, its occupants and anything else on the road. The trouble with the rear torsion bar tube has been largely confined to A and B series cars but is now occurring on later versions. The tube is at the heart of the bodyshell and weaknesses are virtually impossible to detect until the tube suddenly fails. This causes the suspension to bottom out on the shock absorber mountings and the result can be potentially dangerous. In addition, the corners of the chassis legs tend to rust along the whole perimeter of the body.

The main cause of the rampant corrosion that strikes bodywork is the flange inside the front wing at its rearward edge. A perforated flange lets water into the front of the sill and chassis leg bodywork. The first signs of this trouble often manifest themselves in wet carpets. The original mild-steel oil tanks mounted inside the rear wings also tend to be a starting point for corrosion and can cause mechanical disasters. Dirt gets inside rusty oil tanks and finds its way to the engine's bearings, which can result in an expensive blow-up. Stainless steel tanks eliminate this problem. The alloy oil cooler matrix, where fitted, can deteriorate in a similar manner, leading to the same bearing trouble.

The most common fault with Porsche 911 engines is in their hydraulic

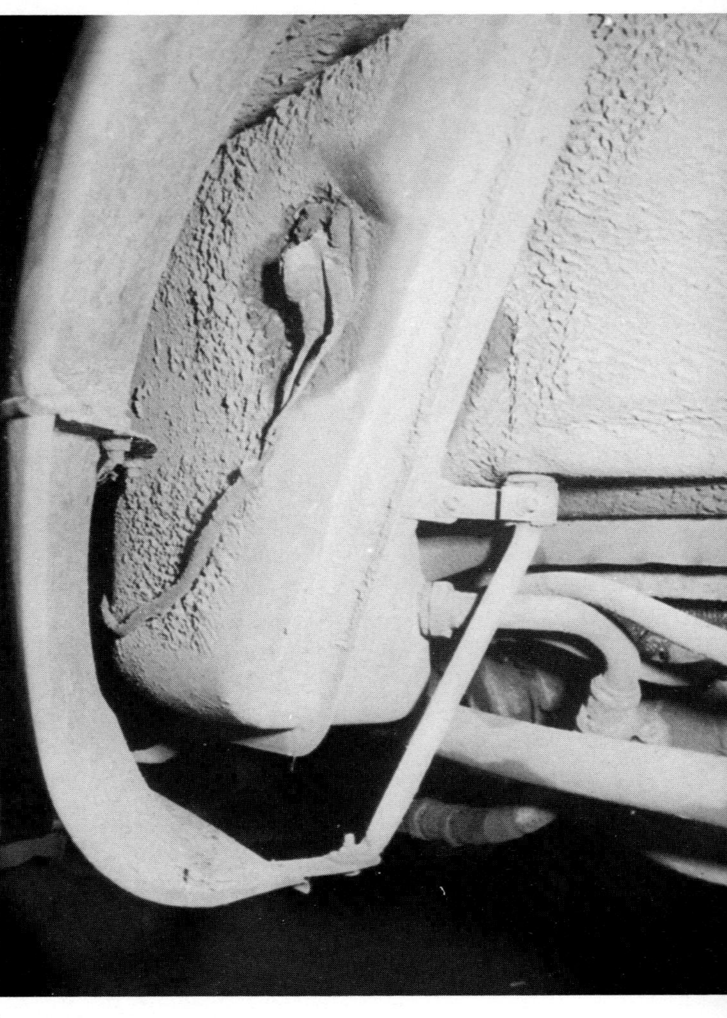

timing chain tensioners. They are designed to work efficiently over the wide range of temperatures common to air-cooled engines. This has the unfortunate effect of limiting their life to around 40,000 to 50,000 miles on average with early examples although this mileage has been improved with the later force-fed variants. The best way to test for such a condition is to run the engine at 2500 rpm in neutral and to listen for noises from the chain. They can often be quite violent, so should not be missed. At higher revs, the tensioner tends to build up enough pressure to reduce the noise. Therefore keeping the revs up can be a way of limping home with such a problem, although the best course is to seek immediate attention. It is really not worth risking blowing up an engine for such a deficiency, which is easily cured. The 2.7-litre cars with high-lift cams are the most susceptible to such trouble, as

The right-hand timing chest cover has been removed on this car to expose its early pattern hydraulic tensioner for replacement.

The oil tank in place behind the right-hand rear wing. Note the accumulation of corrosion-inducing mud.

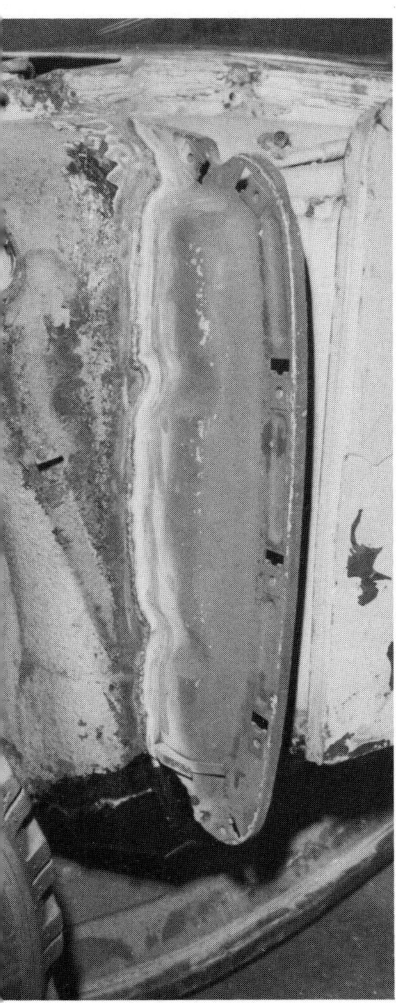

One of the main rust spots in a 911 shell is at the bottom of the front wing rear-mounting flange. A perforated flange lets water into the front of the sill and chassis leg. The body on the example illustrated here, showing the left-hand flange, has been plated ahead of the flange at the bottom.

the tensioner has to work hardest in their case. The timing chain guides are usually made of rubber and can deteriorate in a similar manner. As a result, oilways become blocked, leading to camshaft lubrication problems.

The valve guides, particularly those for the exhaust, also wear, with 60,000 miles as the average life. The result is a smoky engine which burns a lot of oil, but replacements can be put off for a long while providing the oil tank is kept well-filled! Smoke can also be caused by other conditions, such as worn piston rings. A figure of 80,000 miles is a common time for such conditions to manifest themselves. Early blocks can be rebored up to the 2.7-litre capacity and crankshafts reground. Replacement pistons and cylinder barrels are expensive, however.

Early gearboxes can be a source of trouble with a weakness in the input shaft causing breakage on 2-litre cars and the intermediate bearings are subject to failure on 2-litre and 2.2-litre cars. The gearbox fitted to E and F series cars can also suffer from leaking oil seals. These are expensive repairs because rectification entails stripping the gearbox. In the case of the O to D series cars, replacements are expensive and spares are scarce. Engine and gearbox removal is much easier and quicker on a Porsche 911 than on a majority of cars, however, because of the simplicity of their attachment and their light weight. It is essential to make sure that everything is disconnected—particularly the gearbox linkage—before removal if subsequent trouble is to be avoided. Much trouble can emanate from the fuel injection systems fitted from the B series with pump replacements or reconditioning being particularly expensive. Such work is best left to the experts with the proper equipment, however, if frustration and further trouble is to be avoided.

The most common fault on a Porsche 911 is corrosion in the heat exchangers. The earlier pattern lasted only two years on average and rot away easily because of their constant subjection to extreme changes of temperature and exposed position at the tail of the car. Apart from affecting the heating arrangements, prolonged use with a badly corroded heat exchanger on mechanical injection cars can be expensive. When no heat is fed to the automatic choke, it stays on with a resultant high petrol consumption. Factory replacements are expensive, partly due to the exchange rate problems with German-manufactured items, but British firms such as Autofarm are notable for being able to have replacements made at a much lower price and superb-quality American parts are now available.

The suspension on a Porsche 911 takes a hammering but is not usually prone to wear. Corrosion problems are showing up in the wishbones of early cars, however, and must be treated with the utmost respect. A similarly-dangerous defect can be wear in the ball joints at the bottom of the struts of the O, A and B series cars. The clamps wear in a like manner on the B, C and D series cars. These problems were overcome for the E series by using cotter

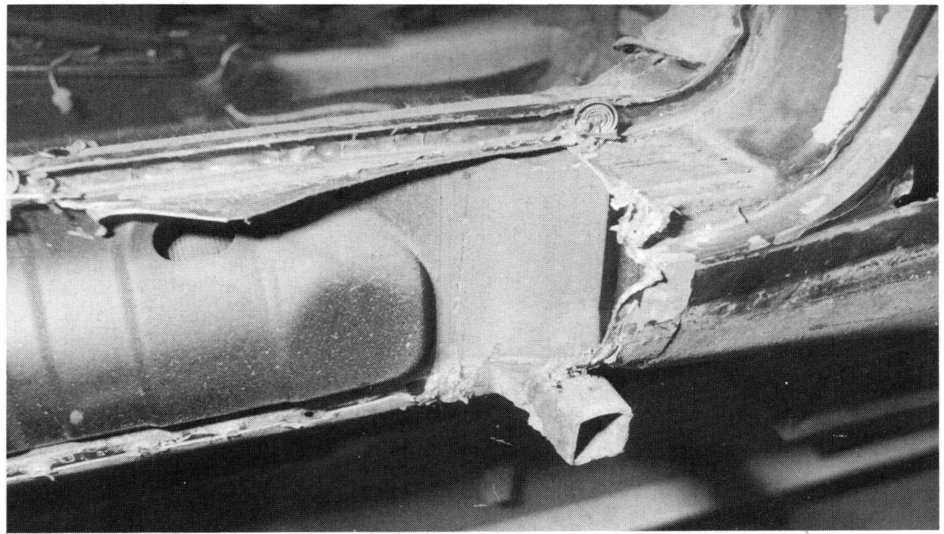

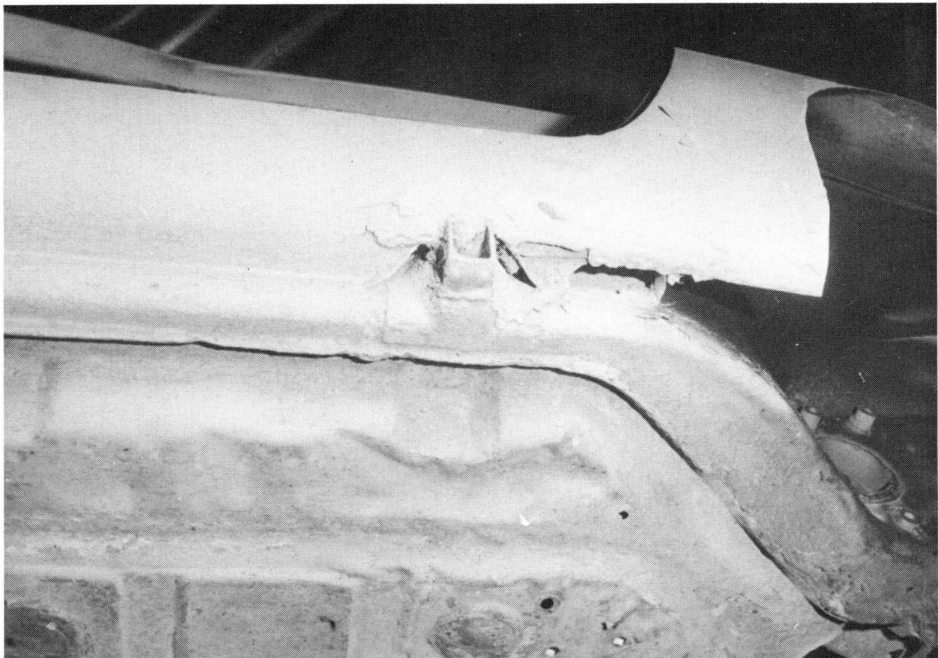

*Right and facing page:* A left-hand jacking point with the outer sill, rear wing and door-closing panels removed in the first picture. A new inner sill, jacking point and bracing tube had to be fitted to complete this repair.

pins to stop the clamps loosening. Corrosion also attacks the torsion bars, which can break near their rear splines. The B, C and D series 911E (and the occasional T and S models) fitted with self-levelling front struts are running into problems as well. These struts are prone to collapse, which results in a sinking suspension. Replacements are expensive and in short supply. It is

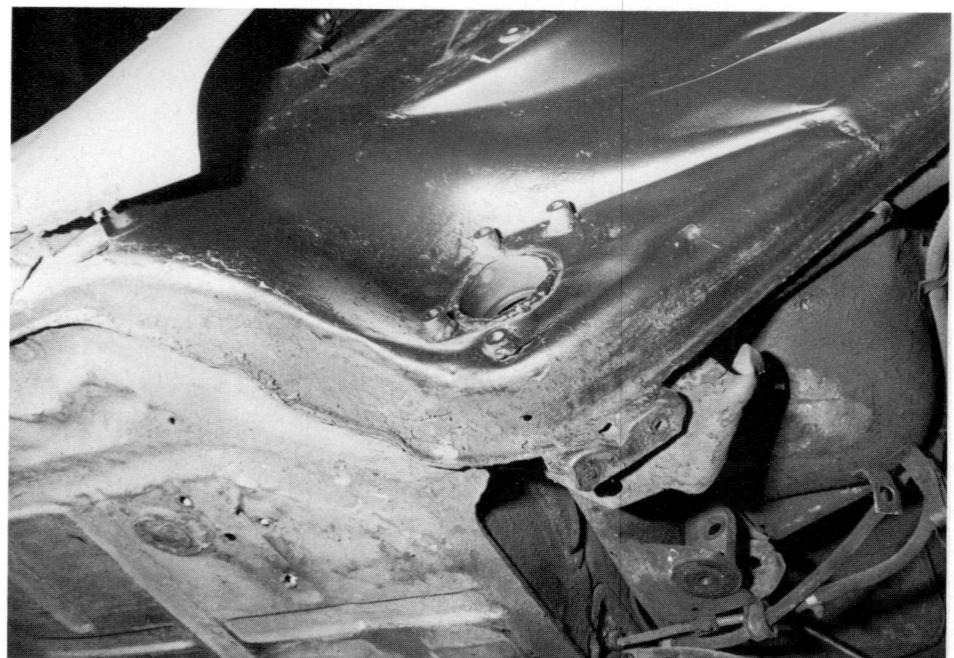

*Left:* Rust points on the 1964-9 O to B series cars; the rear chassis leg, repaired in this case.

*Below right:* Danger spot: rust strikes at door-closing panels and the catch will eventually fall off. This is a right-hand panel.

*Below-left:* The left-hand door-closing panel showing the engine lid catch pull.

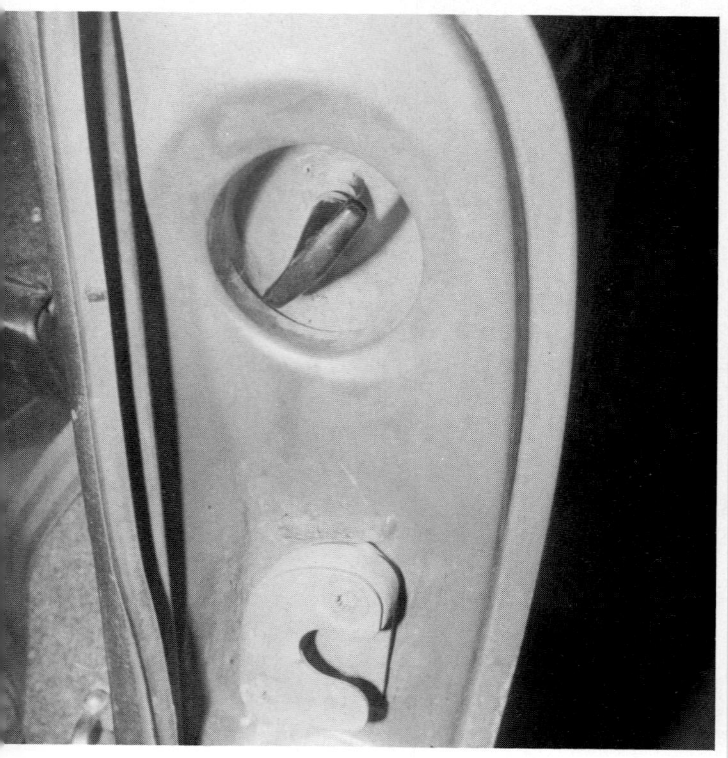

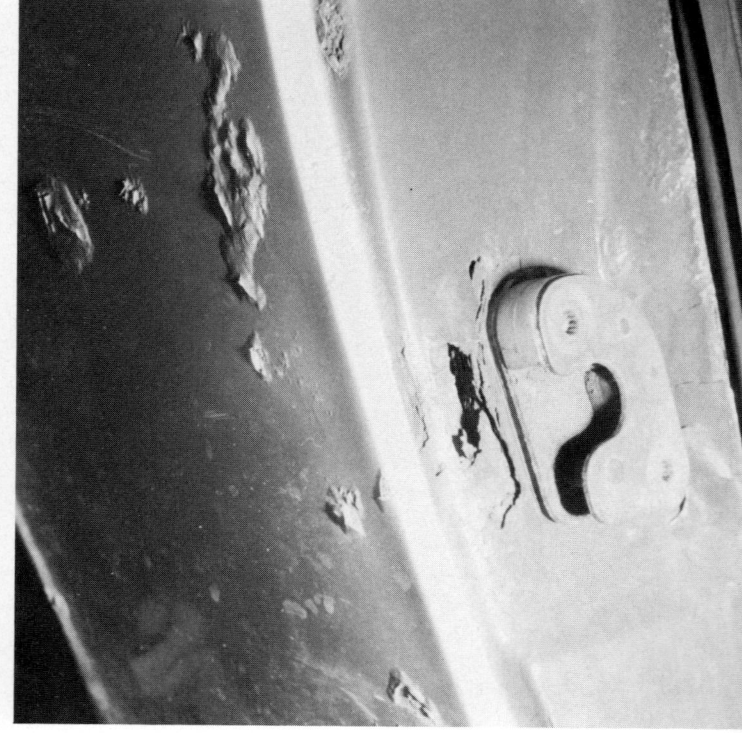

Trouble spot: the rear light. This picture shows a 1964–8 O and A series light which should be mounted inside a metal box behind the wing. However, the box rusts, the mud gets in, the lighting unit fills up because it is not sealed, the lens becomes discoloured and because the lens is bonded on, an entire new unit and mounting box is needed.

*Below right:* Examine the rear flanks of a 911 for rust as there is a mud trap behind this panel.

*Below:* A typically rusty wing on a 1964-8 O and A series car. These front sidelights suffer in the same way as the rear lights and the flanges around the headlights corrode as well.

Find out for yourself . . . the author's 911 undergoing a total restoration.

simple enough to convert the front suspension to the normal torsion bar system, but a lot of expensive new parts are needed. Should a torsion bar fail at the back this can be easily identified by the car having a lop-sided look. Brakes present few problems other than the cost of replacement parts, particularly on cars with alloy calipers, which eventually weaken and expand under pressure. The factory have been quite generous with the thickness of the discs, however, which allows regrinding.

Porsche 911s, such as this Carrera RS, need to be stripped to the bare bones to eliminate all corrosion.

Apart from corrosion and the wear and tear associated with high mileages and age, it is essential to look for accident damage when considering the purchase of a used Porsche 911, because of the high degree of driving skill needed to conduct one to anywhere near the limits of its performance. The most obvious place to look at is any one of the four corners—Porsches are just as likely to leave the road backwards as forwards! The triangular strengthening member is often pushed back in a frontal impact, leaving a wavy floor after even successful repairs. Such a floor need not necessarily adversely affect a car's performance if the rest has been prepared properly, but it is a sign of what the machine has undergone. Door pillars can also be put out of alignment in a big crash, so check the gap around the doors. Marks on the window frames are also a good tell-tale sign of major impacts which have affected the doors. The serious defect in a poorly-repaired car is likely to be misalignment of the track. Avoid such cars like the plague. The same strictures apply to the back of a Porsche 911, plus the common bending of the rear suspension's trailing arms as a result of walloping a wheel on a kerb or similar projection that might leave no other apparent mark. Some late-style alloy wheels are far more likely to crack with such treatment than the earlier ones. Despite this catalogue of potential woes with a Porsche 911 it must be remembered that they are far more practical to run and maintain than almost any other marque providing so much performance!

# Build Your Own 911

The extraordinary versatility of the Porsche 911 and its associated series is demonstrated by the way in which cars to virtually any specification can be built from piles of assorted parts. In theory, one of the first 911s, made in 1964, could be turned into one of the latest Turbos, providing the owner's pocket is deep enough! The price of parts, and the purpose for which the car is intended—road, track, or rallying for instance—are the only limiting factors in this fascinating exercise. A certain degree of skill is necessary in adapting some parts to mate up with others, such as moving suspension mountings to Carrera specifications, but there is nothing that is beyond the ability of the specialist dealers that handle sales and service, and much of the work can be done in enthusiasts' garages. The British firm, Autofarm, are especially well known for building special versions of 911s.

It is also possible to ring a large variety of changes on individual components, such as increasing the capacity of an engine, without changing much of the basic unit. But this is only practical in some engines for the cost and availability of components varies tremendously.

For instance, it is not practical to increase the capacity of the early 2.0-litre and 2.2-litre engines because large bore pistons and cylinders for these engines are no longer available and are unlikely to be made again in view of the ready availability of later, larger-capacity units. Increasing the capacity of these early engines by using a longer stroke—which entails changes to the crankshaft and connecting rods—is impractical in that it costs more than replacing the engine with a ready-made larger-capacity unit. Therefore, potential modifications to the 2.0-litre and 2.2-litre engine should be confined to fitting larger carburettors (or using Webers if the older Solex carburettors are fitted), improving the porting, fitting wilder camshafts and so on. The largest practical carburettors are Weber 46 IDAs, as used on the old 911R. The potential power output attainable on the fuel-injected engines in the early capacity ranges is limited by the size of the system's butterfly valves. Modifying the fuel injection system to take extra-large butterflies can be very expensive, so it is better to think in terms of using carburettors for added performance. The exact choice of cams, timing, exhaust systems and so on is dictated by the purpose for which the car is intended. Full-race engines on megaphone exhaust are obviously impractical for road use, where more torque and legal exhaust systems are necessary.

The 2.4-litre and 2.7-litre engines offer much more scope for modification. They can easily be taken out to 2.8 litres and even up to 3.0

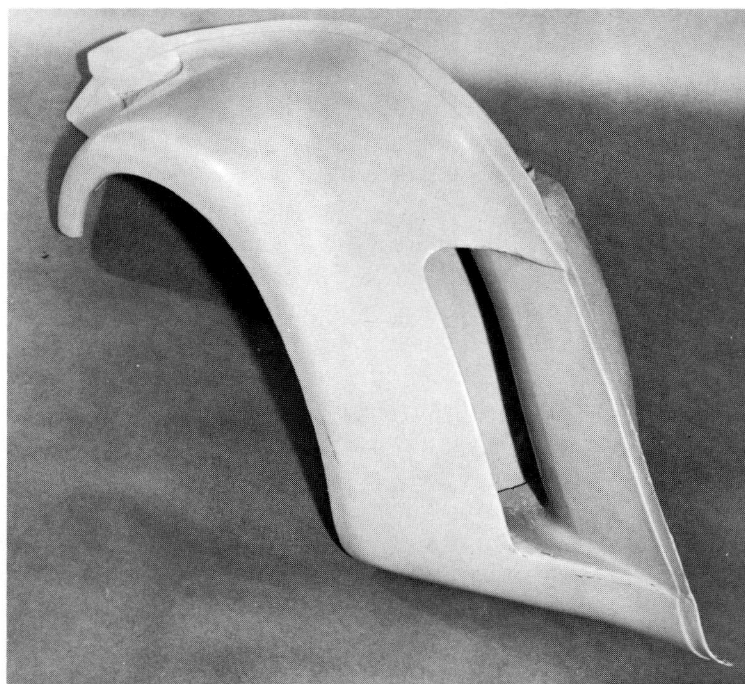

*Right:* A 935-style glass fibre rear wheelarch with front air scoop.

*Above:* A widened wheelarch in glass fibre before final fitting.

litres providing the late crankcase used on all 2.7-litre engines is available. This aluminium crankcase was also used on 2.4-litre engines made from late 1973. All 911s from the 2.4-litre T model to the 1977 3.0 litre used the same bottom end to the engine and cylinder heads. The performance of the engine fitted to the 2.4-litre T model can be readily improved by fitting larger carburettors and that of any fuel-injected 2.4 litre can be easily converted to a 2.7-litre Carrera unit by fitting different cylinders, pistons and associated parts. Carrera units used the same camshafts as the earlier engines fitted to the 911S. The K Jetronic fuel injection fitted from late 1975 is very difficult to modify and enthusiasts are recommended to leave well alone. The balance of this system is extremely delicate and will not tolerate the substantial valve overlap associated with wilder camshafts and higher power ouputs achieved by this means. In fact, engines fitted with this system are subject to a lower rev limit because the fuel injection cannot cope with high revs.

Therefore, if it is intended to increase the performance of K Jetronic engines it is necessary to think in terms of converting to carburettors and fitting wilder camshafts which means changing the pistons to avoid hitting the valves whose travel is liberated by 'hotter' cams. In contrast, the latest Carrera engines readily accept different microchips to vary performance.

The 3.0RS and RSR engines built in 1974 and 1975 were a special case. Their cylinder head securing studs were moved from the old standard of 80 mm apart to 83 mm to allow the increase in capacity. This also meant that they had different heads from those of the earlier engines. Then when the 3.0-litre capacity increase was made standard for production, the stud spacing went up to 86 mm to allow for future capacity increases. This entailed the fitting of yet another batch of cylinders and heads although these retained the same big valves as those fitted to RS and RSR engines.

Modifications up to and above the 3.0-litre capacity are breaking new ground for Porsche enthusiasts. A variety of sizes have been popular, chiefly on competition cars. One of the most common is a 210 bhp unit to Carrera RS specification which can be built up from a 2.4-litre 911E or 911S engine, by using bigger bore cylinders, heads and pistons. A 3.2-litre unit can be built in a similar way using the 83 mm crankcase and a 3.3-litre from the 86 mm crankcase. The 3.3-litre Turbo engine's capacity increase was achieved by making the stroke longer, so a combination of the larger bores and longer strokes can extend these units to 3.5 litres or even 3.7 litres, using a 102 mm stud-spacing crankcase. The 3.5-litre units seem quite reliable but the reliability factor is low at present in the 3.7-litre capacity so the lower capacity would appear to be the present limit of 911 engine development short of turbocharging. The price of these competition parts is also very high.

Engines up to 3.0 RSR specification can use the 2.4-litre and 2.7-litre transmission without trouble providing a larger capacity clutch is fitted. The only problem normally associated with this is on tarmac rallying cars which are habitually lifted off the ground over large bumps by fast-moving drivers, or 'yumped' as the rallymen call it (with apologies to the pronunciation of jumped by the Scandinavians who are so good at it). Normally, when such

*Below:* A Carrera RSR-style replacement front bumper and lip in glass fibre.

*Left:* A 935-style front wheelarch in glass fibre with air outlet at the rear.

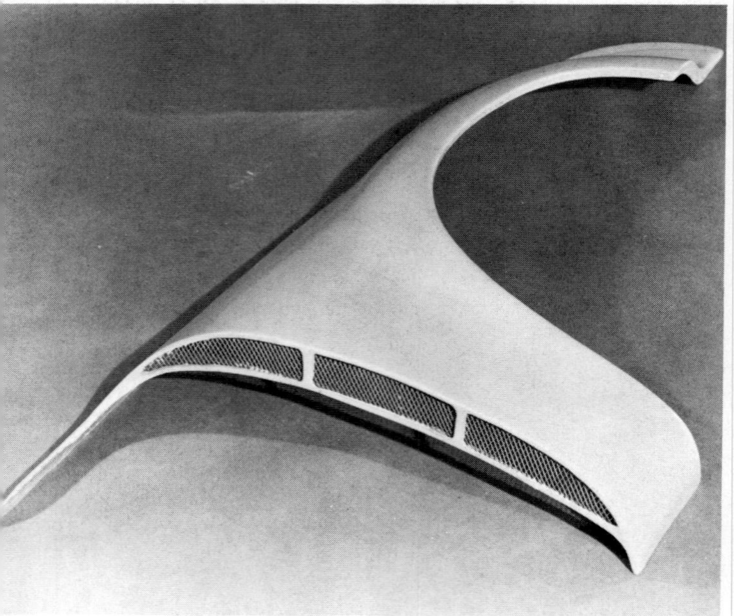

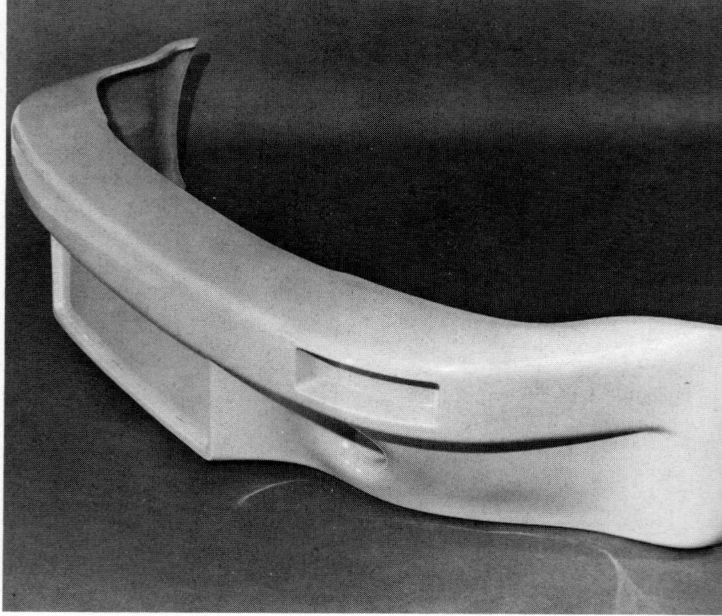

Replacement front wing sections for 911s in glass fibre.

A glass fibre 911 front lid.

units are used with a standard transmission, a stronger clutch is fitted, but in this case it is essential that a standard clutch is retained. Then, if the strain of the tyres biting the tarmac after a jump is too much for the drive line, the clutch suffers rather than the gearbox. It's better to burn a clutch than burst a transmission. The clutch on the earlier 2.0-litre models tends to be an Achilles heel, however, but it is possible to fit a later, larger capacity clutch by modifying the casing. The 2.2-litre cars' transmission can also be used quite successfully on cars with power outputs up to Carrera limits providing they are confined to shorter distance events. The best reasonably-priced transmission other than that fitted to the Turbo, in terms of strength, is that used from the 2.4-litre to the SC. This gearbox—series number 915–can be used on all long wheelbase 911s with only slight body modifications to early cars. It can also be fitted to short wheelbase cars providing the driveshaft flanges are modified.

A popular way of constructing a racing 911 is to buy an early machine that is cheap because it has corroded or the mechanical side is in poor condition, and a late wreck that has suffered front damage. A combination of the parts from both, with suitable repairs to the rusty one, with the addition of competition wheels and tyres, is usually enough to build a racing 911. It is also possible to use the 912 bodyshell for this purpose. It is quite feasible to change the wheelbase of such cars from short to long by swopping around

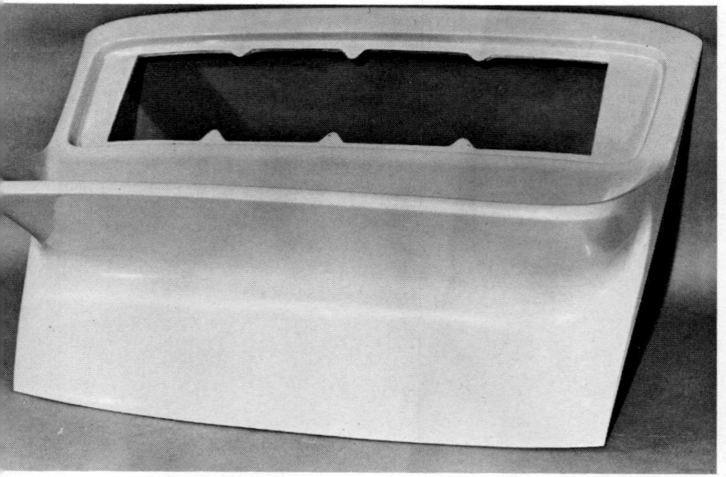

the appropriate parts and fitting new rear wings, although this can be very expensive for road cars where a higher standard of finish is required. There is another school of thought, particularly among hill-climbers, that prefers the short wheelbase for maximum oversteer to help swing their cars through tight hairpins.

The front suspension system of all Porsche 911s can be changed around quite readily although the rear suspension often requires substantial modifications if that of a different series is fitted. With a little bit of 'cutting and shutting' and welding, it is all possible, however. Steering columns are not so readily changeable because of alterations made when the American

*Top left:* A replacement Carrera engine lid in glass fibre with its distinctive duck's tail spoiler.

*Top right:* A 930-style replacement rear lid in glass fibre with 'picnic table' spoiler.

*Bottom left:* Steve Carr of Autofarm surrounded by glass fibre replacement panels.

*Bottom right:* A replacement front cross member—in metal, of course, because it is a stressed part.

Porsches, Porsches everywhere at Autofarm's early premises. Now they have moved to new premises but there are just as many Porsches.

impact bumpers were introduced. Thus it is not practical to fit a late-type steering wheel with its attendant column to an earlier car.

Road wheels can be swopped around with alacrity as there have been no hub changes since 1969. The rear wheel bearings of cars built before 1974 tend to suffer from a limited life, however, when wide wheels are fitted. The only limiting factor when fitting different suspension systems—it is quite possible, for instance, to fit the suspension from a Turbo to the earliest of 911s—is the cost of parts, which can be very high. One of the most popular changes in this area is converting cars with self-levelling struts to the normal front suspension. Early cars fitted with self-levelling struts had different wishbones, which adds to the cost of conversions in their case.

Fuel systems have to be adapted to suit the potential use of the car and the specification of engine. Fitting a K-Jetronic engine to an earlier car, for example, needs alterations to the fuel tank and lines because this system is

An Autofarm 935-style conversion on a 911 Targa.

very sensitive to swirl in the tank. Cars made before 1970 also have smaller oil pipes, so these need to be changed if later engines and gearboxes are fitted.

Brakes can be readily swopped around on all cars made from 1969, although, particularly in the cases of alloy calipers and ventilated discs, everything has to be changed. Ventilated discs are not really necessary on any except the fastest of 911s and Turbos, however.

Almost any type of body can be built up on a 911 providing the owner can afford the price of the panels. This can be minimised by the use of glass fibre parts which are especially popular on competition machines where light weight and cost—in view of potential damage in races and rallies—is of prime importance. The 911 and 912 fixed-head shell is so rigid that it is practical to use glass fibre doors whereas on many rival sports cars steel doors must be retained to maintain overall rigidity. The only real disadvantage to using glass fibre doors is that they are so whippy that they are more difficult to shut from the inside than the normal metal doors.

The only problem area when swopping around body panels is in the bumpers. Various modifications have to be made to accommodate late impact bumpers and there is a problem with short wheelbase cars that had lumps of iron bolted in their bumpers in that they cannot be fitted with modern glass fibre spoilers. It is well worth fitting normal road-going spoilers to earlier cars or those later ones that do not have them if an improvement in straightline stability is desired. The main objection is appearance—some people prefer the older, cleaner, lines—and cost. Racing spoilers are impractical for road use in that they are either wider than the car or grind on the ground when the road dips violently!

It is possible, in theory, to convert a fixed-head coupé into a Targa, although it is hardly worth it as the welding work involved is extensive and it would probably be cheaper to sell the existing car or shell and buy a ready-made Targa. All interior panels can be readily changed for those of later or earlier models. A bodywork conversion that is becoming popular is changing the front of a standard 911 to look like that of the racing 935. This is done by firms such as Autofarm by modifying the front inner wings (with further modifications if impact bumpers are not present) and fitting new front wings and a lighting conversion using parts from the Porsche 928.

# Running and Restoring a 911

A Porsche 911 can be one of the most practical cars to run, and restore even to concours standards, because of the relatively easy way in which it can be dismantled. It is one of the simplest cars to work on because of the superbly engineered way in which it is built and the sheer excellence of its factory workshop manuals. With one of these tomes at your elbow and the knowledge that everything was put together properly in the first place, taking a Porsche 911 to pieces is a much more practical business than at first might be imagined. The only parts that really have to be left to the experts are items such as fuel injection, and the electrical management systems of the latest cars, which require skilled attention. Plus, of course, really exotic machinery like the 959.

One of the most daunting tasks on the majority of cars—whether they need mechanical or cosmetic attention—is taking the engine out. It makes underbonnet preparation for concours, for instance, a major operation. With a Porsche 911 it is quite easy, taking only two or three hours. There's an additional advantage, too. Once all the pipes, lines, gear linkages, and so on, have been disconnected, the engine and transmission is much easier to handle than with most cars, because it is so light.

The interior is also fairly easy to dismantle, so the best way to prepare a 911 for concours, or even to just respray it, is to take the whole car to pieces—reducing it to major components, such as the bodyshell and power train with all ancillaries removed—before you start restoration. In this way, a proper respray can be undertaken without items such as the interior being affected by spray painting.

Before dismantling a 911, to prepare it for concours or to just restore it for everyday use, it is necessary to carry out a detailed examination, noting everything that needs attention or replacement. Photograph or sketch the car from every angle to remind yourself exactly how it was put together in the first place. You might need such aids to memory when you have to re-assemble the car, perhaps months later. In any case, they can save a lot of time wondering which way everything goes back together, even if you have a good knowledge of the car.

Then find out how long it will take to complete the work and how much it will cost. It is then that you can make up your mind whether it is worth doing as much and whether you can afford it. The next stage is to have the car steam cleaned. It is much easier to work on a clean vehicle than a dirty one, and it is also much easier to keep a car clean once preparation of this

A 911 has to be almost completely dismantled to give it a proper respray. This car, a 1976 Targa, has also had wide wheelarches welded on prior to fitting 930-style wheels.

nature has been completed. It must be remembered, however, that a searching steam cleaning can necessitate refinishing, so if the paint is really good, it is worth considering the time-consuming cleaning by hand. The next stage is to collect a lot of boxes, tins and blankets. These will protect the pieces that are removed from the car and help prevent any being lost. You will also need a pile of luggage labels. They save time identifying bits and pieces even if you are sure you know where every last part goes.

While the car is being dismantled, it is essential that the owner, or one person involved in the restoration, is present throughout the whole procedure to make notes on any potential problems. As small parts are removed they should be labelled and filed in separate boxes or tins. It is essential to use a logical sequence here: keep all the left-hand door pieces together, for instance, rather than just putting all the small parts in a box, leaving more room for big pieces in other boxes. Keep the car on its wheels as

Chassis parts reach the Porsche factory at Zuffenhausen ready made from suppliers such as Karmann.

long as possible unless you have a big workshop, so that you can move it around. Take care .) protect exposed parts from corrosion. Many pieces, such as brightwork, must be sent to specialists for restoration—the Porsche Club can help with names and addresses. When they have been returned, wrap them in the blankets and store them somewhere safe and dry until the car is rebuilt.

Many other parts can be restored or checked in the home workshop or garage. Hand clean them meticulously then if they are found to be in excellent condition, wrap them in blankets and store them for later. Otherwise, have them restored, or replace them and assemble them into major components as soon as possible to make sure that everything fits. If the bulk of a major assembly presents a problem—a 911 with its engine removed takes up more than the average lock-up—it can then be dismantled again for storage. But at least you will know at an early point that all the old and new pieces are going to work together. Keep notes of the specialists to whom you have dispatched parts so that you can chase them at appropriate times. A desk diary devoted to the car's restoration is best for this purpose. Mount the photographs taken before restoration in the diary for rapid reference.

When the mechanical cleaning is done and the specialists are well under way you can start on the bodyshell. Sandblasting on steel parts is ideal as it quickly shows up imperfections such as rust holes, while dramatically cutting the cleaning time. It is best to use professional help here as the lightweight panels on a 911 can be damaged badly by the use of a hired sandblaster in amateur hands. Do not let the abrasive sand near glass fibre or alloy components. There's no substitute for removing the paint by hand in this case.

The interior should be relatively easy to remove as it is well made. Interior panels in good condition or just restored are suitable cases for the blanket treatment while the rest of the work is under way because the dirt

The chassis parts are welded into their final form on giant jigs.

*Facing page:* Fixed-head coupés—with or without 930-style wheelarch extensions—are fabricated on the same production lines.

Targas and Cabriolets made separately because they need extra stiffening parts to be welded into the bodyshell before joining the coupés on the same production lines.

raised from body and chassis stripping and the spraying to follow can be ruinous.

Taking a 911 to pieces virtually down to the last nut and bolt is the sure way to prepare it properly for a concours or to restore it to pristine condition, but may be more than is wanted. Perhaps you just want to tidy up your car and to make it as smart as possible for general use without going to such fanatical lengths. Alternatively, you may just want to restore one part of the car, such as its paint, leaving the rest to a later date. In all these cases it is still necessary to clean the car as thoroughly as possible but it is not necessary to go to such lengths as shot blasting. When attempting these super clean-ups, start at the bottom and work your way up. The underside is bound to be the worst part of the car, so that's the best place to start.

The underside can be cleaned in a variety of ways: by a garage with steam cleaning equipment, or by the use of detergent under high pressure. Either of these systems removes oil and grease as well as accumulated road

It takes only five minutes to fit a complete engine and transmission and not much longer to fit the ready-assembled suspension!

dirt. Alternatively, you can get rid of the road dirt by clamping a piece of copper or alloy tube in a garden hose with a Jubilee clip and flattening the end into a megaphone shape to give a high-pressure water jet. It often helps to bend the metal pipe to make the jet more manoeuvrable. Giving the car a thorough washing down once a month with such a device, or more frequently when the roads are salty, can do wonders to prevent corrosion. If possible, site the car near a drain when this is being done because it is a messy business.

When everything has dried out, and you've found out whether you have any holes in the floor or wings, scrape off old underseal and paint and prepare the metal underneath with corrosion-inhibiting material. Then use primer, undercoat and top coat before re-sealing. There's nothing worse than old underseal that has cracked—even with only hairline fractures—for trapping water or saline solution between itself and the metal to which it is attached. Rampant corrosion starts at this point. It can also take hold on patches of primer waiting for their top coat as the primer is porous—so make sure any part of the body gets its top coat as soon as possible.

It's worth treating box sections with anti-rust fluids within two years of their last application to impede corrosion. These solutions can be injected into the box sections with the same sort of sprayer that is used for garden insecticide. Sections of the car which have corroded badly should be replaced with new metal or parts if they are of structural importance, or with new panels or fibreglass replicas if they are not stressed. The front wings and engine lid of a 911 are good examples of unstressed components. Glass fibre panels save a lot of money initially and do not corrode in themselves, but ultimately detract from a car's value if they are not original fittings. Excellent replica panels can be obtained from firms such as Autofarm, and virtually all parts are still available in galvanised steel material from the factory even if they were not made in this material originally. This makes the running and restoration of a Porsche 911 much easier than that of most classic sports cars whose parts are very difficult to obtain.

Engines are built to meticulous standards on the bench.

In some cases it may be cheaper to get a good panel beater to make up part of a wing or similar panel and have it welded in to replace corroded areas. Alternatively tiny holes can be successfully filled with body solder or glass fibre. When respraying areas where there have been local repairs, cover the whole panel rather than just the area which has been repaired and its immediate surroundings as it can be very difficult to match the paint exactly in the middle of a panel.

The best way to deal with the interior of a 911 is to remove the seats as well as the carpets and clean everything thoroughly. First, remove all rubbish and odds and ends and then start on the headlining (assuming the car is a coupé). It is essential that the little clips that secure it at the edges are in good order or you will not be able to refit it properly. For general use, just give the headlining a good brushing and vacuuming; if stains are more deep-seated, remove the headlining and then use carpet shampoo and a sponge. Do not use these while the headlining is in place because the wet fabric will pick up

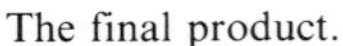

The final product.

The engine is tested for 70 minutes on a dynamometer.

any dirt, or flaky rust, which is behind it and the marks will probably show when it dries. For concours cars, it is best to renew the headlining in any case, as it is easily discoloured.

As long as the rest of the trim around the interior, particularly the doors, is in good order, you can clean it while it is in place. Foam cleaners are the best sort to use here, providing no leather is involved. For cars fitted with leather seats, use saddle soap–readily obtainable from harness shops or coachtrimmers—or a restoration kit from specialists such as the Connolly hide suppliers. If you send them a little bit of the leather from behind the seats they can produce a dye to match it. In company with various coachtrimmers, they can also supply cleaners, leather softeners, lacquer and hide food. You have to remember that leather is really a skin and needs as much attention as your own if it is to be kept in good condition.

Re-upholstering seats should be left to the experts, but it is quite practical to reproduce the other interior panels using the old parts as patterns. Coachtrimmers should be able to supply all the materials.

New carpets can be obtained from the factory or from Porsche specialists, or alternatively, they can be copied using the originals as a pattern in the same manner as the interior panels. If you do not want to sew the new carpeting, you can overlap it and use an adhesive such as Copydex, re-inforcing the joins with carpet binding stuck on with the adhesive. Make sure you do not get the adhesive on the top surface of the carpeting, or you will never get it off.

Use washing-up liquid or window cleaner to restore the glass and don't forget the instruments—it's amazing what a difference they make to a car! Also remember to clean the backs of items such as door handles and interior mirrors as they are easily forgotten, and show up very easily on an otherwise immaculate car, and as such are a potential point-loser in a concours. Very early 911s had wooden fascias and steering wheel rims, and these should be stripped and re-varnished if their finish has deteriorated. Otherwise treat leather-rimmed steering wheels like the seats; cleaining plastic ones is relatively easy.

The best way to clean up mechanical components, such as suspension units, is to remove them *en bloc* and steam clean if rubber bushings are involved or wash them thoroughly in petrol if they are not; paraffin is an abrasive. Once they have dried off, use rubber lubricant on bushes: 911s can be very squeaky without it. Removing major assemblies also gives a good opportunity to inspect them for wear. Always replace rubber parts if there is any doubt as to their durability; their deterioration can lead to rapid wear of the components they protect. It is a good idea, also, to remove alloy wheels and clean them thoroughly from time to time, especially in weather when salt has been used on the roads, as they are especially prone to corrosion. This is essential also with cars fitted with alloy brake calipers as they can be very expensive to replace if they seize up through corrosion. Items such as oil tanks and coolers benefit from periodic external cleaning and refinishing if corrosion and subsequent engine trouble is to be avoided. On very old cars it is also advisable to replace the wiring loom in a major rebuild rather than to make do with the old one, particularly in hot climates where the insulation deteriorates much quicker than in more moderate climes.

With proper attention to cleaning and maintenance, a Porsche 911 is such a well-made car that it should last a lifetime. With little attention to such details, it is tragic the way in which it deteriorates despite every effort made by the manufacturers.

In recent years, it has been possible to buy a new Porsche with what is called a Sport package, composed chiefly of uprated suspension components, more sporting tyres, and seats which provide better location for the occupants—all at the expense of the ultimate refinement associated with the normal specification. The advantage of the Sport options is that the car can be made to perform a good deal better.

Developments highlighted in the British Porsche Production Car Challenge have shown the way in which the earlier cars can be transformed along the same lines. The most dramatic changes can be made at little cost by substituting more modern rubber. BF Goodrich, for instance, market their latest Comp T/A tyres to original dimensions which means that the advantages of modern compounds can be exploited without changing the suspension settings. Other makers, notably Pirelli, Bridgestone and Goodyear, specialise in low-profile tyres that give similar advantages. Using low-profile tyres means, however, that different suspension settings are needed if the car's ride height is to be maintained. Goodrich also manufacture the Comp T/A in the typical 50-section low-profile pattern.

On the author's Carrera RS-specification car, the handling has been dramatically improved at the expense of a harsher ride by lowering the ride height 30 mm, and resetting the back suspension with $1^1/2$ degrees of

Autofarm's engine shop is run on much the same lines as that at Zuffenhausen.

negative camber and toe-in. Stiffer 911SC torsion bars are fitted with the Koni dampers on their hardest settings. The rear anti-roll bar has also been changed to that from a Turbo to further stiffen up the rear end. Corner-weight balancing completes the package. Tyres of 70-section are retained, because they are better suited to rough roads.

There is no need to lower the suspension if low-profile tyres are substituted for the original pattern, providing a reduced ground clearance is not critical. The handling then becomes more responsive—and nervous at the same time.

A further alternative is to fit either the new Porsche Carrera 16-inch wheels with their attendant low-profile rubber, or buy replica 16-inch wheels, such as the Compomotives marketed by the British firm Dage Sport. These wheels have the advantage of being far cheaper than the Porsche originals, and because they are of split-rim pattern, their width can be readily varied should different tyres prove attractive at a later date.

The overall result of packages such as that employed on the author's car is that it still handles like a traditional 911, but everything that happens at, say 60 mph, in a bend now takes place at around 80 mph. The beauty of modifications like this is that you can tailor a car to suit your individual needs. A Porsche 911 really is a racing car for the road, it is so responsive to changes to the running gear.

**Plate Twenty-Four** Hard to tell apart . . . a lightweight Carrera RS in the foreground and a touring model in the background.

**Plate Twenty-Five** One of Porsche's greatest . . . Jody Scheckter in a 3.0RSR at the Nurburgring in 1974.

**Plate Twenty-Six** Luxury racer . . . the Porsche 934.

**Plate Twenty-Seven** Ultimate 935 . . . John Fitzpatrick's spaceframe example at Brands Hatch in 1982.

**Plate Twenty-Eight** Ever popular and practical Porsche . . . the 911SC coupé.

**Plate Twenty-Nine** The open 911SC introduced a new dimension into modern Porsche motoring.

**Plate Thirty** One of the ultimate Porsche road cars . . . a 3.5-litre RSR.

**Plate Thirty-One** Ever popular open-air Porsche . . . the Targa in Carrera form.

**Plate Thirty-Two** Porsche still make great hill-climb cars.

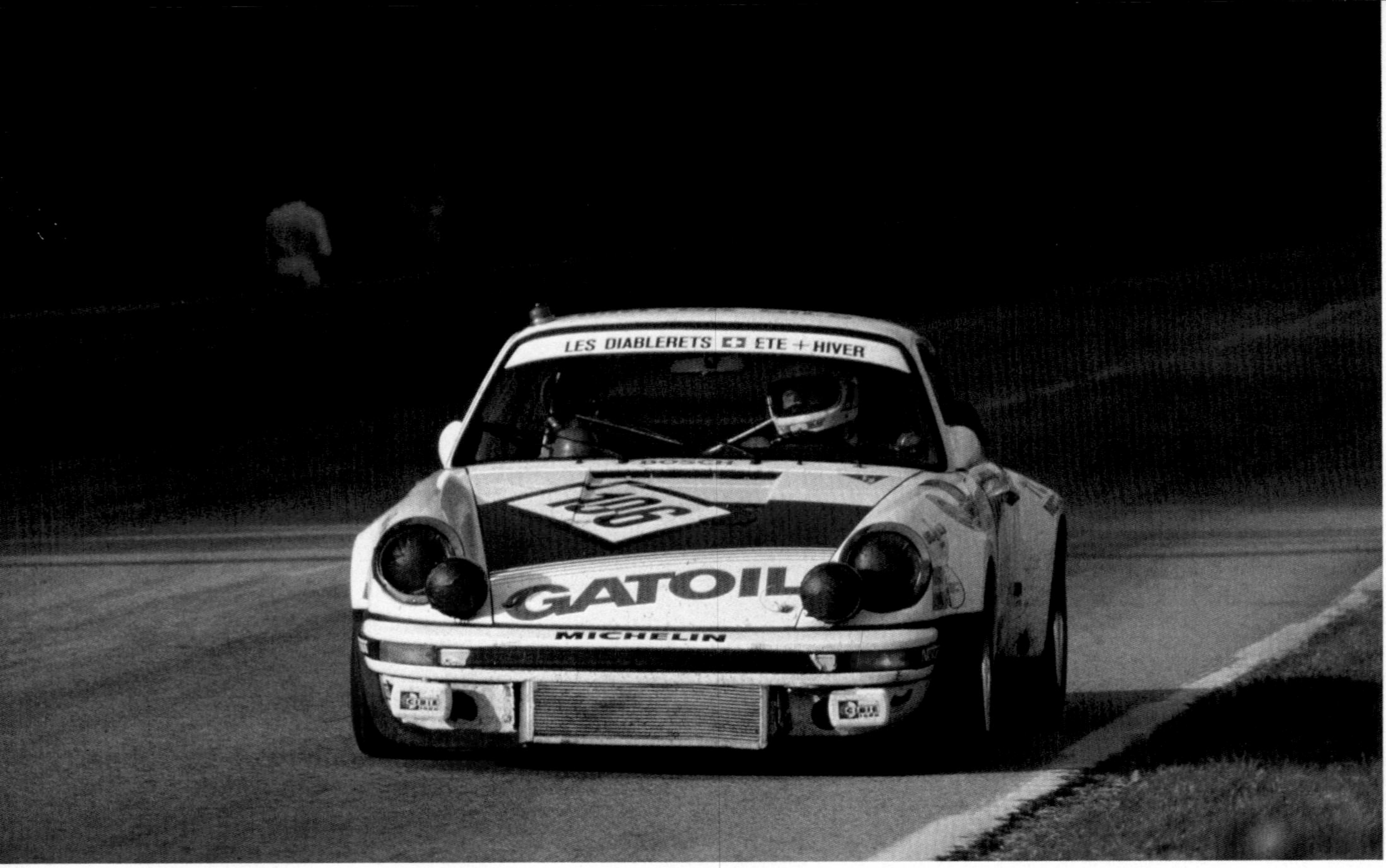
LES DIABLERETS
ETE + HIVER
GATOIL
MICHELIN

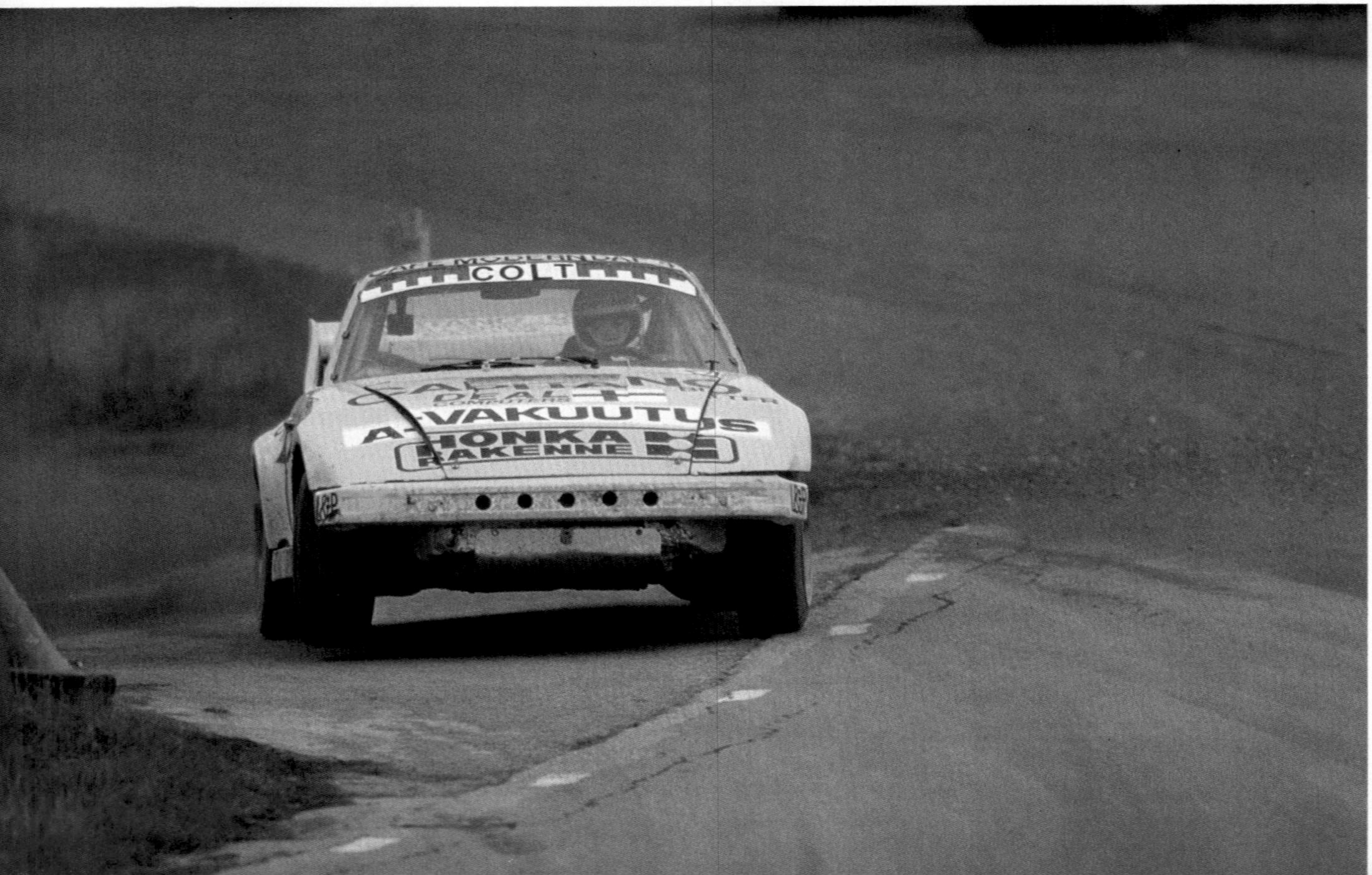
COLT
A-VAKUUTUS
HONKA
RAKENNE

**Plate Thirty-Three** *above left* The Group B Turbo provided superbly economical international racing for drivers like Claude Haldi, pictured at Le Mans in 1983.

**Plate Thirty-Four** *below left* Finland's Matti Alamaki piles on the 750 bhp of his 935-powered rallycross Porsche at Lydden in 1984.

**Plate Thirty-Five** *below* Back in action . . . the historic ex-Elford and Faure 911S driven in the 1985 Coronation Rally at Eppynt by Pete Russell and Steve Foster.

**Plate Thirty-Six** The Carrera RS is still winning in the 1980s . . . with Tony Dron at the wheel in the Porsche Challenge.

**Plate Thirty-Seven** Typically close-packed action in the Porsche Challenge for production cars.

**Plate Thirty-Eight** Modified Porsches have a championship of their own in Britain

FRAISES
FERME
Rothmans
Rothmans
PORSCHE
A451 BJB
Shell Oils
Rothmans 1

**Plate Forty** Exclusive Porsche . . . the Turbo SE.

**Plate Thirty-Nine** *left* Rally supercar . . . the 911SC/RS of Bernard Beguin in the 1985 Rally D'Antibes.

**Plate Forty-One** Wild Porsche . . . the 959 stars in the North African desert.

**Plate Forty-Two** The Porsche 961 charges on at Le Mans in 1987.

**Plate Forty-Three** Economy Porsche . . . Dage Sport's Turbo SE lookalike.

**Plate Forty-Four** Practical and economical powerplant . . . the 1987 Carrera.

**Plate Forty-Five** The 1987 Carrera Sport interior.

A 911

**Plate Forty-Seven** Porsche's greatest road car? The 959

**Plate Forty-Six** *previous page* Benign Porsche . . . the 1987 Carrera Sport.

# The Personalities Behind the Porsche 911

When it comes to considering the personalities behind the Porsche 911, you could call it a family car. In essence, its original conception was that of Professor Ferdinand Porsche II, better known as Ferry Porsche, who is still the firm's chairman. His ideas were based on those of his father, the legendary Professor Ferdinand Porsche, who was responsible for so many cars, particularly the Volkswagen Beetle. He died in 1952 soon after the first car to bear his name, the Porsche Type 356, was established in production. This was the sports car, based on the Volkswagen saloon, that was to endear itself to millions, especially in America, and was to continue in production until 1965.

Throughout this period, the Porsche family firm pursued a policy of steady improvement by development, rather than by dramatic change in the original conception. It can be said that a classic car is one that stays in production without substantial alteration for more than ten years, although this is not the only qualification, of course. But not many designs last that long in the motoring world and cars are a long while in the making before they ever hit the road. So, by 1957, it was apparent that Porsche would have to start designing something to replace the Type 356 which had started as a set of drawings ten years earlier. The year 1957 coincided with the arrival in the family firm of Ferry Porsche's eldest son, Ferdinand Porsche III, known as Butzi. Butzi was a brilliant stylist who cut his teeth on the formula two racing car that had been developed alongside the Type 356. His first years with Porsche were spent working in a variety of departments to see how they were run: a time-honoured practice in family firms, and the first real project of his own was the limited-production Type 904 GT racing car of 1963. The beautiful lines of this mid-engined coupé influenced fellow stylists for years to come. Butzi, who worked with a small staff of his own, turned his attention next to the Type 695 project, which was the forerunner of the 911.

Meanwhile, another member of the Porsche clan, Ferdinand Piëch, had started work in 1963 on the development of the flat six engine and five-speed transmission that was used in the Type 904 and ultimately found its way into the 911. Ferdinand Piëch was the son of Louise Piëch, Ferry's sister. When the first Professor Porsche died in 1952, the Porsche company had become known as Dr Ing. h.c.F. Porsche A.G., which in Germany implies a limited partnership. The shareholdings were divided equally between Ferry and

Porsche men at the helm—from the left: Dr Ernst Fuhrmann with board member Helmut Bott research and development manager Wolfgang Eyb and body designer Wolfgang Mobius.

Louise and later were split into ten equal parts for themselves and each of their four children. Thus the three people chiefly responsible for the 911, Ferry and Butzi Porsche and Ferdinand Piëch were equal shareholders, with Ferry the more senior. They worked well together despite tensions between the Porsche and Piëch sides of the family that were united chiefly by a desire to see their firm succeed. These tensions were inevitable because of the Porsche way of doing things. Each member of a design team was responsible for a particular area of a car under development. Should one fail to allow for the needs of the others, everybody was called together so that the whole problem could be thrashed out from beginning to end. In a thoroughly German manner, every conceivable alternative was examined before a final compromise was reached. Ferry Porsche usually had the last say, but it was design by committee rather than by any one person, which was bound to cause friction with a large number of people being involved. One of the principal problems was that members of the design teams engaged on a particular project, such as the prototypes that became the 911, often felt that nepotism was involved if a decision went in favour of one side of the Porsche clan or the other. It would be years before Ferry Porsche could sort out that problem.

It was fortunate for the Porsche firm that Ferry had a good idea of what he wanted and what he considered best for the family's fortunes as a whole. He believed firmly in his father's old-established support of the German cartel policy which developed into a system where Volkswagen built the cheap, small cars, Ford and Opel made the medium-sized vehicles, Mercedes the big, expensive ones and Porsche the sports cars. When confronted with committee suggestions that the Type 356's replacement might be a four-seater, Ferry Porsche has been oft-quoted as saying: 'Shoemaker, stick to your last.' The new Porsche might have to be a two-plus-two seater to broaden its marketing appeal and please the sales people at Porsche, but it would be a sports car first and foremost, not a four-seater saloon. Ferry Porsche would compromise only so far. Butzi and Ferdinand Piëch were made in the same mould. Butzi was convinced—with justification—that his styling was the best, and Ferdinand Piëch was a fanatic for technical perfection. Much credit must go to him for the way in which the original engine has been able to be stretched to 3.3 litres, although Ferry Porsche was later to say that if he had realised this was possible he would have said that it was too heavy for a start! Perhaps if Ferry Porsche had realised this, the early 911s would have handled more easily, but as it was, Ferdinand Piëch got his way and ultimately the car was developed to cope with the extra power and turbocharging. Commendably, Ferry Porsche then said he was glad it had worked out that way.

Once Butzi Porsche had completed the styling exercises, the body project was handed over to Erwin Komenda, whose association with the

Porsche company dated to its earliest days. He had been responsible for the definitive Type 356 shape and body, and his opinions carried a lot of weight. One of them was that people generally were getting bigger and that cars should be enlarged to cater for them. He didn't like the restricted back seats of a two-plus-two and registered his objections in the strongest manner. When it became apparent that he felt so deeply that the body project should be a four-seater, Ferry Porsche shuffled the job of turning Butzi's styling into solid metal to engineers at the Reutter factory, who were to build the body. Komenda realised which way the wind was blowing and promptly buckled down to doing the job himself. This example illustrates how the Porsche company allowed their most respected employees to develop their own lines of thought before Ferry Porsche made up his mind which way it should work out in the end; it also showed that even the oldest-established engineers and designers had to recognise who was in charge and how frustrations could build up with younger men than Komenda. Later Ferry Porsche was to say that more than any other car, the 911 was 'his' because by the time he was responsible for its conception he could afford to design anything he wanted.

Engine development had started under technical director Klaus von Rücker, who left Porsche early in 1962 in the wake of an expensive and not very satisfactory season in Formula One racing. His job was taken over by Hans Tomala, who had worked his way up from Porsche's tractor engineering department. Tomala took over responsibility for everything to do with engineering in the production, experimental and design departments during the gestation period of the 911. He was also responsible for the design of the 904, styled by Butzi Porsche.

Tomala backed development of the new six-cylinder engine from the Grand Prix eight-cylinder he had inherited against the old four-cylinder racing engine that was used at first in the 904. The four-cylinder was at the limit of its development from a unit which had originally been designed by Dr Ernst Fuhrmann, who was later to figure most prominently in the 911 story. One of Tomala's key decisions, on which he was supported by Ferry Porsche, was to use chain drives for the camshafts of the new engine. This entailed the use of the hydraulic tensioners the early examples of which gave trouble in extended service. Ironically, he opted for chain, rather than bevel drive, which he considered to be too noisy, or new rubber belts pioneered by the tiny German firm of Glas, in keeping with his 'company man' image. He considered that the rubber belt drives, which were ideal in theory for the new engine, had not been sufficiently well tried to meet Porsche standards of reliability. Ferdinand Piëch was his development engineer in charge of the new engine from 1963. Like Piëch, Tomala was a perfectionist. When confronted with the problem of the erratic handling of early 911 production cars, he was emphatic that no adjustment facilities were needed at the top end

*Facing page:* Porsche 911 personalities in clockwise order: Rico Steinemann, Hans Tomala, Huschke von Hanstein, Butzi Porsche, Ferdinand Piëch and Peter Falk.

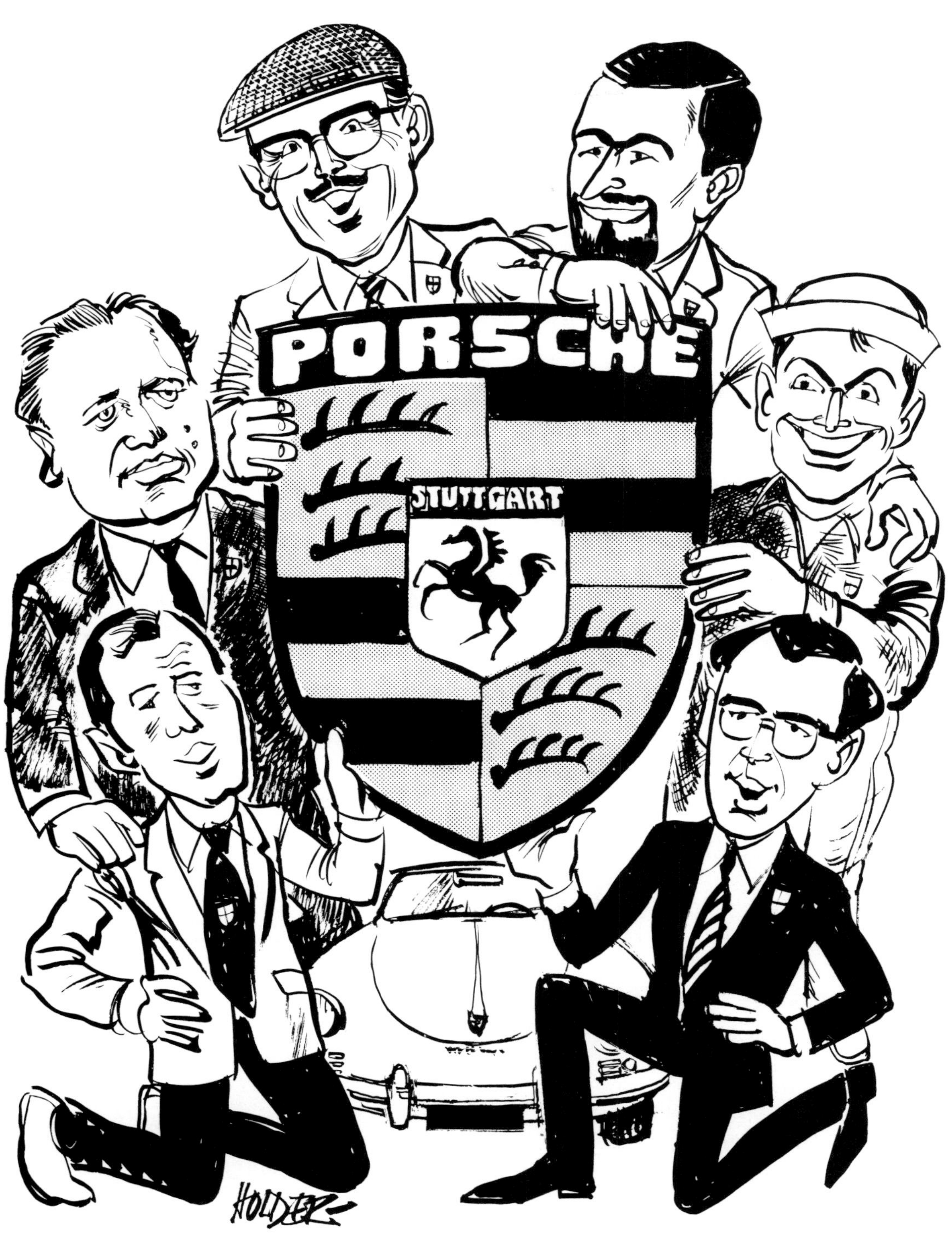
PORSCHE
STUTTGART
HOLDER

The bold Carrera lettering was a product of the Porsche design department.

of the front suspension's MacPherson struts. He pointed out that the bodyshells were made to very fine tolerances and if the mounting holes were drilled in exactly the right places everything would be all right. This was feasible on prototypes built by highly-skilled engineers but did not work out in practice on the production line. Tomala soon lost this battle and Porsche had to resort to bolting iron lumps into the ends of the front bumpers to make the 911 more stable in a straight line and less susceptible to the pressures of side winds. Later, adjustment facilities were built in for the front struts, but the rather agricultural solution of bolting lumps of iron into the front bumpers was hardly in the Porsche idiom and Tomala left in 1966. He was succeeded as chief of development by Ferdinand Piëch, who had a much more scientific approach to such problems.

Under Piëch, technical development almost ran riot. The 911's wheelbase was lengthened, its engine enlarged, the induction changed, and grams were pared off here and there. A magnesium crankcase—the largest casting ever made in this material at the time—replaced aluminium, extra centimetres were squeezed into the rear seat pan, and oil tanks, coolers and batteries were swopped back and forth. At the same time as he was doing this, he was generating extraordinary racing cars such as Types 908 and 917. Butzi Porsche concentrated on simpler issues, such as the Targa top with its brightwork hoop to emphasise, rather than try to hide, a strong shape. It is not what Butzi wanted, however. He thought an open version of the 911 should have a special rear body shape rather than just an adaptation of the existing coupé.

He was overruled by other members of the committees involved, who thought that Porsche could not sell enough open cars to justify the expense involved with a special body. The popularity of the open Porsche since proved Butzi to be right, and the Targa top remains as an option. Butzi's department was also responsible for some extraordinary and often psychedelic, colour schemes on competition Porsches; these developed into the Carrera lettering and so on for 911s.

Throughout his life, Ferry Porsche favoured competition as a way of improving a car, designing a new one, and generating the publicity to sell existing machines.

He frequently allowed almost the entire publicity budget to be ploughed into competition activities. Thus the men behind the Porsche 911's competition history are important, too.

The incredible figure of Fritz Sittig Huschke Baron von Hanstein played a dominant role during the early period of the Porsche 911's competition history. Huschke von Hanstein's association with Porsche dated to the days when the first Professor Porsche designed the pre-war Auto Union Grand Prix cars. Von Hanstein joined the firm as a salesman in 1952, soon becoming a works driver, press officer and competitions director. He did these three jobs with great flair for sixteen years, being responsible for the 911's early success in rallying. Although always charming and very persuasive, von Hanstein was a past master at political intrigue and represented Porsche's interests well in international racing circles. He effectively relinquished control of racing activities to Ferdinand Piëch in 1966, but continued to serve Porsche as a talent spotter—luring Vic Elford away from Fords in 1967—and as an organiser for Porsche's highly-successful rally programme in 1968. He was deeply involved in the inner circles of the company, giving wise counsel on the design of engines, transmissions and the cars themselves. Karl Ludvigsen described him in *Porsche—Excellence was Expected (Automobile Quarterly)* as: 'One of the great personalities of Porsche history, this Baron whose stiff right arm was never at ease unless it was shaking hands, embracing a beautiful woman, wielding a massive cine camera, or punching through fast upshifts in a record-breaking Porsche car.' He loved breaking records, and even at the age of sixty-two, he set new standards for international ten-kilometre and ten-mile classes at 153.1 mph and 161.6 mph with a Carrera RS in 1974. Von Hanstein was first and foremost a close ally of Ferry Porsche and was eventually replaced in 1969 as press officer and official racing director by a Piëch man, Rico Steinemann, as the young Ferdinand continued his sweeping wind of change throughout the company. Steinemann, a twenty-nine-year-old Swiss journalist, was as charming as von Hanstein—who went into public relations on the product side with Porsche—and very ambitious.

Like Piëch, he was more interested in the cars than the drivers, whereas von Hanstein always thought of the drivers first and viewed the cars as merely a means to an end to win competitions for Porsche. Steinemann, who had driven a works 911R in 1967, achieved a tremendous amount with Porsche in the three years he was in charge of competition activities. He was chiefly concerned with the glamorous 917 racing project but, when necessary, devoted just as much time to the 911's interests. Steinemann ran his works team like a machine, which was to prove especially valuable in the Marathons de là Route where his dictates were of equal importance to the drivers' flair in making sure the 911s lasted the course to win. He also fought hard, but in vain, to get the 911S accepted as a touring car in international racing in 1970 despite von Hanstein's warning three years earlier that its victories in such events were tarnished by resentment that such a machine could be qualified as a saloon car. Steinemann left Porsche at the end of the 1971 season when his contract expired because he wanted to get into Grand Prix racing, but returned in 1975 to edit the house magazine *Christophorus* for four years.

During the early years of the 911, the political scene at Porsche was becoming very tense. Production had run at a steady 14,000-plus for the A series and B series cars, before falling to just under 12,000 with the D series as inflation started to grip the world. Turnover fell by 25 per cent at the same time and the Porsche company faced its first cash crisis for twenty years in 1971. It came at a time when the young Porsches and Piëchs were vying for better positions within the firm, which was frustrating other employees who saw no way to the top on sheer ability when there were so many members of the family to accommodate. But no matter how much they tried to outmanoeuvre each other, the Porsches and Piëchs both wanted what was best for the company as a whole and injected a substantial amount of capital into the firm from joint resources to overcome the cash crisis. The only point on which they really clashed was on who should run the firm, so they tried doing it through a management committee set up in 1971. Ferdinand Porsche was chairman, Ferdinand Piëch and Butzi Porsche were members, Dr Michael Piëch was appointed to look after administration, with a fifth member, Heinz Branitzki, as a neutral. Branitzki, a marketing man, was in charge of finances. This formula failed to work satisfactorily, however, so Ferry Porsche decided to try something new. In the same manner as when there were problems with design, he called the Porsches and Piëchs together and suggested that they all step down and leave the way clear for executives appointed purely on ability rather than family ties. A Porsche or a Piëch could still occupy a top job, providing all the other Porsches and Piëchs agreed. After a period of consideration, all members of the clan agreed that this was the best solution for the company and Ernst Fuhrmann was brought back to take over purchasing and production, with Ferdinand Piëch's deputy, Helmuth Bott, in charge of development. A holding company was set up to run Porsche enterprises, which included all manner of engineering and design work apart from building cars, with Ferry Porsche and Louise Piëch as joint heads. Fuhrmann became chairman of a management committee to run car building, which included the 911, with Branitski in charge of commercial activities. Butzi Porsche left to set up his own design firm, with Ferdinand Piëch rising to the top at the Audi branch of Volkswagen. Ferry Porsche remained as chairman of the Board of Directors, lending assistance to the car side in a consultative capacity. To complete these far-reaching changes, on the car-making side Porsche KG was turned into Porsche AG (for Aktiengesellschaft), a stock company, in 1972. Ferry Porsche's final word on the subject, in his biography, *We At Porsche* (Haynes) was: 'Disagreements at management level benefit no one. They are like sand in a well-oiled machine.' And later he explained that his overall philosophy was—so long as he had ultimate control—he would always try to give executives a lot of latitude, otherwise their creativity might be suppressed.

Peter Schutz . . . the car enthusiast whose gamble nearly paid off.

One of Fuhrmann's first important decisions had a profound influence on the 911's destiny. With Ferry Porsche's support, he decided to back the 911 in competition rather than the very expensive turbocharged 917 project, which he considered had departed too far from any kind of car that could be driven on the road and hence identified with it. Although the cost of developing and racing the 917 had been justified both in terms of the publicity it brought Porsche and design experience, Fuhrmann was of the opinion that an all-out racing version of the 911 would bring the same rewards for a fraction of the outlay. Hence the Carrera RS and RSR, which not only boosted the firm's image but sold very well, too.

With hindsight, it is possible to see the inspired leadership Fuhrmann gave to Porsche. He was a little-known quantity when he took over in 1972, having remained in the background as the man who designed the famous four-cam engine soon after joining the firm at its start. In the late 1950s, he left to become technical director of the Goetze piston ring firm before being called back, doubtless at Ferry Porsche's behest as they had always worked well together. Although Fuhrmann had designed a famous engine, he viewed it as his first and last, preferring not to interfere with his engineers' work, provided he was satisfied that they were following the right lines. Only when they hit snags, such as the cooling of the turbocharged engine, would he step in—and with inspiration suggested the intercooler that solved the problem. He defended competition vigorously, explaining that it gave young designers more experience in any one year than in five or six in the normal way, and this was in addition to its benefits from publicity. The modern-day 911s well reflect Fuhrmann's personality, a mixture of emotional, practical, adventurous and conservative ideals. He loved speed, saying: 'He who chops off the speed to cure the disease of accidents is like a doctor who amputates a leg to cure a blister on the foot. Before that, all other means of healing, above all the most specific ones, should be brought to bear.' He was a practical man, having promoted savage economies during the depressed year of 1975 which saw Porsche make a small profit when everybody else thought that they would lose a fortune, selling only 8177 H series cars. This was largely because of their high price and performance, which some people considered almost indecent in a year of severe economic cutbacks. He was also an adventurous man, introducing the Turbo in the same year; and a superstitious man, keeping a candle burning at home when a Porsche was in an important race. But, above all, he was a conservative man, keeping the 911 in production because it was selling well, when he was planning to replace it with the new 924 and 928 ranges in 1975.

Fuhrmann was the man who led the revolution in Porsches, changing them from stark, medium-priced sports cars to expensive exotics when that was the most profitable thing to do. He was responsible for the high level of luxurious fittings in the Turbo because of its inevitably high price.

On the competition side, Manfred Jantke, a journalist who took over Stienemann's job in 1973 after Klaus Reichard had held the fort in 1972, organised the Carrera's dominance in GT racing and inspired the highly-successful 935 programme, which was carried on so successfully by the Kremer brothers. Tony Lapine is the man responsible for the smooth way in which Porsches got round the American bumper regulations that ruined the appearance of so many sports cars. Lapine, a Latvian who used to work as a stylist for General Motors, is typical of Porsche men. When they were celebrating the centenary of the first Professor Ferdinand Porsche's birth in 1975, he drove his Porsche to Maffersdorf, formerly in Austria, now in Czechoslovakia, where the old professor was born to bring back to Stuttgart a container full of its soil.

Fuhrmann was disappointed, however, that the 928 could never match 911 sales, often running at less than half the older car's production rate. The 924, for which he was also responsible, sold well but was not very profitable because it was produced by Audi, rather than Porsche. It is understandable that he tried to promote his own cars, but found that Ferry Porsche would allow only so much latitude with what had become the firm's most vital product. Inevitably their relationship became strained as Fuhrmann resisted moves to develop the 911, preferring to concentrate resources on the 924 and 928.

By 1978, Ferry Porsche had moved his office out of Zuffenhausen, away from Fuhrmann's side, preferring the company of the marketing men at Ludwigsburg. Late he told journalist Edouard Seidler:

> 'Fuhrmann had no contact with the market. When I was running the company, I had the advantage of being able to build what I liked, knowing that others would like it too. I was in symbiosis with a specific slot in the market. Fuhrmann was not.'

He added that everybody at Porsche expected the 928—a luxury touring car rather than a sports car—to take over from the 911, until they saw the final product. Ferry Porsche said:

> 'Originally is was supposed to be more spacious in the back, and hardly more expensive than the 911. The 928 is a good car, but it does not correspond to the market slot we were aiming at. It is always a mistake to want to do something new for reasons of pride or vanity.'

Inevitably, in his entrenched position, Fuhrmann had to go. The final blow to his relationship with Ferry Porsche came in 1979 when he planned to produce a cheaper version of the 928, which would compete directly with the 911. His long-term plan was then to run down 911 production with the introduction of the 944 in 1981, stopping it for good in 1984 when the 944 Turbo would be launched in the same price bracket with a similar performance. Ferry Porsche was horrified, not in the least because the front-engined cars were still failing to make a significant advance in total sales. Fuhrmann was duly retired and German-born American truck engineer Peter Schutz—a declared car enthusiast, rather than purely an

Porsche's new leader . . . Heinz Branitzki

engineer or accountant—became his replacement on January 1, 1981. With his biggest market in mind, Ferry Porsche said:

> 'I was looking for a manager who was a technician with a feeling for business and marketing, and who could be a leader. Porsche does not need inventors; we have lots of those. We needed a man who could motivate all the others and lead them to the highest performance level.'

Schutz, who was 50 at the time, carried out his brief to promote the 911 with enthusiasm—and Ferry Porsche moved back to Zuffenhausen. He was accompanied by his youngest son, Wolfgang, then 36; his brothers, Butzi and Hans-Peter, were, by then, completely involved in the allied business of Porsche Design, while a further brother, Gerhard, preferred farming. Ferdinand Piëch still represented his family interests on the supervisory board, but was concentrating on his career—via the spectacular four-wheel-drive Quattro—at Audi.

For a time, all looked well as Schutz revitalised the 911 range and introduced an uprated 924—the 944—with a Porsche, rather than an Audi engine. But he suffered from the financial handicap of having to develop three distinct lines—the entry-level 924, the mid-range 944 (Turbo versions of which occupied exactly the same price and performance bracket as the Carrera), the expensive 928, plus what would be a very costly exercise, the 959. The 959, in particular, represented many of the ideals which Ferry Porsche had wanted, but not necessarily been able to afford, to put into production: for years, for instance, he had encouraged the study of four-wheel-drive. Ever conscious of the American market, Schutz followed a lone course among supercar makers by insisting that any new engines—and there were three, for the 944, 928 and 959—would have to run on lead-free petrol. The investment was immense, but he looked to have won his gamble as Porsche enjoyed record profits in 1985.

The 959's development took far longer than expected, however, so much so that it was dramatically under-priced on its introduction because Porsche had pre-sold the entire production run. At the same time, the strength of the mark had sent the price of their normal products soaring and long-term development of the four-cylinder cars had taken a back seat. It needed only a major recession in the American market—and to a certain extent in Europe—to hit the sales of the four-cylinder cars especially hard. The Japanese yen also soared against the dollar, but rival Oriental products, which were initially only slightly cheaper than Porsche's four-cylinder cars, became much cheaper as these larger manufacturers managed to spread price increases over their entire range, including high-selling saloon cars.

The 911 soared in price as well, and sales fell, but not so dramatically because there was nothing else in the world quite like it. Sadly, Schutz the car enthusiast had to go, to be replaced on January 1, 1988, by accountant Heinz

Branitski, deputy chairman of the executive board since 1976. He was 58 at the time of his appointment, however, so speculation was rife that he would be replaced by somebody else in a couple of years or so when he came to the normal retirement age.

Meanwhile, Wolfgang Porsche, an economist, was ever at his father's side, occupying an adjoining office at Zuffenhausen and deputising for him at many functions. The potential situation had been best summed up some months earlier in *Motor* by former Porsche publicity man Michael Cotton:

> 'Until 1981, Porsche's emphasis was always engineering orientated. The consultancy flourished at Weissach, and the marketing department had the job of selling the products. That changed with Peter Schutz's appointment, not just because he said so, but because Professor Porsche [Ferry Porsche had been awarded the title his father held by the University of Stuttgart in 1984] could see that the future of his company was inextricably tied to economics and marketing. Today Porsche have engineers aplenty—some of them nearing genius level—and it doesn't need another to command the ship. The third generation of management, it seems most likely, will be prominent in the economic field.'

# Porsche Clubs

As is only to be expected from a car which attracts such a fanatical following, Porsche clubs throughout the world are made up chiefly of 911 owners.

Porsche Club events vary from racing . . . to touring, with everyone welcome, even a Ferrari owner who preferred the company on a gastronomic trip to France.

There is also an extraordinary number of Porsche clubs because the cars are so durable and find themselves in all corners of the world. In addition, many Porsche owners tend to be individualists, so there are clubs and branches in a fantastic number of areas, arranging meetings, runs, barbecues, trips abroad, publishing magazines and news letters, and providing technical assistance among all the usual activities of motor clubs. In keeping with cars that have such a strong sporting tradition, Porsche owners are also prone to travel *en masse* to motor races, especially endurance events in which the marque has long starred, historic events, and rounds of the rapidly-spreading series for production Porsches. Because the cars need so little adaptation for competition, many of the national clubs also have special facilities for owners who want to compete. The addresses of the main national clubs are listed below, but because secretaries are often voluntary, such information is likely to change frequently within the lifespan of a book. Happily, the parent Porsche factory—along with their dealers—are great supporters of the clubs, so information can often be obtained from local importers or the Porsche Clubs Co-ordinator, at Dr Ing hc F Porsche AG, Porschestrasse 15-19, D-7140, Ludwigsburg, West Germany.

**Porsche Club of America,**
Sec: Sandi Misura,
1753 Las Gallina,
San Rafael,
California 94903, USA

**Porsche Club Argentina,**
Sec: David Santana,
Avenida Santa Fe 950
1640 Acussuso,
Buenos Aires,
Argentina

**Porsche Club of NSW,**
Sec: John Clark,
PO Box 183
Lindfield NSW 2070
Australia

**Porsche Club of Western Australia,**
Sec: Rob Jones,
PO Box 447,
South Perth,
Western Australia 6151

**Austria: Porsche Club Wien,**
Sec: Ing Udo Poeschmann,
Mariahilfer Str 19-21,
A-1060 Vienna

**Porsche Club Belgique,**
50 rue du Mail,
B-1050,
Brussels, Belgium

**Porsche Club of Brazil,**
Sec: Claudio Tozzi,
Rua Nigeria 121,
BR-04538 Sao Paulo, Brazil

**Porsche Club Great Britain,**
Executive director: Roy Gillham,
Ayton House,
West End,
Northleach,
Gloucestershire GL54 3HG,
Great Britain

**Porsche Club Denmark,**
Sec: Flemming L. Nielsem,
Ved Jaegerdiget 9A,
DK-2670 Greye Strand,
Denmark

**Porsche Club Deutschland,**
Sec: Manfred Pfeiffer,
Podbielskiallee 25-27,
D-1000 Berlin 33,
West Germany

**Porsche Club Suomi-Finland,**
Sec: Klaus Kingelin,
Sipilan Kartano,
SF-12380 Lappakoski,
Finland

**Porsche Club de France,**
Sec: Marc Tripels,
c/o Sonauto SA,
1 Avenue du Fief,
BP 479,
F-95005 Cergy Pontoise Cedex,
France

**Porsche Club Holland,**
Sec: P. Polle,
Wim Sonneveldlaan 227,
NL-3584 ZS Utrecht,
Netherlands

**Porsche Club Hong Kong,**
Sec: Wong Chuk Hang,
No 1 Yip Fat Street,
PO Box 24539,
Aberdeen Post Office,
Aberdeen,
Hong Kong

**Porsche Club Italia,**
Sec: Gabriella Bigontina,
Via Carlo Osma 2,
I-201151 Milano,
Italy

**Porsche Club of Japan,**
Sec: H Sumitani,
c/o Mitsuwa Motor co Ltd,
No 18-6 Roppongi 3-Chome,
Miniato-Ku,
Tokyo 106,
Japan

**Porsche Club Luxembourg,**
Sec: J Frast,
c/o Novotel,
E42-route d'Echternach,
L-1453 Luxembourg-Dommeldang

**Nederlandse Porsche Club,**
Van Alkemadelaan 878,
Den Haag,
Netherlands

**Porsche Club of New Zealand,**
Sec: J Robertson,
204 Beach Road,
Campbell's Bay,
Auckland,
New Zealand

**Porsche Club Norway,**
Sec: Johannes Bidesbol,
Postboks 32,
Lysejordet,
N-Oslo 7,
Norway

**Porsche Club of South Africa,**
Sec: Angela Hausler,
PO Box 9834,
Johannesburg 2000,
South Africa

**Porsche Club Spain,**
Sec: Immaculada Sanz,
Paseo de la Castellana 240,
Madrid 16,
Spain

**Porsche Club Sweden,**
Sec: Stina Liljeberg,
Postbox 340 25,
S-10026 Stockholm,
Sweden

**Porsche Club Romand,**
Sec: Philippe Collet,
Chateau 13,
CH-18-6 St Legier,
Switzerland

**Porsche Club Zurich,**
Sec: Roland Studer,
c/o Oscar Senn-Bucher,
Boldistrasse 76,
CH-5414 Rieden-Bussbaumen,
Switzerland

# Your Porsche 911 Log Book

Mechanical specifications, dimensions, and production figures:

## Porsche 911 0 series (early models)

16,634 built between September 1964 and August 1966, chassis numbers from 300001 to 300235 (1964/5); 300236 to 305100 (1965/6).

### Engine

Six-cylinder, CUBIC CAPACITY 1991 cc; BORE AND STROKE 80 mm x 66 mm; MAX POWER 130 bhp at 6100 rpm; MAX TORQUE 128 lb/ft at 4,200 rpm; COMPRESSION RATIO 9:1; CARBURETTORS (September 1964—February 1966) 2 Solex triple-choke, (February 1966—September 1966) 2 Weber triple-choke.

### Chassis

WEIGHT (dry) 2183 lb; WHEELBASE 7 ft 3.05 ins; FRONT TRACK 4 ft 5.3 ins; REAR TRACK 4 ft 4 ins; LENGTH 13 ft 7.9 ins; WIDTH 5 ft 3.4 ins: HEIGHT 4 ft 4 ins: TURNING CIRCLE 32.8 ft; FRONT SUSPENSION independent MacPherson telescopic damper struts, lower wishbones, longitudinal torsion bars; REAR SUSPENSION independent, trailing radius arms, transverse torsion bars, telescopic dampers; BRAKES disc all round, front diameter 9.25 ins, rear 9.57 ins; GEARBOX five-speed (ratios 3.09, 1.89, 1.32, 1, 0.76, final drive 4.43, other ratios available); STEERING rack and pinion; WHEELS 15 ins x 4.5 ins all round.

Three 911 cars were built to 'Monte' specification, chassis numbers 303075–77, using 1,991 cc engines producing 160 bhp at 6,600 rpm with 134 lb/ft of torque at 5,200 rpm, at an overall weight of 2,271 lb.

## Porsche 911 0 series (late models)

12,148 built between September 1966 and August 1967, chassis numbers 305101 to 308552 (fixed-head coupé), 500001 to 500718 (Targa), 305101S to 308523S (911S coupé), 500001S to 500718S (911S Targa).

### Engine

Six-cylinder, CUBIC CAPACITY 1991 cc; BORE AND STROKE 80 mm x 66 mm; MAX POWER (911 model) 130 bhp at 6,100 rpm, (911S model) 160 bhp at 6,600 rpm; MAX TORQUE (911) 128 lb/ft at 4,200 rpm, (911S)

133 lb/ft at 5,200 rpm; COMPRESSION RATIO (911) 9:1, (911S) 9.8:1; CARBURETTORS 2 Weber triple-choke.

### Chassis

WEIGHT (dry) 2183 lb; WHEELBASE 7 ft 3.05 ins; FRONT TRACK 4 ft 5.3 ins; REAR TRACK 4 ft 4 ins; LENGTH 13 ft 7.9 ins; WIDTH 5 ft 3.4 ins; HEIGHT 4 ft 4 ins; TURNING CIRCLE 32.8 ft; FRONT SUSPENSION independent MacPherson telescopic damper struts, lower wishbones longitudinal torsion bars; REAR SUSPENSION independent, trailing radius arms, transverse torsion bars, telescopic dampers; BRAKES disc all round, front diameter 9.25 ins, rear 9.57 ins (ventilated on 911S); GEARBOX five-speed (ratios 3.09, 1.89, 1.32, 1.04, 0.79 final drive 4.43, other ratios available), STEERING rack and pinion; WHEELS (911) 15 ins x 4.5 ins all round, (911S) 15 ins x 5 ins all round.

Three 911 cars were built to 'Rally' specification, chassis numbers 306655S to 57S, using 1,991 cc engines producing 170 bhp at 7,300 rpm with 134 lb/ft of torque at 5,200 rpm, at an overall weight of 2,271 lb. Four 911R racing cars were also built, using chassis numbers 305876, 30767 to 71, and 118990001R, using 1,991 cc engines producing 210 bhp at 8,000 rpm with 152 lb/ft of torque at 6,000 rpm, at an overall weight of 1,764 lb.

## Porsche 911 A series

14,159 built between September 1967 and August 1968, chassis numbers 11830001 to 11830473 (911 fixed-head, US specification, body made by Porsche), 11835001 to 11835742 (911 fixed-head, body made by Karmann), 11880001 to 11880268 (911 Targa, Porsche body), 11810001 to 11810720 (911L fixed-head, Porsche body), 11805001 to 11805449 (911L fixed-head US specification, Porsche body), 11860001 to 11860307 (911L Targa, Porsche body), 11855001 to 11855134 (911L Targa US specification, Porsche body), 11820001 to 11820928 (911T fixed head, Porsche body), 11825001 to 11825683 (911T fixed-head, Karmann body), 11870001 to 11870521 (911T Targa, Porsche body), 11800001 to 11801267 (911S fixed-head, Porsche body), 11850001 to 11850442 (911S Targa, Porsche body).

### Engine

Six-cylinder, CUBIC CAPACITY 1991 cc; BORE AND STROKE 80 mm x 66 mm; MAX POWER (911) 130 bhp at 6100 rpm, (911L) 130 bhp at 6,100 rpm, (911T) 110 bhp at 5,800 rpm, (911S) 160 bhp at 6600 rpm; MAX TORQUE (911) 130 lb/ft at 4,200 rpm (911L) 130 lb/ft at 6,100 rpm, (911T) 115 lb/ft at 4,200 rpm, (911S) 133 lb/ft at 5,200 rpm; COMPRESSION RATIO (911) 9:1; (911L) 9:1, (911T) 8.6:1, (911S) 9.8:1; CARBURETTORS 2 Weber triple-choke.

### Chassis

WEIGHT (dry) 2381 lb (911 Targa), 2271 lb (911S fixed-head); WHEELBASE 7 ft 3.05 ins; FRONT TRACK 4 ft 5.3 ins; REAR TRACK 4 ft 4 ins; LENGTH 13 ft 7.9 ins; WIDTH 5 ft 3.4 ins: HEIGHT 4 ft 4 ins; TURNING CIRCLE 32.8 ft; FRONT SUSPENSION independent MacPherson telescopic damper struts, lower wishbones, longitudinal torsion bars; REAR SUSPENSION independent, trailing radius arms, transverse torsion bars, telescopic dampers; BRAKES disc all round, front diameter 9.25 ins, rear 9.57 ins; (ventilated on 911S); GEARBOX (911 and 911T) four-speed (ratios 3.09, 1.63, 1.04, 0.79, (911L and 911S), five-speed (ratios 3.09, 1.89, 1.32, 1.04, 0.79, final drive 4.43, other ratios available; optional Sportomatic transmission (ratios) 2.4, 1.63, 1.22, 0.93; STEERING rack and pinion; WHEELS 15 ins x 5.5 ins all round.

## Porsche 911 B series

14,822 built between September 1968 and August 1969, chassis numbers 119000001 to 119000343 (911T fixed-head, Porsche body), 119120001 to 119123561 (911T fixed-head, Karmann body), 119100001 to 119111282 (911T Targa, Porsche body), 119200001 to 119200954 (911E fixed-head, Porsche body), 119220001 to 119221014 (911E fixed-head, Karmann body), 119210001 to 119210858 (911E Targa, Porsche Body), 119300001 to 119301492 (911S fixed-head, Porshe body), 119310001 to 119310614 (911S Targa, Porsche body).

### Engine

Six-cylinder, CUBIC CAPACITY 1991 cc; BORE AND STROKE 80 mm x 66 mm; MAX POWER (911T) 110 bhp at 5,800 rpm, (911E) 140 bhp at 6,500 rpm (911S) 170 bhp at 6,500 rpm; MAX TORQUE (911T) 115 lb/ft at 4,200 rpm, (911E) 130 lb/ft at 4,500 rpm (911S) 130 lb/ft at 5,500 rpm; COMPRESSION RATIO (911T) 8.6:1, (911E) 9.1:1 (911S) 9.9:1; FUEL INJECTION (911E and 911S) Bosch mechanical; CARBURETTORS (911T) 2 Weber triple-choke.

### Chassis

WEIGHT (dry) 2249 lb (911E Targa), 2194 lb (911S fixed head); WHEELBASE 7 ft 5 ins; FRONT TRACK 4 ft 6.4 ins; REAR TRACK 4 ft 5.3 ins; LENGTH 13 ft 7.9 ins; WIDTH 5 ft 3.4 ins; HEIGHT 4 ft 4 ins; TURNING CIRCLE 35.1 ft; FRONT SUSPENSION (911T and 911S) independent MacPherson telescopic damper struts, lower wishbones, longitudinal torsion bars, (911E) independent MacPherson telescopic self-levelling damper struts, lower wishbones, longitudinal torsion bars; REAR SUSPENSION independent, trailing radius arms, transverse torsion bars, telescopic dampers; BRAKES disc all round, front diameter 8.98 ins, rear 9.61 ins (ventilated on 911S); GEARBOX (911T) four-speed (ratios) 3.09, 1.63, 1.04, 0.79, (911E and 911S) five-speed (ratios) 3.09, 1.89, 1.32, 1.04. 0.86, final drive 4.43, other ratios available; optional Sportomatic transmission (ratios) 2.4, 1.63, 1.22, 0.93; STEERING rack and pinion; WHEELS (911T) 15 ins x 5.5 ins all round, (911E and 911S) 15 ins x 6 ins all round, 14 ins x 5.5 ins all round optional.

## Porsche 911C series

14,388 built between September 1969 and August 1970, chassis numbers 9110100001 to 9110102418 (911T fixed-head, Porsche body), 9110120001 to 9110124126 (911T fixed-head, Karmann body), 9110110001 to 9110112545 (911T Targa, Porsche body) 9110200001 to 9110201304 (911E fixed-head, Porsche body), 9110220001 to 9110220667 (911E fixed-head, Karmann body), 9110210001 to 9110210933 (911 Targa, Porsche body) 911300001 to 9110301744 (911S fixed-head, Porsche body).

### Engine

Six-cylinder, CUBIC CAPACITY 2195 cc; BORE AND STROKE 84 mm x 66 mm; MAX POWER (911T) 125 bhp at 5,800 rpm, (911E) 155 bhp at 6,200 rpm, (911S) 180 bhp at 6,500 rpm; MAX TORQUE (911T) 131 lb/ft at 4,200 rpm, (911E) 141 lb/ft at 4,500 rpm; (911S) 147 lb/ft at 5,200 rpm; COMPRESSION RATIO (911T) 8.6:1, (911E) 9.1:1, (911S) 9.8:1; FUEL INJECTION (911E and 911S) Bosch mechanical; CARBURETTORS (911T) 2 Solex triple-choke.

### Chassis

WEIGHT (dry) 2,249 lb (911 fixed-head); WHEELBASE 7 ft 5 ins; FRONT TRACK 4 ft 6.4 ins; REAR TRACK 4 ft 5.3 ins; LENGTH 13 ft 7.9 ins; WIDTH 5 ft 3.4 ins; HEIGHT 4 ft 4 ins; TURNING CIRCLE 35.1 ft; FRONT SUSPENSION (911T and 911S) independent MacPherson telescopic damper struts, lower wishbones, longitudinal torsion bars, (911E) independent MacPherson telescopic self-levelling damper struts, lower wishbones, longitudinal torsion bars, REAR SUSPENSION independent, trailing radius arms, transverse torsion bars, telescopic dampers; BRAKES ventilated disc all round, front diameter 8.98 ins, rear 9.67 ins; GEARBOX (911T) four-speed (ratios) 3.09, 1.63, 1.04, 0.79, (911E and 911S) five-speed (ratios) 3.09, 1.89, 1.32, 1.04, 0.86 final drive 4.43, other ratios available; optional Sportomatic transmission (ratios) 2.4; 1.63, 1.22, 0.93; STEERING rack and pinion; WHEELS (911T) 15 ins x 5.5 ins all round, (911E and 911S) 15 ins x 6 ins all round, 14 ins x 5.5 ins optional.

Five 911S cars were built to 'Rally' specification, chassis numbers 9110300001 to 3, 9110300949 to 50, using 2,195-cc 911S engines, at an overall weight of 2,116 lb. Three 911S racing cars, chassis numbers 9110300001–3, were built with 2,247-cc engines using a bore and stroke of 85 mm x 66 mm, producing 240 bhp at 7,800 rpm and 166 lb/ft of torque at 6,300 rpm, at an overall weight of 1,852 lb. Later one of the rally cars, chassis number 9110300949, was rebuilt with a 2,395-cc engine using a bore and stroke of 85 mm x 70.4 mm, producing 260 bhp at 8,000 rpm and 181 lb/ft of torque at 6,500 rpm at an overall weight of 1,742 lb.

## Porsche 911 D series

11,928 built between September 1970 and August 1971, chassis numbers 9111100001 to 9111110583 (911T fixed-head, Porsche body), 9111120001 to 9111121934 (911T fixed-head, Karmann body), 9111119991 to 9111113476 (911T Targa, Porsche body), 9111200001 to 9111201088 (911E fixed-head, Porsche body), 911210001 to 9111210935 (911E Targa, Porsche body), 9111300001 to 9111301430 (911S fixed-head, Porsche body), 9111310001 to 9111310788 (911S Targa, Porsche body).

### Engine

Six-cylinder, CUBIC CAPACITY 2195 cc; BORE AND STROKE 84 mm x 66 mm; MAX POWER (911T) 125 bhp at 5,800 rpm, (911E) 155 bhp at 6,200 rpm, (911S) 180 bhp at 6,500 rpm MAX TORQUE (911T) 131 lb/ft at 4,200 rpm, (911E) 141 lb/ft at 4,500 rpm, (911S) 147 lb/ft at 5200 rpm; COMPRESSION RATIO (911T) 8.6:1, (911E) 9.1:1, (911S) 9.8:1; FUEL INJECTION (911E AND 911S) Bosch mechanical; CARBURETORS (911T) 2 Solex triple-choke.

### Chassis

WEIGHT (dry) 2249 lb (911E fixed-head); WHEELBASE 7 ft 5 ins; FRONT TRACK 4 ft 6.4 ins; REAR TRACK 4 ft 5.3 ins; LENGTH 13 ft 7.9 ins; WIDTH 5 ft 3.4 ins; HEIGHT 4 ft 4 ins; TURNING CIRCLE 35.1 ft; FRONT SUSPENSION (911T and 911S) independent MacPherson telescopic damper struts, lower wishbones, longitudinal torsion bars, (911E) independent MacPherson telescopic self-levelling damper struts, lower wishbones, longitudinal torsion bars; REAR SUSPENSION independent, trailing radius arms, transverse torsion bars, telescopic dampers, BRAKES ventilated disc all round, front diameter 8.98 ins, rear 9.61 ins; GEARBOX (911T) four-speed (ratios) 3.09, 1.63, 1.04 0.79, (911E and 911S) five-speed (ratios) 3.09, 1.89, 1.32, 1.04, 0.86 final drive 4.3, other ratios available; optional Sportomatic transmission (ratios) 2.4, 1.63, 1.22, 0.93; STEERING rack and pinion; WHEELS (911T) 15 ins x 5.5 ins all round, (911E and 911S) 15 ins x 6 ins all round, 14 ins x 5.5 ins optional.

Two 911S cars were built to 'rally' specification, chassis number

9111300637 and 9111300683 with 2,195-cc 911S engines at an overall weight of 2,161 lb.

Three 911S cars, chassis numbers 9111300561, 9111300589 and 9111300612, were built to 'Safari' specification with 2,195 cc 911S engines at an overall weight of 2,161 lb.

## Porsche 911 E series

12,883 built between September 1971 and August 1972, chassis numbers 9112500001 to 9112501963 (911T fixed-head), 9112510001 to 9112511523 (911T Targa), 9112200001 to 9112201124 (911E fixed-head), 9112210001 to 9112210861 (911E Targa), 9112300001 to 911230750 (911S fixed-head), 9112310001 to 9112310989 (911S Targa), 9112100001 to 9112102931 (911T fixed-head US specification), 9112110001 to 9112111821 (911T Targa US specification).

### Engine

Six-cylinder, CUBIC CAPACITY 2341 cc; BORE AND STROKE 84 mm x 70.4 mm; MAX POWER (911T) 130 bhp at 5,600 rmp, (911TV) 130 bhp at 5,600 rpm, (911TE) 14— bhp at 5600 rpm, (911E) 154 bhp at 6,200 rpm, (911S) 190 bhp at 6,500 rpm; MAX TORQUE (911T) 145 lb/ft at 4,000 rpm, (911TV) 145 lb/ft at 4,000 rpm, (911TE) 145 lb/ft at 4,000 rpm, (911E) 152 lb/ft at 4,500 rpm, (911S) 159 lb/ft at 5,200 rpm; COMPRESSION RATIO (911T, 911TV and 911TE) 7.5:1, (911E) 8:1, (911S) 8.4L1; FUEL INJECTION (911TE, 911E and 911S) Bosch mechanical; CARBURETTORS (911T and 911TV) 2 Solex triple-choke.

### Chassis

WEIGHT (dry) 2215 lb (911T fixed-head); WHEELBASE 7 ft 5 ins; FRONT TRACK 4 ft 6.4 ins; REAR TRACK 4 ft 5.3 ins; LENGTH 13 ft 7.9 ins; WIDTH 5 ft 3.4 ins; HEIGHT 4 ft 4 ins; TURNING CIRCLE 35.1 ft; FRONT SUSPENSION independent MacPherson telescopic damper struts, lower wishbones, longitudinal torsion bars; REAR SUSPENSION independent, trailing radius arms, transverse torsion bars, telescopic dampers; BRAKES ventilated disc all round, front diameter 8.98 ins, rear 9.61 ins; GEARBOX (911T) four-speed (ratios) 3.18, 1.78, 1.13, 0.82 (911E and 911S) five-speed (ratios) 3.18, 1.83, 1.26, 0.96, 0.76, final drive 4.43, other ratios available; optional Sportomatic transmission, four-speed (ratios) 2.4, 1.56, 1.13, 0.86; STEERING rack and pinion; WHEELS (911T) 15 ins x 5.5 ins all round, (911E and 911S) 15 ins x 6 ins all round, 14 ins x 5.5 ins optional.

Seven 911S cars were built to racing specification, chassis numbers 9112300041 to 47, using engines either of 2,466 cc (with bore and stroke of 89 mm x 6 mm) or 2,492 cc (with bore and stroke of 86.7 mm x 70.4 mm) each producing 270 bhp at 8,000 rpm and 192 lb/ft of torque at 6,300 rpm at an overall weight of 2,116 lb.

## Porsche 911 F series

15,000 built between September 1972 and August 1973, chassis numbers 9113500001 to 9113510001 (911T fixd-head), 9113510001 to 9113511541 (911T Targa), 9113200001 to 9113201366 (911E fixed-head), 9113219991 to 9113211055 (911E Targa), 9113300001 to 9113301430 (911S fixed-head), 9113310001 to 9113310925 (91S Targa), 9113600001 to 9113601036 (Carrera RS fixed-head), 91136013037 to 9113601590) (911SC fixed-head as Carrera RS), 9113100001 to 9113101252 (911T fixed-head US specification), 9113110001 to 9113119781 (911T Targa US specification).

### Engine

Six-cylinder, CUBIC CAPACITY (911T, 911E, 911S) 2341 cc, (Carrera) 2687 cc; BORE AND STROKE (911T, 911E, 911S) 84 mm x 70.4 mm, (Carrera) 90 mm x 70.4 mm; MAX POWER (911T) 130 bhp at 5,600 rpm, (911TV) 130 bhp at 5,600 rpm, (911TE early models) 140 bhp at 5,600 rpm, (911TE late models) 140 bhp at 5,700 rpm, (911E) 165 bhp at 6,2000 rpm, (911S) 190 bhp at 6,500 rpm, (Carrera RS) 210bhp at 6300 rpm; MAX TORQUE (911T) 145 lb/ft at 4,000 rpm, (911TV) 145 lb/ft at 4,000 rpm (911TE early models) 145 lb/ft at 4,000 rpm, (911TE late models) 148 lb/ft at 4,000 rpm, (911E) 152 lb/ft at 4,500 rpm, (911S) 159lb/ft at 5,2000 rpm, (Carrera RS) 188 lb/ft at 5,1000 rpm, COMPRESSION RATIO (911T, 911TV and 911TE early and late models) 7.5:1, (911E) 8:1, (911S) 8.5:1, (Carrera) 8.5:1 FUEL INJECTION (911E, 911S and 911TE early models) Bosch mechanical, (911TE late models) K-Jetronic; CARBURETTORS (911T and 911TV) 2 Solex triple-choke.

### Chassis

WEIGHT (dry) 2215 lb (911T fixed head), 2370 lb (911E fixed head), 2117 lb (Carrera); WHEELBASE 7 ft 5 ins; FRONT TRACK 4 ft 6.4 ins; REAR TRACK (911T, 911E and 911S) 4 ft 5.3 ins, (Carrera RS and 911SC) 4 ft 6.9 ins; LENGTH 13 ft 7.9 ins; WIDTH (911T, 911E and 911S) 5 ft 3.4 ins, (Carrera RS) 5 ft 5.4 ins; HEIGHT 4 ft 4 ins; TURNING CIRCLE 35.1 ft; FRONT SUSPENSION independent MacPherson telescopic damper struts, lower wishbones, longitudinal torsion bars; REAR SUSPENSION independent, trailing radius arms, transverse torsion bars, telescopic dampers; BRAKES ventilated discs all round, front diameter 8.98 ins, rear 9.61 ins; GEARBOX (911T) four-speed (ratios) 3.18, 1.78, 1.13, 0.82, (911E, 911S,

Carrera RS and 911SC) five-speed (ratios) 3.18, 1.83, 1.26, 0.96, 0.76, final drive 4.43, other ratios available; optional Sportomatic transmission on 911T, 911E, 911S, four-speed (ratios) 2.4, 1.56, 1.13, 0.86; STEERING rack and pinion; WHEELS (911T) 15 ins x 5.5 ins all round, (911E and 922S) 15 ins x 6 ins all round, 14 ins x 5.5 ins optional, (Carrera RS and 911SC) 15 ins x 6 ins front, 15 ins x 7 ins rear.

Two Carrera RS cars were built to Safari rally specification, chassis numbers 9113600285 and 9113600288, using 2,687-cc Carrera RA engines at an overall weight of 2,161 lb. Forty-nine Carrera RS cars, chassis numbers between 9113600386 and 9113601549, were built with engines of 2,808 cc using a bore and stroke of 92 mm x 70.4 mm giving 300 bhp at 8,000 rpm with 216 lb/ft of torque at 6,500 rpm at an overall weight of 1,984 lb. Eight Carrera RSR cars, chassis numbers 911360019R1, 911360020R2, 911360307R3, 911360328R4, 911360576R5, 911360588R6, 911360686R7 and 911360974R8, were built with engines of either 2,808 cc (with bore and stroke of 92 mm x 70.4 mm) giving 300 bhp at 8,000 rpm and 217 lb/ft of torque at 6,500 rpm, or 2,993 cc (with bore and stroke of 95 mm x 70.4 mm) giving either 315 bhp at 8,000 rpm and 213 lb/ft of torque at 6,500 rpm of 300 bhp at 8,000 rpm and 231 lb/ft of torque at 6,500 rpm, at an overall weight of 1,874 lb.

## Porsche 911 G series

11,649 built between September 1973 and August 1974, chassis numbers 9114100001 to 9114104014 (911 fixed-head), 9114110001 to 9114113110 (911 Targa), 9114300001 to 9114301359 (911S fixed-head), 9114310001 to 9114310898 (911S Targa), 9114600001 to 9114601036 (Carrera fixed-head), 9114610001 to 9114610433 (Carrera Targa), 9114400001 to 9114400528 (Carrera fixed-head US specification).

### Engine

Six-cylinder, CUBIC CAPACITY 2687 cc; BORE AND STROKE 90 mm x 70.4 mm; MAX POWER (911) 150 bhp at 5700 rpm, (911S) 175 bhp at 5,800 rpm, (Carrera) 210 bhp at 6,300 rpm, (Carrera US specification) 175 bhp at 5,800 rpm; MAX TORQUE (911) 174 lb/ft at 3,800 rpm, (911S) 174 lb/ft at 4,000 rpm, (Carrera) 188 lb/ft at 5,100 rpm, (Carrera US specification) 174 lb/ft at 4,000 rpm; COMPRESSION RATIO (911) 8:1, (911S) 8.5:1, (Carrera) 8.5:1, (Carrera US specification) 8.5:1; FUEL INJECTION (911 and 911S) K-Jetronic, (Carrera) Bosch mechanical.

### Chassis

WEIGHT (dry) 2380 lb (911S fixed-head); WHEELBASE 7 ft 5 ins; FRONT TRACK 4 ft 4.6 ins; REAR TRACK (911 and 911S), 4 ft 5.3 ins, (Carrera) 4 ft 6.9 ins; LENGTH 14 ft 0.9 ins; WIDTH (911 and 911S) 5 ft 3.4 ins, (Carrera) 5 ft 5.4 ins; HEIGHT 4 ft 4 ins; TURNING CIRCLE

35.1 ft; FRONT SUSPENSION independent MacPherson telescopic damper struts, lower wishbones, longitudinal torsion bars; REAR SUSPENSION independent, trailing radius arms, transverse torsion bars; telescopic dampers; BRAKES ventilated discs all round, front diameter 8.98 ins, rear 9.61 ins; GEARBOX (911 and 911S) four-speed (ratios) 3.18, 1.6, 1.04, 0.72, (Carrera) five-speed (ratios) 3.18, 1.83, 1.26, 0.93, 0.72, final drive 4.43, other ratios available; optional Sportomatic transmission (911 and 911S), four-speed (ratios) 2.4, 1.56, 1.13, 0.86; STEERING rack and pinion; WHEELS (911 and 911S) 15 ins x 6 ins all round, 14 ins x 5.5 ins optional, (Carrera) 15 ins x 6 ins front, 15 ins x 7 ins rear.

One hundred and eight Carrera RS 3.0 cars were built to GT racing specification, on chassis numbers between 9114609001 and 9114609109, with 2,993-cc engines using a bore and stroke of 95 mm x 70.4 mm, producing 230 bhp at 6,200 rpm with 202 lb/ft of torque at 5,000 rpm, at an overall weight of 2,028 lb. One Carrera RSR 3.0 car among these chassis numbers was built with a 2,993-cc engine producing 330 bhp at 8,000 rpm and 231 lb/ft of torque at 6,500 rpm, at an overall weight of 1,984 lb. One of the Carrera RSR cars, chassis number 9113600576R5 was rebuilt as a Turbo RSR car with another, chassis number 9114609016R9, with a 2,142-cc engine using a bore and stroke of 83 mm x 66 mm, producing 450 bhp at 8,000 rpm and 333 lb/ft of torque at 5,500 rpm, at an overall weight of 1,653 lb. Two Turbo RSRs, chassis numbers 9114609101R12 and 911409102R13, were built with 2,142-cc engines using a bore and stroke of 83 mm x 66 mm producing 500 bhp at 8,000 rpm and 405 lb/ft of torque at 5,500 rpm at an overall weight of 1,808 lb.

## Porsche 911 and 930 H series

8,177 built between September 1974 and August 1975, chassis numbers 911510001 to 9115101238 (911 fixed-head), 9115110001 to 9115110998 (911 Targa), 9115300001 to 9115300385 (911S fixed-head), 9115310001 to 9115310266 (911S Targa), 9115600001 to 9115600518 (Carrera fixed-head), 9115610001 to 9115610197 (Carrera Targa), 9115200001 to 9115202310 (911S fixed-head US specification), 9115210001 to 9115211517 (911S Targa US specification), 9115400001 to 9115400395 (Carrera fixed-head US specification), 9305700001 to 9305700284 (930)

### Engine

Six-cylinder, CUBIC CAPACITY (911, 911S and Carrera) 2,687 cc, (930) 2,994 cc turbocharged; BORE AND STROKE (911, 911S and Carrera) 90 mm x 70.4 mm, (930) 95 mm x 70.4 mm; MAX POWER (911) 150 bhp at 5,700 rpm, (911S) 175 bhp at 5,800 rpm, (Carrera) 210 bhp at 6,300 rpm, (911S US specification) 165 bhp at 5,800 rpm, (Carrera, US specification)

165 bhp at 5,800 rpm, (930) 260 bhp at 5,500 rpm; MAX TORQUE (911) 174 lb/ft at 3,800 rpm, (911S) 174 lb/ft at 4,000rpm, (Carrera) 188 lb/ft at 5,100 rpm, (911S US specification) 166 lb/ft at 4,000 rpm, (Carrera US specification) 166 lb/ft at 4,000 rpm, (930) 253 lb/ft at 4,000 rpm; COMPRESSION RATIO (911) 8:1, (911S) 8.5:1 (930) 6.5:1; FUEL INJECTION (911, 911S, 911S US specification, Carrera US specification and 930) K-Jetronic, (Carrera) Bosch mechanical.

### Chassis

WEIGHT (dry) 2,370 lb (911 fixed-head) 2,514 lb (930); WHEELBASE 7 ft 5 ins; FRONT TRACK (911, 911S, Carrera) 4 ft 6.4 ins; (930) 4 ft 8.3 ins; REAR TRACK (911, 911S) 4 ft 5.3 ins, (Carrera) 4 ft 6.9 ins, (930) 4 ft 11.06 ins; LENGTH 14 ft 0.9 ins; WIDTH (911 and 911S) 5 ft 3.4 ins, (Carrera) 5 ft 5.4 ins, (930) 5 ft 9.7 ins; HEIGHT 4 ft 4 ins; TURNING CIRCLE 35.1 ft; FRONT SUSPENSION independent MacPherson telescopic damper struts, lower wishbones, longitudinal torsion bars; REAR SUSPENSION independent, trailing radius arms, transverse torsion bars, telescopic dampers; BRAKES ventilated discs all round, front diameter 8.98 ins, rear 9.61 ins; GEARBOX (911 and 911S) four-speed (ratios) 3.18, 1.6, 1.04, 0.72, (Carrera) five-speed (ratios) 3.18, 1.83, 1.26, 0.93, 0.72, final drive 4.43, other ratios available, (930) four-speed 2.25, 1.3, 0.89, 0.656, final drive 4.2; optional Sportomatic transmission on 911 and 911S, four-speed (ratios) 2.4, 1.56, 1.13, 0.86 STEERING rack and pinion; WHEELS (911 and 911S) 15 ins x 6 ins all round, 14 ins x 5.5 ins optional, (Carrera) 15 ins x 6 ins front, 15 ins x 7 ins rear, (930) 15 ins x 7 ins front, 15 ins x 8 ins rear.

## Porsche 911 and 930 I series

12,726 built between September 1975 and August 1976, chassis numbers 9116300001 to 9116301868 (911 fixed-head), 9116310001 to 9116311576 (911 Targa), 9116600001 to 9116601093 (Carrera 3 fixed-head), 9116610001 to 9116610479 (Carrera 3 Targa), 930670001 to 9306700157 (930), 9116200001 to 9116202079 (911S fixed-head US specification), 9116210001 to 9116212175 (911S Targa US specification), 9306800001 to 9306800530 (930 US specification).

### Engine

Six-cylinder CUBIC CAPACITY (911 and 911S US specification) 2,687 cc, (Carrera 3) 2,994 cc, (930) 2,994 cc turbocharged; BORE AND STROKE (911 and 911S US specification) 90 mm x 70.4 mm (Carrera 3 and 930) 95 mm x 70.4 mm; MAX POWER (911 and 911S US specification) 165 bhp at 5,800 rpm, (Carrera 3) 200 bhp at 6,000 rpm, (930) 260 bhp at 5,500 rpm, (930 US specification) 245 bhp at 5,500 rpm; MAX TORQUE (911 and 911S

US specification) 174 lb/ft at 4,000 rpm, (Carrera 3) 188 lb/ft at 4,200 rpm, (930 and 930 US specification) 253 lb/ft at 4,200 rpm; COMPRESSION RATIO (911 and 911S US specification) 8.5:1, (Carrera 3) 8.5:1, (930 and 930 US specification) 6.5:1; fuel injection K-Jetronic

**Chassis**
WEIGHT (dry) 2,470 lb (911 fixed-head) 2,514 lb (930); WHEELBASE 7 ft 5 ins; FRONT TRACK (911, 911S US specification and Carrera 3) 4 ft 6.4 ins, (930 and 930 US specification) 4 ft 8.3 ins; REAR TRACK (911 and 911 US specifcation) 4 ft 5.3 ins, (Carrera 3) 4 ft 6.9 ins, (930 and 930 US specification) 4 ft 11.06 ins; LENGTH 14 ft 0.9 in; WIDTH (911 and 911S US specification) 5 ft 3.4 ins, (Carrera 3) 5 ft 5.4 ins, (930 and 930 US specification) 5 ft 9.7 ins; HEIGHT 4 ft 2.1 ins; TURNING CIRCLE 35.1 ft; FRONT SUSPENSION independent MacPherson telescopic damper struts, lower wishbones, longitudinal torsion bars; REAR SUSPENSION independent, trailing radius arms, transverse torsion bars; telescopic dampers; BRAKES ventilated discs all round, front diamter 8.98 ins, rear 9.61 ins; GEARBOX (911 and 911S US specification) four-speed (ratios) 3.18, 1.6, 1.04, 0.72, (Carrera 3) five-speed (ratios) 3.18, 1.83, 1.26, 0.93, 0.72, final drive 4.43, other ratios available, (930) four-speed (ratios) 2.25, 1.3, 0.893, 0.656, final drive 4.2; optional Sportomatic transmission on 911, 911S US specification, Carrera 3, four-speed (ratios) 2.4, 1.56, 1.13, 0.86; STEERING rack and pinion; WHEELS (911 and 911S US specification) 15 in x 6 ins all round, 14 ins x 5.5 ins optional, (Carrera 3) 15 ins x 6 ins front, 15 ins x 7 ins rear, (930) 15 ins x 8 ins rear.

Thirty-one 934 cars were built, chassis numbers 9306700151 to 180 and 9306700540, with engines of 2,993 cc using a bore and stroke of 95 mm x 70.4 mm, producing 485 bhp at 7,000 rpm and 434 lb/ft of torque at 5,400 rpm, at an overall weight of 2,469 lb. Three 935 cars were built, chassis numbers 930570002R15, 935001 and 935002 with engines of 2,808 cc using a bore and stroke of 92 mm x 70.4 mm, producing 590 bhp at 7,900 rpm and 434 lb/ft of torque at 5,400 rpm, at an overall weight of 2,138 lb.

## Porsche 911 and 930 J series

13,792 built between Spetember 1976 and August 1977, chassis numbers 9117300001 to 9117302449 (911 fixed-head), 9117310001 to 9117311724 (911 Targa), 9117600001 to 9117601473 (Carrera 3 fixed-head), 9117610001 to 9117610646 (Carrera 3 Targa), 93007700001 to 9307700695 (930), 9117200001 to 9117203388 (911S fixed-head US specification) 9117210001 to 9117212747 (911S Targa US specification), 9307800001 to 9307800727 (930 US specification).

## Engine

Six-cylinder CUBIC CAPACITY (911 and 911S US specification) 2,687 cc, (Carrera 3) 2,994 cc, (930) 2,994 cc turbocharged; BORE AND STROKE (911 and 911S US specification) 90 mm x 70.4 mm, (Carrera 3,930) 95 mm x 70.4 mm; MAX POWER (911 and 911S US specification) 165 bhp at 5,800 rpm; (Carrera 3) 200 bhp at 6,000 rpm, (930) 260 bhp at 5,500 rpm, (930 US specification) 245 bhp at 5,500 rpm; MAX TORQUE (911 and 911S US specification) 174 lb/ft at 4,000 rpm, (Carrera 3) 188 lb/ft at 4,200 rpm, (930 and 930 US specification) 253 lb/ft at 4,200 rpm: COMPRESSION RATIO (911 and 911S US specification) 8.5:1, (Carrera 3) 8.5:1, (930 and 930 US specification) 6.5:1 FUEL INJECTION K-Jetronic.

## Chassis

WEIGHT (dry) 2,470 lb (911 fixed-head), 2,514 lb (930); WHEELBASE 7 ft 5 ins; FRONT TRACK (911, 911S US specification and Carrera 3) 4 ft 6.4 ins, (930 and 930 US specification) 4 ft 8.3 ins; REAR TRACK (911 and 911S US specification) 4 ft 5.3 ins, (Carrera 3) 4 ft 6.9 ins, (930 and 930 US specification) 4 ft 11.06 ins; LENGTH 14 ft 0.9 ins; WIDTH (911 and 911S US specification) 5 ft 3.4 ins, (Carrera 3) 5 ft 4.96 ins, (930 and 930 US specification) 5 ft 9.7 ins; HEIGHT 4 ft 2.1 ins; TURNING CIRCLE 35.1 ft; FRONT SUSPENSION independent MacPherson telescopic damper struts, lower wishbones, longitudinal torsion bars; REAR SUSPENSION independent, trailing radius arms, transverse torsion bars, telescopic dampers; BRAKES ventilated discs all round, front diameter 8.98 ins, rear 9.61 ins; GEARBOX (911 and 911S US specification) four-speed (ratios) 3.18, 1.6, 1.04, 0.72, (Carrera 3) five-speed (ratios) 3.18, 1.83, 1.26, 0.93, 0.72, final drive 4.43, other ratios available, (930) four-speed (ratios) 2.25, 1.3, 0.893, 0.656, final drive 4.2; optional Sportomatic transmission on 911 and 911S US specification, Carrera 3, four-speed (ratios) 2.4, 1.56, 1.13, 0.86; STEERING rack and pinion; WHEELS (911 and 911S US specification) 15 ins x 6 ins all round, 14 ins x 5.5 ins optional, (Carrera 3) 15 ins x 6 ins front, 15 ins x 7 ins rear, (930) 15 ins x 8 ins rear.

Ten 934 US-specification cars were built, chassis numbers 9307700951 to 960, with 2.993-cc engines using a bore and stroke of 95 mm x 70.4 mm, producing 540 bhp at 7,000 rpm, with 434 lb/ft of torque at 5,400 rpm, at an overall weight of 2,469 lb. Thirteen 935 cars were built, chassis numbers 9307700901 to 913, with 2,857 cc using a bore and stroke of 92 mm x 70.4 mm, producing 590 bhp at 8,000 rpm with 434 lb/ft of torque at 5,400 rpm, at an overall weight of 2,138 lb. Three 935–77 cars were built, chassis numbers 93577003 to 5, using 2,867-cc engines producing 630 bhp at 8,000 rpm with 434 lb/ft of torque at 5,400 rpm, at an overall weight of 2,138 lb. One 935-77 'Baby', chassis number 93502001, was built, with a

1,425-cc engine using a bore and stroke of 71 mm x 60 mm, producing 370 bhp at 8,000 rpm, at an overall weight of 1,609 lb.

## Porsche 911 and 930 K series

10,665 built between September 1977 and August 1978, 9118300001 to 9118302438 (911SC fixed-head), 9118310001 to 9118311729 (911SC Targa), 9308700001 to 9308700735 (930), 9118200001 to 930202436 (911SC fixed-head US specification), 9118210001 to 9118212579 (911SC Targa US specification), 9308800001 to 9308800461 (930 US specification).

### Engine

Six-cylinder CUBIC CAPACITY (911SC and 911SC US specification) 2,994 cc, (930 and 930 US specification 3,299 cc; BORE AND STROKE (911SC and 911SC US specification) 95 mm x 70.4 mm, (930 and 930 US specification) 97 mm x 74.4 mm; MAX POWER (911SC and 911SC US specification) 180 bhp at 5,500 rpm, (930) 300 bhp at 5,500 rpm, (930 US specification) 265 bhp at 5,500 rpm; MAX TORQUE (911SC) 195 lb/ft at 4,200 rpm, (911SC US specification) 187 lb/ft at 4,200 rpm, (930) 304 lb/ft at 4,000 rpm, (930 US specification) 290 lb/ft at 4,000 rpm; COMPRESSION RATIO (911SC and 911SC US specification) 8.5:1, (930 and 930 US specification) 7:1; FUEL INJECTION K-Jetronic.

### Chassis

WEIGHT (dry) 2,558 lb (911SC fixed-head) 2,867 lb (930); WHEELBASE 7 ft 5 ins; FRONT TRACK (911SC) 4 ft 6.4 ins, (930) 4 ft 8.3 ins; REAR TRACK (911SC) 4 ft 6.9 ins, (930) 4 ft 11.06 ins; LENGTH 14 ft 0.9 in; WIDTH (911SC) 5 ft 4.96 ins, (930) 5 ft 9.7 ins; HEIGHT (911SC) 4 ft 4 ins, (930) 4 ft 3.5 ins; TURNING CIRCLE 35.1 ft; FRONT SUSPENSION independent MacPherson telescopic damper struts, lower wishbones, longitudinal torsion bars; REAR SUSPENSION independent trailing radius arms, transverse torsion bars, telescopic dampers; BRAKES ventilated discs all round, front diameter 9.25 ins, rear 9.61 ins; GEARBOX (911SC) five-speed (ratios) 3.18, 1.83, 1.26, 1, 0.82, final drive 3.9, (930) four-speed (ratios) 2.25, 1.30, 0.89, 0.66, final drive 4.2; optional Sportomatic transmission on 911SC, three-speed (ratios) 2.4, 1.43, 0.93; STEERING rack and pinion; WHEELS (911SC) 15 ins x 6 ins front, 15 ins x 7 ins rear, (930) 16 ins x 7 ins front, 16 ins x 8 ins rear.

Four 911SC Safari cars were built, chassis numbers 9118300789, 9118301416, 9118301474, and 9118301476 with 911SC engines producing 250 bhp at 6,800 rpm and 220 lb/ft of torque at 5,500 rpm, at an overall weight of 2,866 lb. One 935-78 car was built with a 2,857-cc engine using a bore and stroke of 92.8 mm x 70.4 mm, producing 600 bhp at 8,000 rpm and

434 lb/ft of torque at 5,400 rpm, at an overall weight of 2,138 lb. One 935-78 car was built with a 2,994 cc engine, using a bore and stroke of 95 mm x 70.4 mm, producing 675 bhp at 8,000 rpm and 528 lb/ft of torque at 5,600 rpm, at an overall weight of 2,260 lb. Alternative engines of 3,124 cc using a bore and stroke of 97 mm x 70.4 mm, producing 680 bhp at 8,000 rpm, with 520 lb/ft of torque at 5,600 rpm, and 3,160 cc using a bore and stroke of 95 mm x 74.4 mm, producing 720 bhp at 8,000 rpm with 542 lb/ft of torque at 5,500 rpm, were available. Two 935-78 'Moby Dick' cars were built, chassis numbers 935006-007, with a 3,211-cc engine using a bore and stroke of 95.7 mm x 74.4 mm, producing 750 bhp at 8,200 rpm with 615 lb/ft of torque at 6,500 rpm, at a weight of 2,260 lb.

## Porsche 911 and 930 L series

11,069 built between September 1978 and August 1979, 9119300001 to 9119303318 (911SC fixed-head), 9119310001 to 9119311874 (911SC Targa), 9309700001 to 9309700820 (930), 9309200001 to 9309202013 (911SC fixed-head US specification) 9119210001 to 9119211965 (911SC Targa US specification), 93098000001 to 9309800781 (930 US specification)

### Engine

Six-cylinder CUBIC CAPACITY (911SC and 911SC US specification) 2,994 cc, (930 and 930 US specification), 3,299 cc; BORE AND STROKE (911SC and 911SC US specification) 95 mm x 70.4 mm, (930 and 930 US specification) 97 mm x 74.4 mm; MAX POWER (911SC and 911SC US specification) 180 bhp at 5,500 rpm, (930) 300 bhp at 5,500 rpm, (930 US specification) 265 bhp at 5,500 rpm; MAX TORQUE (911SC) 188 lb/ft at 4,200 rpm, (911SC US specification) 175 lb/ft at 4,200 rpm, (930) 304 lb/ft at 4,000 rpm, (930 US specification) 290 lb/ft at 4,000 rpm, COMPRESSION RATIO (911SC and 911SC US specification) 8.5:1, (930 and 930 US specification) 7:1; fuel injection K-Jetronic.

### Chassis

WEIGHT (dry) 2,558 lb (911SC fixed-head) 2,867 lb (930); WHEELBASE 7 ft 5 ins; FRONT TRACK (911SC) 4 ft 6.4 ins, (930) 4 ft 8.3 ins; REAR TRACK (911SC) 4 ft 6.9 ins, (930) 4 ft 11.06 ins; LENGTH 14 ft 0.9 ins; WIDTH (911SC) 5 ft 4.96 ins, (930) 5 ft 9.7 ins; HEIGHT (911SC) 4 ft 4 ins, (930) 4 ft 3.5 ins; TURNING CIRCLE 35.1 ft; FRONT SUSPENSION independent MacPherson telescopic damper struts, lower wishbones, longitudinal torsion bars, REAR SUSPENSION telescopic dampers; BRAKES ventilated discs all round, front diameter 9.25 ins, rear 9.61 ins; GEARBOX (911SC) five-speed (ratios) 3.18, 1.83, 1.26, 1, 0.82, final drive 3.9, (930) four-speed (ratios) 2.25, 1.3, 0.89, 0.66, final drive 4.2; STEERING rack and pinion; WHEELS (911SC) 15 ins x 6 ins front, 16 ins x 7 ins rear,

(930) 15 ins x 7 ins front, 16 ins x 8 ins rear.

Nine 935-79 cars were built, chassis numbers 93500016 to 17, 93500022 to 28, with engines of 3,160 cc using a bore and stroke of 95 mm x 74.4 mm, producing 720 bhp at 8,000 rpm and 542 lb/ft of torque at 5,500 rpm, at an overall weight of 2,260 lb.

## Porsche 911 and 930 new A series

9,943 built between September 1979 and August 1980, chassis numbers 91A0130001 to 91A0134831 (911SC fixed-head and Targa), 91A0140001 to 91A0144272 (911SC fixed-head US specification), 93A0070001 to 93A0070840 (930).

### Engine

Six-cylinder CUBIC CAPACITY (911SC and 911SC US specification) 2,994 cc, (930) 3,299 cc; BORE AND STROKE (911SC and 911SC US specification) 95 mm x 70.4 mm, (930) 97 mm x 74.4 mm; MAX POWER (911SC) 188 bhp at 5,500 rpm, (911SC US specification) 180 bhp at 5,500 rpm, (930) 300 bhp at 5,500 rpm; MAX TORQUE (911SC) 195 lb/ft at 4,300 rpm, (911SC US specification) 180 lb/ft at 4,200 rpm, (930) 304 lb/ft at 4,000 rpm; COMPRESSION RATIO (911SC) 8.6:1, (911SC US specification) 9.3:1, (930) 7:1; fuel injection K-Jetronic.

### Chassis

WEIGHT (dry) 2,558 lb (911SC fixed-head), 2,867 lb (930); WHEELBASE 7 ft 5 ins; FRONT TRACK (911SC) 4 ft 6.4 ins, (930) 4 ft 8.3 ins; REAR TRACK (911SC) 4 ft 6.9 ins, (930) 4 ft 11.06 ins; LENGTH 14 ft 0.9 ins; WIDTH (911SC) 5 ft 4.96 ins, (930) 5 ft 9.7 ins; HEIGHT (911SC) 4 ft 4 ins, (930) 4 ft 3.5 ins; TURNING CIRCLE 35.1 ft; FRONT SUSPENSION independent MacPherson telescopic damper struts, lower wishbones, longitudinal torsion bars, REAR SUSPENSION telescopic dampers; BRAKES ventilated discs all round, front diameter 9.25 ins, rear 9.61 ins; GEARBOX (911SC) five-speed (ratios) 3.18, 1.83, 1.26, 1, 0.82, final drive 3.9, (930) four-speed (ratios) 2.25, 1.3, 0.89, 0.66, final drive 4.2; STEERING rack and pinion; WHEELS (911SC) 15 ins x 6 ins front, 15 ins x 7 ins rear, (930) 16 ins x 6 ins front, 16 ins x 8 ins rear.

## Porsche 911 and 930 new B series

8.757 built between September 1979 and August 1980, chassis numbers WPO22291ZBS100001 to WPO22291ZBS103181 (911SC fixed-head), WPO22291ZBS140001 to WPO22291ZBS141703 (911SC Targa), WPOAA091BS120001 to WPOAA091BS121573 (911SC fixed-head US specification), WPOEA091BS160001 to WPOEA091BS161407 (911SC Targa US specification), WPO22291ZBS129500 to WPO22291ZBS129622

(911SC fixed-head Japanese specification), WPO22291ZBS169500 to WPO22291ZBS169510 (911SC Targa Japanese specification), WPO22293ZBS000001 to WPO22293ZBS000698 (930), WPO-JA093BS050001 to WPOJA093BS050063 (930 Canadian specification).

### Engine

Six-cylinder CUBIC CAPACITY (911SC and 911SC US and Japanese-specification) 2,994 cc, (930 and 930 Canadian specification) 3,229 cc; BORE AND STROKE (911SC and 911SC US and Japanese specification) 95 mm x 70.4 mm, (930 and 930 Canadian specification) 97 mm x 74.4 mm; MAX POWER (911SC) 204 bhp at 5,900 rpm, (911SC US and Japanese specification) 180 bhp at 5,500 rpm, (930 and 930 Canadan specification) 300 bhp at 5,500 rpm; MAX TORQUE (911SC) 195 lb/ft at 4,300 rpm, (911SC US and Japanese specification) 180 lb/ft at 4,200 rpm, (930 and 930 Canadian specification) 304 lb/ft at 4,000 rpm; COMPRESSION RATIO (911SC) 9.8:1 (911SC US and Japanese specification) 9.3:1, (930 and 930 Canadian specification) 7:1; fuel injection K-Jetronic

### Chassis

WEIGHT (dry) 2,558 lb (911SC fixed-head), 2,867 lb (930); WHEELBASE 7 ft 5 ins; FRONT TRACK (911SC) 4 ft 6.4 ins, (930) 4 ft 8.3 ins; REAR TRACK (911SC) 4 ft 6.9 ins, (930) 4 ft 11.06 ins; LENGTH 14 ft 0.9 ins; WIDTH (911SC) 5 ft 4.96 ins, (930) 5 ft 9.7 ins; HEIGHT (911SC) 4 ft 4 ins, (930) 4 ft 3.5 ins; TURNING CIRCLE 35.1 ft; FRONT SUSPENSION independent MacPherson telescopic damper struts, lower wishbones, longitudinal torsion bars, REAR SUSPENSION telescopic dampers: BRAKES ventilated discs all round, front diameter 9.25 ins, rear 9.61 ins; GEARBOX (911SC) five-speed (ratios) 3.18, 1.83, 1.26, 1, 0.82, final drive 3.9, (930) four-speed (ratios) 2.25, 1.3, 0.89, 0.66, final drive 4.2; STEERING rack and pinion; WHEELS (911SC) 15 ins x 6 ins front, 15 ins x 7 ins rear, (930) 16 ins x 7 ins front, 16 ins x 8 ins rear.

## Porsche 911 and 930 new C series

11,082 built between September 1980 and August 1981, chassis numbers WPO22291ZCS100001 to WPO22291ZCS103307 (911SC fixed-head), WPO22291ZCS14001 to WPO22291ZCS141737 (911SC Targa), WPOAA91CS120001 to WPOAA091CS122457 (911SC fixed-head US specification), WPOEA091CS160001 to WPOEA091CS162426 (911SC Targa US-specification), WPO22291ZCS109501 to WPO22291ZCS109628 (911SC fixed-head Japanese specification), WPO22293ZCS000001 to WPO22293ZCS000938 (930), WPO22293ZCS000001 to WPO22293ZCS000938 (930), WPOJA093CS050001 to WPO-JA093CS050089 (930 Canadian specification).

### Engine

Six-cylinder CUBIC CAPACITY (911SC and 911SC US and Japanese specification) 2,994 cc, (930 and 930 Canadian specification), 3,299 cc; BORE AND STROKE (911SC and 911SC US and Japanese-specification) 95 mm x 70.4 mm, (930 and 930 Canadian specification) 97 mm x 74.4 mm; MAX POWER (911SC) 204 bhp at 5,900 rpm, (911SC US and Japanese specification) 180 bhp at 5,500 rpm, (930 and 930 Canadian specification) 300 bhp at 5,500 rpm; MAX TORQUE (911SC) 195 lb/ft at 4,300 rpm, (911SC US and Japanese specification) 180 lb/ft at 4,200 rpm, (930 and 930 Canadian-specification) 304 lb/ft at 4,000 rpm; COMPRESSION RATIO (911SC) 9.8:1 (911SC US and Japanese specification) 9.3:1, (930 and 930 Canadian specification) 7:11; fuel injection K-Jetronic.

### Chassis

WEIGHT (dry) 2,558 lb (911SC fixed-head), 2,867 lb (930); WHEELBASE 7 ft 5 ins; FRONT TRACK (911SC) 4 ft 6.4 ins, (930) 4 ft 8.3 ins; REAR TRACK (911SC) 4 ft 6.9 ins, (930) 4 ft 11.06 ins; LENGTH 14 ft 0.9 ins; WIDTH (911SC) 5 ft 4.96 ins, (930) 5 ft 9.7 ins; HEIGHT (911SC) 4 ft 4 ins, (930) 4 ft 3.5 ins; TURNING CIRCLE 35.1 ft; FRONT SUSPENSION independent MacPherson telescopic damper struts, lower wishbones, longitudinal torsion bars, REAR SUSPENSION telescopic dampers; BRAKES ventilated discs all round, front diameter 9.25 ins, rear 9.61 ins; GEARBOX (911SC) five-speed (ratios) 3.18, 1.83, 1.26, 1, 0.82, final drive 3.9, (930) four-speed (ratios) 2.25, 1.3, 0.89, 0.66, final drive 4.2; STEERING rack and pinion; WHEELS (911SC) 15 ins x 6 ins front, 15 ins x 7 ins rear, (930) 16 ins x 7 ins front, 16 ins x 8 ins rear.

One 911SC 3.0 rally car was built, chassis number WPO22291ZCS100338, with a 911SC engine producing 230 bhp at 7,800 rpm with 200 lb/ft of torque at 5,600 rpm, at an overall weight of 2,359 lb.

## Porsche 911 and 930 new D series

13,906 built between September 1981 and August 1982, WPO22291ZDS100001 to WPO22291ZDS102995 (911SC fixed-head), WPO22291ZDS140001 to WPO22291ZDS141258 (911SC Targa), WPO22291ZDS15001 to WPO2291ZDS152406 (911SC Cabriolet), WPOAA091DS120001 to WPOAA091DS122559 (911SC fixed-head US specification), WPOEA091DS160001 to WPOEA091DS161430 (911SC Targa US specification), WPOEA091DS170001 to WPOEA091DS171781 (911SC Cabriolet US specification), WPO22291ZDS10951 to WPO22291ZDS109645 (911SC fixed-head Japanese specification), WPO22291ZDS149501 to WPO2291ZDS149562 (911SC Targa Japanese specification WPO22291ZDS159501 to WPO22291ZDS159590 (911SC

Cabriolet Japanese specification) WPO22293ZDS000001 to WPO222932ZDS001015 (930), WPOJA093DS050001 to WPO-JA093DS050065 (930 Canadian specification.

### Engine

Six-cylinder CUBIC CAPACITY (911SC and 911SC US and Japanese specification) 2,994 cc, (930 and 930 Canadian specification) 3,299 cc; BORE AND STROKE (911SC and 911SC US and Japanese specification) 95 mm x 70.4 mm (930 and 930 Canadian specification) 97 mm x 74.4 mm; MAX POWER (911SC) 204 bhp at 5,900 rpm, (911SC US and Japanese specification) 180 bhp at 5,500 rpm, (930 and 930 Canadian specification) 300 bhp at 5,500 rpm; MAX TORQUE (911SC) 195 lb/ft at 4,300 rpm, (911SC US and Japanese specification) 180 lb/ft at 4,200 rpm, (930 and 930 Canadian specification) 318 lb/ft at 4,000 rpm; COMPRESSION RATIO (911SC) 9.8:1, (911SC US and Japanese specification) 9.3:1, (930 and 930 Canadian specification) 7:1; fuel injection K-Jetronic.

### Chassis

WEIGHT (dry) 2,558 lb (911SC fixed-head), 2,867 lb (930); WHEELBASE 7 ft 5 ins; FRONT TRACK (911SC) 4 ft 6.4 ins, (930) 4 ft 8.3 ins; REAR TRACK (911SC) 4 ft 6.9 ins, (930) 4 ft 11.06 ins; LENGTH 14 ft 0.9 ins; WIDTH (911SC) 5 ft 4.96 ins, (930) 5 ft 9.7 ins; HEIGHT (911SC) 4 ft 4 ins, (930) 4 ft 3.5 ins; TURNING CIRCLE 35.1 ft; FRONT SUSPENSION independent MacPherson telescopic damper struts, lower wishbones, longitudinal torsion bars, REAR SUSPENSION telescopic dampers; BRAKES ventilated discs all round, front diameter 9.25 ins, rear 9.61 ins; GEARBOX (911SC) five-speed (ratios) 3.18, 1.83, 1.26, 1. 0.82, final drive 3.9, (930) four-speed (ratios) 2.25, 1.3, 0.89, 0.66, final drive 4.2; STEERING rack and pinion; WHEELS (911SC) 15 ins x 6 ins front, 15 ins x 7 ins rear, (930) 16 ins x 7 ins front, 16 ins x 8 ins rear.

## Porsche 911 and 930 new E series

14,309 built between September 1982 and August 1983, chassis numbers WPO22291ZES100001 to WPO22291ZES14033 (Carrera fixed-head), WPO22291ZES140001 to WPO22291ZES141469 (Carrera Targa), WPO22291ZES150001 to WPO22291ZES151835 (Carrera Cabriolet), WPOABO91ES120001 to WPOAB091ES122282 (Carrera fixed-head US-specification), WPOEB091ES160001 to WPOEB091ES162260 (Carrera Targa US specification), WPOEB091ES170001 to WPOEB091ES171191 (Carrera Cabriolet US specification), WPO22291ZES109501 to WPO22291-ZES109717 (Carrera fixed-head Japanese specification), WPO22291-ZES149501 to WPO2291ZES149564 (Carrera Targa Japanese specification) WPO22291ZES159501 to WP022195ZES159577 (Carrera Cabriolet

Japanese specification), WPO22295ZES000001 to WPO22293ZES000804 (930), WPOJA093ES00001 to WPOJA093ES050077 (930 Canadian specification).

### Engine

Six-cylinder CUBIC CAPACITY (Carrera and Carrera US and Japanese specification) 3,164 cc, (930 and 930 Canadian specification), 3,299 cc; BORE AND STROKE (Carrera and Carrera US and Japanese specification) 95 mm x 74.4 mm, (930 and 930 Canadian specification) 97 mm x 74.4 mm; MAX POWER (Carrera) 231 bhp at 5,900 rpm, (Carrera US and Japanese specification) 202 bhp at 5,900 rpm, (930 and 930 Canadian specification) 300 bhp at 5,500 rpm; MAX TORQUE (Carrera) 209 lb/ft at 4,800 rpm, (Carrera US and Japanese specification) 185 lb/ft at 4,800 rpm, (930 and 930 Canadian specification) 318 lb/ft at 4,000 rpm; COMPRESSION RATIO (Carrera) 10.3:1, (Carrera US and Japanese specification) 9.5:1, (930 and 930 Canadian specification) 7:1; fuel injection DME.

### Chassis

WEIGHT (dry) 2,558 lb (Carrera fixed-head) 2,867 lb (930); WHEELBASE 7 ft 5 ins; FRONT TRACK (Carrera) 4 ft 6.4 ins, (930 and Carrera with M491 option) 4 ft 8.3 ins; REAR TRACK (Carrera) 4 ft 6.9 ins, (930 Carrera with M491 option) 4 ft 11.06 ins; LENGTH 14 ft 0.9 ins; WIDTH (Carrera) 5 ft 4.96 ins, (930 and Carrera with M491 option) 5 ft 9.7 ins; HEIGHT (Carrera) 4 ft 4 ins, (930 and Carrera with M491 option) 4 ft 3.5 ins; TURNING CIRCLE 35.1 ft; FRONT SUSPENSION independent MacPherson telescopic damper struts, lower wishbones, longitudinal torsion bars, REAR SUSPENSION telescopic dampers; BRAKES ventilated discs all round, front diameter 9.25 ins, rear 9.61 ins; GEARBOX (Carrera) five-speed (ratio) 3.18, 1.83, 1.26, 0.966, 0.786, (Carrera US and Japanese specification) 3.18, 1.83, 1.26, 1, 0.82, final drive 3.9, (930) four-speed (ratios) 2.25, 1.3, 0.89, 0.66, final drive 4.2; STEERING rack and pinion; WHEELS (Carrera) 15 ins x 6 ins front, 15 ins x 7 ins rear, optional 16 ins x 6 ins front, 16 ins x 7 ins rear, (930 and Carrera with M491 option) 16 ins x 7 ins front, 16 ins x 8 ins rear.

Three 911 Paris-Dakar cars were built, chassis numbers WPO22291-ZES100020 to 22, using Carrera engines producing 225 bhp at 6,000 rpm and 203 lb/ft of torque at 4,700 rpm at an overall weight of 2,679 lb.

# Index

# Index of Illustrations

# Acknowledgements

The author is grateful to the following photographers, firms and libraries for allowing their pictures to be used:

*Autocar,* 13 left, 14, 15, 16 left and right, 17 top, 18 left and right, 20 left and right, 29 top left and right, bottom, 30, 36, 37 top right, 40 left and right, 79 top and bottom, 80 left, 100 top and bottom, 101, 150 right, 158, 164, 165 top and bottom, 186, 196, 197, 199 right

*Autofarm,* 247 left and right, 248 left and right, 249 left and right, 250 top left and right, bottom left and right, 251, 252

Bradbury, Nick, 128

FF Publishing, **colour plates 40, 47,** black and white, page 10 top

Hilton Press Services, **colour plates 18, 23, 24, 25, 26, 27, 30, 31, 32, 33, 34, 35, 36, 37, 38, 39, 42, 43, 44, 45, 46,** black and white, pages 54 bottom, 65, 86 bottom, 87 top and bottom, 88, 89, 91, 92, 94 top, 120, 129, 131 top, 132, 133, 134 top and bottom, 135 bottom, 136, 137, 138, 139, 140, 142, 143, 144, 145, 146, 179, 180 left, 201, 207, 210, 211, 212 top and bottom, 215, 217, 220, 223, 228, 231, 244 top and bottom, 245, 279 top and bottom

Holder, Tim, 268, 271

London Art-Technical, **colour plates 1, 2, 3, 4, 5, 6, 7, 8, 9, 10, 11, 12, 13, 14, 15, 16, 17, 19, 20, 21, 22,** black and white, pages 3 top and bottom, 7 top and bottom, 8 top and bottom, 17 bottom, 31 left and right, 32, 37 top left, bottom, 38, 39 top, 41, 44 top and bottom, 70 top and bottom, 71, 73, 75 top, bottom left and right, 76, 77, 78 top and bottom, 80 right, 82, 83 top, middle, bottom left and right, 85, 103 top and bottom, 104, 105, 106 main picture, 107, 108, 109, 110 top and bottom, 111 top and bottom, 112, 113, 114, 115, 116 top and bottom, 117, 118 top and bottom, 119, 121, 123 top and bottom, 124 top and bottom, 126, 127 top and bottom, 131 bottom, 148, 151, 153 bottom, 155 top and bottom, 157, 166, 170, 171, 172, 173 left and right, 181, 182, 185, 188, 189, 191, 192, 199 left, 204 top, middle, bottom left and right, 257, 258 top and bottom, 259, 260, 261, 262, 263, 272

*Motor*, 12, 13 right, 24, 27 top and bottom, 39 bottom, 106 inset, 149, 150 left, 153 top and middle, 168, 169, 174 left and right, 180 right

Skilleter, Paul, 233, 234 top and bottom, 235 top, middle and bottom, 236 top left and right, bottom, 238 left and right, 239, 240 top and bottom, 241 top and bottom, 242 top, bottom left and right, 243 top, bottom left and right, 255, 265

Porsche Cars GB, **colour plates 29, 41** black and white, pages 4, 5, 9, 10 middle and bottom, 42, 46, 50 top and bottom, 51, 52 top and bottom, 54 top, 56, 57, 58 top and bottom, 59, 60, 61, 62 top and bottom, 63, 64, 66, 68, 94 bottom, 202, 208 top and bottom, 213 top and bottom, 221, 224, 227, 256, 274, 277

Valente, Mike, **cover**

Young, Bob, **colour plate 28,** black and white, pages 86 top, 97 top and bottom, 135 top